BLOOM'S

HOW TO WRITE ABOUT

Stephen Crane

JOYCE CALDWELL SMITH

INTRODUCTION BY HAROLD BLOOM

BLOOM'S
LITERARY CRITICISM
An imprint of Infobase Publishing

Bloom's How to Write about Stephen Crane

Copyright © 2012 by Infobase Learning

Introduction © 2012 by Harold Bloom

Bloom's Literary Criticism
An imprint of Infobase Learning
132 West 31st Street
New York NY 10001

Library of Congress Cataloging-in-Publication Data

Smith, Joyce Caldwell.
  Bloom's how to write about Stephen Crane / by Joyce Caldwell Smith ; introduction by Harold Bloom.
      p. cm. — (Bloom's how to write about literature)
  Includes bibliographical references and index.
  ISBN 978-1-60413-751-4 (alk. paper)
    1. Crane, Stephen, 1871-1900—Criticism and interpretation. 2. Criticism—Authorship. 3. Report writing. I. Title. II. Title: How to write about Stephen Crane. III. Title: Stephen Crane.
PS1449.C85Z83 2011
813'.4—dc22   2011025760

Cover design by Ben Peterson
Composition by Erika K. Arroyo
Cover printed by Yurchak Printing, Landisville PA
Book printed and bound by Yurchak Printing, Landisville PA
Date printed: November 2011
Printed in the United States of America

10 9 8 7 6 5 4 3 2 1

CONTENTS

SERIES
INTRODUCTION

Bloom's How to Write about Literature series is designed to inspire students to write fine essays on great writers and their works. Each volume in the series begins with an introduction by Harold Bloom, meditating on the challenges and rewards of writing about the volume's subject author. The first chapter then provides detailed instructions on how to write a good essay, including how to find a thesis; how to develop an outline; how to write a good introduction, body text, and conclusion; how to cite sources; and more. The second chapter provides a brief overview of the issues involved in writing about the subject author and then a number of suggestions for paper topics, with accompanying strategies for addressing each topic. Succeeding chapters cover the author's major works.

The paper topics suggested within this book are open-ended, and the brief strategies provided are designed to give students a push forward in the writing process rather than a road map to success. The aim of the book is to pose questions, not answer them. Many different kinds of papers could result from each topic. As always, the success of each paper will depend completely on the writer's skill and imagination.

HOW TO WRITE ABOUT STEPHEN CRANE: INTRODUCTION

by Harold Bloom

Stephen Crane's contribution to the canon of American literature is fairly slight in bulk: one classic short novel, three vivid stories, and two or three ironic lyrics. *The Red Badge of Courage*; "The Open Boat," "The Blue Hotel," and "The Bride Comes to Yellow Sky"; "War Is Kind" and "A man adrift on a slim spar"—a single small volume can hold them all. Crane was dead at twenty-eight, after a frantic life, but a longer existence probably would not have enhanced his achievement. He was an exemplary American writer, flaring in the forehead of the morning sky and vanishing in the high noon of our evening land. An original, if not quite a Great Original, he prophesied Hemingway and our other journalist-novelists and still seems a forerunner of much to come.

The Red Badge of Courage is Crane's undoubted masterwork. Each time I reread it, I am surprised afresh, particularly by the book's originality, which requires a reader's act of recovery, because Crane's novel has been so influential. To write about battle in English, since Crane, is to be shadowed by Crane. Yet Crane, who later saw warfare in Cuba and between the Greeks and the Turks in his work as a correspondent, had experienced no fighting when he wrote *The Red Badge of Courage*. There is no actual experience that informs Crane's version of the Battle of Chancellorsville, one of the most terrible carnages of the American

Civil War. Yet anyone who has gone through warfare, from the time of the novel's publication (1895) until now, has testified to Crane's uncanny accuracy at the representation of battle. *The Red Badge of Courage* is an impressionist's triumph, in the particular sense that "impressionist" had in the literature of the nineties, a Paterian sense that went back to the emphasis upon *seeing* in Carlyle, Emerson, and Ruskin. Conrad and Henry James, both of whom befriended Crane, had their own relation to the impressionist mode, and each realized that Crane was a pure or natural impressionist, indeed the only one, according to Conrad.

Pater, deftly countering Matthew Arnold, stated the credo of literary impressionism:

> The first step towards seeing one's object as it really is, is to know one's impression as it really is, to discriminate it, to realize it distinctly.

Pater's "object" is a work of art, verbal or visual, but the critic here has stated Stephen Crane's quest to see the object of experience as it is, to know one's impression of it, and to realize that impression in narrative fiction. Scholarly arguments as to whether and to what degree *The Red Badge of Courage* is naturalistic, symbolist, or impressionist, can be set aside quickly. Joyce's *Ulysses* is both naturalistic and symbolist within the general perspective of the Paterian or impressionistic "epiphany" or privileged moment, but juxtapose the *Red Badge* to *Ulysses* and Crane is scarcely naturalistic or symbolist in comparison. Crane is altogether an impressionist, in his "vivid impressionistic description of action on that woodland battlefield," as Conrad phrased it, or, again in Conrad's wording, in "the imaginative analysis of his own temperament tried by the emotions of a battlefield."

If Crane's impressionism had a single literary origin, as to some extent is almost inevitable, Kipling is that likely forerunner. The puzzles of literary ancestry are most ironical here, since Kipling's precursor was Mark Twain. Hemingway's famous observation that all modern American literature comes out of the one book *Huckleberry Finn* is only true of Crane, the indubitable beginning of our modern literature, insofar as Crane took from Kipling precisely what the author of *The Light That*

Failed and *Kim* owed to Twain. Michael Fried's association of Crane with the painter Eakins is peculiarly persuasive, since Crane's visual impressionism is so oddly American, without much resembling Whistler's. Crane is almost the archetype of the writer as a child of experience, yet I think this tends to mean that then there are a few strong artistic precursors, rather than a tradition that makes itself available. Associate Crane with Kipling and Eakins, on the way to, but still a distance from, Conrad and the French Post-Impressionists, and you probably have stationed him accurately enough.

The Red Badge of Courage is necessarily a story about fear. Crane's Young Soldier, again as Conrad noted, "dreads not danger but fear itself. . . . In this he stands for the symbol of all untried men." Henry Fleming, as eventually we come to know the Young Soldier, moves ironically from a dangerous self-doubt to what may be an even more dangerous dignity. This is the novel's famous yet perhaps equivocal conclusion:

> For a time this pursuing recollection of the tattered man took all elation from the youth's veins. He saw his vivid error, and he was afraid that it would stand before him all his life. He took no share in the chatter of his comrades, nor did he look at them or know them, save when he felt sudden suspicion that they were seeing his thoughts and scrutinizing each detail of the scene with the tattered soldier.
>
> Yet gradually he mustered force to put the sin at a distance. And at last his eyes seemed to open to some new ways. He found that he could look back upon the brass and bombast of his earlier gospels and see them truly. He was gleeful when he discovered that he now despised them.
>
> With this conviction came a store of assurance. He felt a quiet manhood, nonassertive but of sturdy and strong blood. He knew that he would no more quail before his guides wherever they should point. He had been to touch the great

death, and found that, after all, it was but the great death. He was a man.

So it came to pass that as he trudged from the place of blood and wrath his soul changed. He came from hot plowshares to prospects of clover tranquilly, and it was as if hot plowshares were not. Scars faded as flowers.

It rained. The procession of weary soldiers became a bedraggled train, despondent and muttering, marching with churning effort in a trough of liquid brown mud under a low, wretched sky. Yet the youth smiled, for he saw that the world was a world for him, though many discovered it to be made of oaths and walking sticks. He had rid himself of the red sickness of battle. The sultry nightmare was in the past. He had been an animal blistered and sweating in the heat and pain of war. He turned now with a lover's thirst to images of tranquil skies, fresh meadows, cool brooks—an existence of soft and eternal peace.

Over the river a golden ray of sun came through the hosts of leaden rain clouds.

More Hemingway than Hemingway is that very American sentence: "He had been to touch the great death, and found that, after all, it was but the great death. He was a man." Is the irony of that dialectical enough to suffice? In context, the power of the irony is beyond question, since Crane's prose is strong enough to bear rephrasing as: "He had been to touch the great fear, and found that, after all, it was still the great fear. He was not yet a man." Crane's saving nuance is that the fear of being afraid dehumanizes, while accepting one's own mortality bestows upon one the association with others that grants the dignity of the human. How does Crane's prose find the strength to sustain a vision that primary and normative? The answer, I suspect, is the Bible and Bunyan, both of them being deeply at work in this unbelieving son of a Methodist minister: "He

came from hot plowshares to prospects of clover tranquilly, and it was
as if hot plowshares were not." The great trope of Isaiah is assimilated in
the homely and unassuming manner of Bunyan, and we see the Young
Soldier, Henry Fleming, as an American Pilgrim, anticipating when both
sides of the Civil War "shall beat their swords into plowshares, and their
spears into pruning hooks."

Crane's accurate apprehension of the phantasmagoria that is battle
has been compared to Tolstoy's. There is something to such a parallel, perhaps because Tolstoy even more massively is a biblical writer.
What is uniquely Crane's, what parts him from all prior visionaries of
warfare, is difficult to define, but is of the highest importance for establishing his astonishing originality. Many examples might be chosen, but
I give the death of the color sergeant from the conclusion of Chapter 19:

> Over the field went the scurrying mass. It was a handful
> of men splattered into the faces of the enemy. Toward it
> instantly sprang the yellow tongues. A vast quantity of blue
> smoke hung before them. A mighty banging made ears
> valueless.
>
> The youth ran like a madman to reach the woods before a
> bullet could discover him. He ducked his head low, like a
> football player. In his haste his eyes almost closed, and the
> scene was a wild blur. Pulsating saliva stood at the corners
> of his mouth.
>
> Within him, as he hurled himself forward, was born a love, a
> despairing fondness for this flag which was near him. It was
> a creation of beauty and invulnerability. It was a goddess,
> radiant, that bended its form with an imperious gesture to
> him. It was a woman, red and white, hating and loving, that
> called him with the voice of his hopes. Because no harm
> could come to it he endowed it with power. He kept near, as
> if it could be a saver of lives, and an imploring cry went from
> his mind.

> In the mad scramble he was aware that the color sergeant
> flinched suddenly, as if struck by a bludgeon. He faltered,
> and then became motionless, save for his quivering knees.
>
> He made a spring and a clutch at the pole. At the same
> instant his friend grabbed it from the other side. They jerked
> at it, stout and furious, but the color sergeant was dead, and
> the corpse would not relinquish its trust. For a moment there
> was a grim encounter. The dead man, swinging with bended
> back, seemed to be obstinately tugging, in ludicrous and
> awful ways, for the possession of the flag.
>
> It was past in an instant of time. They wrenched the flag
> furiously from the dead man, and, as they turned again, the
> corpse swayed forward with bowed head. One arm swung
> high, and the curved hand fell with heavy protest on the
> friend's unheeding shoulder.

In the "wild blur" of this phantasmagoria, there are two images of
pathos, the flag and the corpse of the color sergeant. Are they not to some
degree assimilated to one another, so that the corpse becomes a flagpole,
and the flag a corpse? Yet so dialectical is the interplay of Crane's biblical irony that the assimilation, however incomplete, itself constitutes a
figure of doubt as to the normative intensities of patriotism and group
solidarity that the scene exemplifies, both in the consciousness of Henry
Fleming and in that of the rapt reader. The "despairing fondness" for the
flag is both a Platonic and a Freudian Eros, but finally more Freudian. It
possesses "invulnerability" for which the soldier under fire has that Platonic desire for what he himself does not possess and quite desperately
needs, but it manifests even more a Freudian sense of the ambivalence
both of and towards the woman as object of the drive, at once a radi-
ant goddess sexually bending her form though imperiously, yet also a
woman, red and white, hating and loving, destroying and healing.

The corpse of the color sergeant, an emblem of devotion to the flag
and the group even beyond death, nevertheless keeps Fleming and his
friend from the possibility of survival as men, compelling them to clutch
and jerk at the pole, stout and furious. Life-in-death incarnate, the corpse

obstinately tugs for the staff of its lost life. Homer surely would have appreciated the extraordinary closing gesture, as the corpse sways forward, head bowed but arm swung high for a final stroke, as "the curved hand fell with heavy protest on the friend's unheeding shoulder."

Crane is hardly the American Homer; Walt Whitman occupies that place forever. Still, *The Red Badge of Courage* is certainly the most Homeric prose narrative ever written by an American. One wants to salute it with Whitman's most Homeric trope, when he says of the grass:

And now it seems to me the beautiful uncut hair of graves.

HOW TO WRITE
A GOOD ESSAY

By Laurie A. Sterling and Joyce Caldwell Smith

While there are many ways to write about literature, most assignments for high school and college English classes call for analytical papers. In these assignments, you are presenting your interpretation of a text to your reader. Your objective is to interpret the text's meaning in order to enhance your reader's understanding and enjoyment of the work. Without exception, strong papers about the meaning of a literary work are built upon a careful, close reading of the text or texts. Careful, analytical reading should always be the first step in your writing process. This volume provides models of such close, analytical reading, and these should help you develop your own skills as a reader and as a writer.

As the examples throughout this book demonstrate, attentive reading entails thinking about and evaluating the formal (textual) aspects of the author's works: theme, character, form, and language. In addition, when writing about a work, many readers choose to move beyond the text itself to consider the work's cultural context. In these instances, writers might explore the historical circumstances of the time period in which the work was written. Alternatively, they might examine the philosophies and ideas that a work addresses. Even in cases where writers explore a work's cultural context, though, papers must still address the more formal aspects of the work itself. A good interpretative essay that evaluates Charles Dickens's use of the philosophy of utilitarianism in his novel *Hard Times,* for example, cannot adequately address the author's treatment of the philosophy without firmly grounding this discussion in the book itself. In other words, any analytical paper about a text, even one that seeks to evaluate the work's cultural context, must also have a firm handle on the work's themes, characters, and language. You must look for and evaluate these aspects of a work, then, as you read a text and as you prepare to write about it.

WRITING ABOUT THEMES

Literary themes are more than just topics or subjects treated in a work; they are attitudes or points about these topics that often structure other elements in a work. Writing about theme therefore requires that you not just identify a topic that a literary work addresses but also discuss what the work says about that topic. For example, if you were writing about the culture of the American South in William Faulkner's famous story "A Rose for Emily," you would need to discuss what Faulkner says, argues, or implies about that culture and its passing.

When you prepare to write about thematic concerns in a work of literature, you will probably discover that, like most works of literature, your text touches upon other themes in addition to its central theme. These secondary themes also provide rich ground for paper topics. A thematic paper on "A Rose for Emily" might consider gender or race in the story. While neither of these could be said to be the central theme of the story, they are clearly related to the passing of the "old South" and could provide plenty of good material for papers.

As you prepare to write about themes in literature, you might find a number of strategies helpful. After you identify a theme or themes in the story, you should begin by evaluating how other elements of the story—such as character, point of view, imagery, and symbolism—help develop the theme. You might ask yourself what your own responses are to the author's treatment of the subject matter. Do not neglect the obvious, either: What expectations does the title set up? How does the title help develop thematic concerns? Clearly, the title "A Rose for Emily" says something about the narrator's attitude toward the title character, Emily Grierson, and all she represents.

WRITING ABOUT CHARACTER

Generally, characters are essential components of fiction and drama. (This is not always the case, though; Ray Bradbury's "August 2026: There Will Come Soft Rains" is technically a story without characters, at least any human characters.) Often, you can discuss character in poetry, as in T. S. Eliot's "The Love Song of J. Alfred Prufrock" or Robert Browning's "My Last Duchess." Many writers find that analyzing character is one of the most interesting and engaging ways to work with a piece of literature and to shape a paper. After all, characters generally are human, and we all know something about being human and living in the world. While it is always important to remember that these figures are not real people but creations of the writer's imagination, it can be fruitful to begin evaluating them as you might evaluate a real person. Often you can start with your own response to a character. Did you like or dislike the character? Did you sympathize with the character? Why or why not?

Keep in mind, though, that emotional responses like these are just starting places. To truly explore and evaluate literary characters, you need to return to the formal aspects of the text and evaluate how the author has drawn these characters. The twentieth-century writer E. M. Forster coined the terms *flat* characters and *round* characters. Flat characters are static, one-dimensional characters that frequently represent a particular concept or idea. In contrast, round characters are fully drawn and much more realistic characters that frequently change and develop over the course of a work. Are the characters you are studying flat or round? What elements of the characters lead you to this conclusion? Why might the author have drawn characters like this? How does their development affect the meaning of the work? Similarly, you should explore the techniques the author uses to develop characters. Do we hear a character's own words, or do we hear only other characters' assessments of him or her? Or, does the author use an omniscient or limited omniscient narrator to allow us access to the workings of the characters' minds? If so, how does that help develop the characterization? Often you can even evaluate the narrator as a character. How trustworthy are the opinions and assessments of the narrator? You should also think about characters' names. Do they mean anything? If you encounter a hero named Sophia or Sophie, you should probably think about her wisdom (or lack thereof), since *sophia* means "wisdom" in Greek. Similarly, since the name Sylvia is derived from the word *sylvan,* meaning "of the wood," you might want to evaluate that character's relationship with nature. Once again, you might look to the title of the work. Does Herman Melville's "Bartleby, the Scrivener" signal anything about Bartleby himself? Is Bartleby adequately defined by his job as scrivener? Is this part of Melville's point? Pursuing questions such as these can help you develop thorough papers about characters from psychological, sociological, or more formalistic perspectives.

WRITING ABOUT FORM AND GENRE

Genre, a word derived from French, means "type" or "class." Literary genres are distinctive classes or categories of literary composition. On the most general level, literary works can be divided into the genres of drama, poetry, fiction, and essays, yet within those genres there are classifications that are also referred to as genres. Tragedy and comedy, for example, are genres of drama. Epic, lyric, and pastoral are genres of poetry. *Form,* on the other hand, generally refers to the shape or structure of a work. There are many clearly defined forms of poetry that follow specific patterns of meter, rhyme, and stanza. Sonnets, for example, are poems that follow a fixed form of 14 lines. Sonnets generally follow one of two basic sonnet forms, each with its own distinct rhyme scheme. Haiku is another example of poetic form, traditionally consisting of three unrhymed lines of five, seven, and five syllables.

While you might think that writing about form or genre might leave little room for argument, many of these forms and genres are very fluid. Remember that literature is evolving and ever changing, and so are its forms. As you study poetry, you may find that poets, especially more modern poets, play with traditional poetic forms, bringing about new effects. Similarly, dramatic tragedy was once quite narrowly defined, but over the centuries playwrights have broadened and challenged traditional definitions, changing the shape of tragedy.

When Arthur Miller wrote *Death of a Salesman,* many critics challenged the idea that tragic drama could encompass a common man like Willy Loman.

Evaluating how a work of literature fits into or challenges the boundaries of its form or genre can provide you with fruitful avenues of investigation. You might find it helpful to ask why the work does or does not fit into traditional categories. Why might Miller have thought it fitting to write a tragedy of the common man? Similarly, you might compare the content or theme of a work with its form. How well do they work together? Many of Emily Dickinson's poems, for instance, follow the meter of traditional hymns. While some of her poems seem to express traditional religious doctrines, many seem to challenge or strain against traditional conceptions of God and theology. What is the effect, then, of her use of traditional hymn meter?

WRITING ABOUT LANGUAGE, SYMBOLS, AND IMAGERY

No matter what the genre, writers use words as their most basic tool. Language is the most fundamental building block of literature. It is essential that you pay careful attention to the author's language and word choice as you read, reread, and analyze a text. Imagery is language that appeals to the senses. Most commonly, imagery appeals to our sense of vision, creating a mental picture, but authors also use language that appeals to our other senses. Images can be literal or figurative. Literal images use sensory language to describe an actual thing. In the broadest terms, figurative language uses one thing to speak about something else. For example, if I call my boss a snake, I am not saying that he is literally a reptile. Instead, I am using figurative language to communicate my opinions about him. Since we think of snakes as sneaky, slimy, and sinister, I am using the concrete image of a snake to communicate these abstract opinions and impressions.

The two most common figures of speech are similes and metaphors. Both are comparisons between two apparently dissimilar things. Similes are explicit comparisons using the words *like* or *as*; metaphors are implicit comparisons. To return to the previous example, if I say, "My boss, Bob, was waiting for me when I showed up to work five minutes late today—the snake!" I have constructed a metaphor. Writing about his experiences fighting in World War I, Wilfred Owen begins his poem "Dulce et decorum est" with a string of similes: "Bent double, like old beggars under sacks, / Knock-kneed, coughing like hags, we cursed through sludge." Owen's goal was to undercut clichéd notions that war and dying in battle were glorious. Certainly, comparing soldiers to coughing hags and to beggars underscores his point.

"Fog," a short poem by Carl Sandburg, provides a clear example of a metaphor. Sandburg's poem reads:

> The fog comes
> on little cat feet.
>
> It sits looking
> over harbor and city
> on silent haunches
> and then moves on.

Notice how effectively Sandburg conveys surprising impressions of the fog by comparing two seemingly disparate things—the fog and a cat.

Symbols, by contrast, are things that stand for, or represent, other things. Often they represent something intangible, such as concepts or ideas. In everyday life we use and understand symbols easily. Babies at christenings and brides at weddings wear white to represent purity. Think, too, of a dollar bill. The paper itself has no value in and of itself. Instead, that paper bill is a symbol of something else, the precious metal in a nation's coffers. Symbols in literature work similarly. Authors use symbols to evoke more than a simple, straightforward, literal meaning. Characters, objects, and places can all function as symbols. Famous literary examples of symbols include Moby Dick, the white whale of Herman Melville's novel, and the scarlet *A* of Nathaniel Hawthorne's *The Scarlet Letter*. As both of these symbols suggest, a literary symbol cannot be adequately defined or explained by any one meaning. Hester Prynne's Puritan community clearly intends her scarlet *A* as a symbol of her adultery, but as the novel progresses, even her own community reads the letter as representing not just *adultery*, but *able, angel*, and a host of other meanings.

Writing about imagery and symbols requires close attention to the author's language. To prepare a paper on symbolism or imagery in a work, identify and trace the images and symbols and then try to draw some conclusions about how they function. Ask yourself how any symbols or images help contribute to the themes or meanings of the work. What connotations do they carry? How do they affect your reception of the work? Do they shed light on characters or settings? A strong paper on imagery or symbolism will thoroughly consider the use of figures in the text and will try to reach some conclusions about how or why the author uses them.

WRITING ABOUT HISTORY AND CONTEXT

As noted above, it is possible to write an analytical paper that also considers the work's context. After all, the text was not created in a vacuum. The author lived and wrote in a specific time period and in a specific cultural context and, like all of us, was shaped by that environment. Learning more about the historical and cultural circumstances that surround the author and the work can help illuminate a text and provide you with productive material for a paper. Remember, though, that when you write analytical papers, you should use the context to illuminate the text. Do not lose sight of your goal—to interpret the meaning of the literary work. Use historical or philosophical research as a tool to develop your textual evaluation.

Thoughtful readers often consider how history and culture affected the author's choice and treatment of his or her subject matter. Investigations into the history and context of a work could examine the work's relation to specific historical events, such as the Salem witch trials in seventeenth-century Massachusetts or the restoration of Charles II to the English throne in 1660. Bear in mind that historical context is not limited to politics and world events. While knowing about the Vietnam War is certainly helpful in interpreting much of Tim O'Brien's fiction, and some knowledge of the French Revolution clearly illuminates the dynamics of Charles Dickens's *A Tale of Two Cities,* historical context also entails the fabric of daily life. Examining a text in light of gender roles, race relations, class boundaries, or working conditions can give rise to thoughtful and compelling papers. Exploring the conditions of the working class in nineteenth-century England, for example, can provide a particularly effective avenue for writing about Dickens's *Hard Times.*

You can begin thinking about these issues by asking broad questions at first. What do you know about the time period and about the author? What does the editorial apparatus in your text tell you? Similarly, when specific historical events or dynamics are particularly important to understanding a work but might be somewhat obscure to modern readers, textbooks usually provide notes to explain historical background. With this information, ask yourself how these historical facts and circumstances might have affected the author, the presentation of theme, and the presentation of character. How does knowing more about the work's specific historical context illuminate the work? To take a well-known example, understanding the complex attitudes toward slavery during the time Mark Twain wrote *Adventures of Huckleberry Finn* should help you begin to examine issues of race in the text. Additionally, you might compare these attitudes to those of the time in which the novel was set. How might this comparison affect your interpretation of a work written after the abolition of slavery but set before the Civil War?

WRITING ABOUT PHILOSOPHY AND IDEAS

Philosophical concerns are closely related to both historical context and thematic issues. Like historical investigation, philosophical research can provide a useful tool as you analyze a text. For example, an investigation into the working class in Dickens's England might lead you to a topic on the philosophical doctrine of utilitarianism in *Hard Times*. Many other works explore philosophies and ideas quite explicitly. Mary Shelley's famous novel *Frankenstein*, for example, explores John Locke's tabula rasa theory of human knowledge as she portrays the intellectual and emotional development of Victor Frankenstein's creature. As this example indicates, philosophical issues are more abstract than investigations of theme or historical context. Some other examples of philosophical issues include human free will, the formation of human identity, the nature of sin, or questions of ethics.

Writing about philosophy and ideas might require some outside research, but usually the notes or other material in your text will provide you with basic information, and often footnotes and bibliographies suggest places you can go to read further about the subject. If you have identified a philosophical theme that runs through a text, you might ask yourself how the author develops this theme. Look at character development and the interactions of characters, for example. Similarly, you might examine whether the narrative voice in a work of fiction addresses the philosophical concerns of the text.

WRITING COMPARISON AND CONTRAST ESSAYS

Finally, you might find that comparing and contrasting the works or techniques of an author provides a useful tool for literary analysis. A comparison and contrast essay might compare two characters or themes in a single work, or it might compare the author's treatment of a theme in two works. It might also contrast methods of character development or analyze an author's differing treatment of a philosophical concern in two works. Writing comparison and contrast essays, though, requires some special consideration. While they generally provide you with plenty of material to use, they also come with a built-in trap: the laundry list. These papers often become mere lists of connections between the works. As this chapter will discuss, a strong thesis must make an assertion that you want to prove or validate. A strong comparison/contrast thesis, then, needs to comment on the significance of the similarities and differences you observe. It is not enough merely to assert that the works contain similarities and differences. You might, for example, assert why the similarities and differences are important and explain how they illuminate the works' treatment of theme. Remember, too, that a thesis should not be a statement of the obvious. A comparison/contrast paper that focuses only on very obvious similarities or differences does little to illuminate the connections between the works. Often, an effective method of shaping a strong thesis and argument is to begin your paper by noting the similarities between the works but then to develop a thesis that asserts how these apparently similar elements are different. If, for example, you observe that Emily Dickinson wrote a number of poems about spiders, you might analyze how she uses spider imagery differently in two poems. Similarly, many scholars have noted that Hawthorne created many "mad scientist" characters, men who are so devoted to their science or their art that they lose perspective on all else. A good thesis comparing two of these characters—Aylmer of "The Birth-mark" and Dr. Rappaccini of "Rappaccini's Daughter," for example—might initially identify both characters as examples of Hawthorne's mad scientist type but then argue that their motivations for scientific experimentation differ. If you strive to analyze the similarities or differences, discuss significances, and move beyond the obvious, your paper should move beyond the laundry list trap.

PREPARING TO WRITE

Armed with a clear sense of your task—illuminating the text—and with an understanding of theme, character, language, history, and philosophy, you are ready to approach the writing process. Remember that good writing is grounded in good reading and that close reading takes time, attention, and more than one reading of your text. Read for comprehension first. As you go back and review the work, mark the text to chart the details of the work as well as your reactions. Highlight important passages, repeated words, and image patterns. "Converse" with the text through marginal notes. Mark turns in the plot, ask questions, and make observations about characters, themes, and language. If you are reading from a book that does not belong to you, keep a record of your reactions in a journal or notebook. If you have read a work of literature carefully, paying attention to both the text and the context of the work, you have a leg up on the writing process. Admittedly, at this point, your ideas are probably very broad and undefined, but you have taken an important first step toward writing a strong paper.

Your next step is to focus, to take a broad, perhaps fuzzy, topic and define it more clearly. Even a topic provided by your instructor will need to be focused appropriately. Remember that good writers make the topic their own. There are a number of strategies—often called "invention"—that you can use to develop your own focus. In one such strategy, called *freewriting,* you spend 10 minutes or so just writing about your topic without referring back to the text or your notes. Write whatever comes to mind; the important thing is that you just keep writing. Often this process allows you to develop fresh ideas or approaches to your subject matter. You could also try *brainstorming*: Write down your topic and then list all the related points or ideas you can think of. Include questions, comments, words, important passages or events, and anything else that comes to mind. Let one idea lead to another. In the related technique of *clustering,* or *mapping,* write your topic on a sheet of paper and write related ideas around it. Then list related subpoints under each of these main ideas. Many people then draw arrows to show connections between points. This technique helps you narrow your topic and can also help you organize your ideas. Similarly, asking journalistic questions— Who? What? Where? When? Why? and How?—can lead to ideas for topic development.

Thesis Statements

Once you have developed a focused topic, you can begin to think about your thesis statement, the main point or purpose of your paper. It is imperative that you craft a strong thesis; otherwise, your paper will likely be little more than random, disorganized observations about the text. Think of your thesis statement as a kind of road map for your paper. It tells your reader where you are going and how you are going to get there.

To craft a good thesis, you must keep a number of points in mind. First, as the title of this subsection indicates, your paper's thesis should be a statement, an assertion about the text that you want to prove or validate. Beginning writers often formulate a question that they attempt to use as a thesis. For example, a writer exploring the theme of courage in Crane's *Red Badge of Courage* might ask, How does Henry's idea of courage in battle change during the novel? While a question like this is a good strategy to use in the invention process to help narrow your topic and find your thesis, it cannot serve as the thesis statement because it does not tell your reader what you want to assert about courage. You might shape this question into a thesis by instead proposing an answer to that question: In *The Red Badge of Courage*, the young soldiers all want to be brave in battle, but the protagonist himself runs from the first skirmish. The novel ultimately argues that courage relies not on specific actions but on putting others' welfare above one's own. Notice that this thesis provides an initial plan or structure for the rest of the paper, and notice, too, that the thesis statement does not necessarily have to fit into one sentence. After discussing Henry's early ideas of courage, you could examine the ways in which Henry and the other recruits act in battle and then theorize about what Crane says about courage more generally; perhaps you could discuss how courage in this instance is not so much what others see Henry accomplish but what his motivations are during the fighting.

Second, remember that a good thesis makes an assertion that you need to support. In other words, a good thesis does not state the obvious. If you tried to formulate a thesis about courage by simply saying, The definition of courage is important in The Red Badge of Courage, you have done nothing but rephrase the obvious. Since Crane's novel is centered on Henry and his fear of looking like a coward, there would be no point in spending three to five pages supporting that assertion. You might try to develop a thesis from that point by asking yourself some further questions: What does it mean for Henry to feel like a hero as the trains pull into various stations on the trip from his home town to Washington: "The regiment was fed and caressed at station after station until the youth had believed that he must be a hero" (Crane 8)? Does the novel seem to indicate that courage is a result of enlistment and wearing a uniform? Does it present courage as a quality that comes from not being afraid, or is it more dependent on caring for others in times of vulnerability? Such a line of questioning might lead you to a more viable thesis, like the one in the preceding paragraph.

As the comparison with the road map also suggests, your thesis should appear near the beginning of the paper. In relatively short papers (three to six pages) the thesis almost always appears in the first paragraph. Some writers fall into the trap of saving their thesis for the end, trying to provide a surprise or a big moment of revelation, as if to say, "TA-DA! I've just proved that in 'The Open Boat' Crane uses the small dinghy to symbolize the problems of community in the world." Placing a thesis at the end of an essay can seriously mar the essay's effectiveness. If you fail to define your essay's point and purpose clearly at the beginning, your reader will find it difficult to assess the clarity of your argument and understand the points you are making. When your argument comes as a surprise at the end, you force your reader to reread your essay in order to assess its logic and effectiveness.

Finally, you should avoid using the first person ("I") as you present your thesis. Though it is not strictly wrong to write in the first person, it is difficult to do so gracefully. While writing in the first person, beginning writers often fall into the trap of writing self-reflexive prose (writing *about* their paper *in* their paper). Often this leads to the most dreaded of opening lines: "In this paper I am going to discuss. . . ." Not only does this self-reflexive voice make for very awkward prose, but it frequently allows writers to announce a topic boldly while completely avoiding a thesis statement. An example might be a paper that begins as follows: "The Open Boat," Crane's most famous short story, takes place in a small dinghy, which serves as a lifeboat for four shipwrecked men. In this paper I am going to discuss how these men get along with one another. The author of this paper has done little more than announce a general topic for the paper (how the men in the boat get along). While the last sentence might be a thesis, the writer fails to present an opinion about the significance of their reactions to one another. To improve this thesis, the writer would need to back up a couple of steps. First, the announced topic of the paper is too broad; it largely summarizes the events in the story, without saying anything about the ideas in the story. The writer should highlight what she considers the meaning of the story: What is the story about? The writer might conclude that the men learn to get along even though they are very different. From here, the author could select the means by which Crane communicates these ideas and then begin to craft a specific thesis. A writer who chooses to explore the boat as a microcosm of the world might, for example, craft a thesis that reads, "The Open Boat" is a story that explores the effects of a correspondent's confinement in a small boat with three other men, all of whom must learn to be cooperative and supportive in the face of danger. The physical closeness, the fight for survival, and the eventual encounter with land encourage the correspondent to develop and foster a sense of community in a hostile world.

Outlines

While developing a strong, thoughtful thesis early in your writing process should help focus your paper, outlining provides an essential tool for logically shaping that paper. A good outline helps you see—and develop—

the relationships among the points in your argument and assures you that your paper flows logically and coherently. Outlining not only helps place your points in a logical order but also helps you subordinate supporting points, weed out any irrelevant points, and decide if there are any necessary points that are missing from your argument. Most of us are familiar with formal outlines that use numerical and letter designations for each point. However, there are different types of outlines; you may find that an informal outline is a more useful tool for you. What is important, though, is that you spend the time to develop some sort of outline—formal or informal.

Remember that an outline is a tool to help you shape and write a strong paper. If you do not spend sufficient time planning your supporting points and shaping the arrangement of those points, you will most likely construct a vague, unfocused outline that provides little, if any, help with the writing of the paper. Consider the following example of a faulty outline using the thesis from above.

"The Open Boat" is a story that explores the effects of a correspondent's confinement in a small boat with three other men, all of whom must learn to be cooperative and supportive in the face of danger. The physical closeness, the fight for survival, and the eventual encounter with land encourage the correspondent to develop and foster a sense of community in a hostile world.

    I. Introduction and thesis

   II. The correspondent
       A. Shipwrecked
       B. Alone in a dinghy with three other men
       C. Threatened by outside forces
       D. Community

  III. The oiler, one of the other three

   IV. Images of Nature
       A. The shark circling the boat

```
    V. Conclusion
        A. The correspondent learns to appreciate
           the other three men and we see this by
           observing his ideas and his cooperation
```

This outline has a number of flaws. *First,* the major topics labeled with the Roman numerals are not logical. Sections II and III refer to two of the story's four characters, not to the importance of community. Section IV refers to images of Nature, which may be relevant to the correspondent's sense of community, but these images do not logically merit a major section. *Second,* the subdivisions of section II are illogical. That section's A, B, and C all refer to specific threats that bring the men closer together, but Section D, "community," does not belong in this list. The writer could argue that community is the idea that results from the circumstances (therefore, it is the idea that results from all the threats in the situation), but it itself is not an example of a threat. *Third,* there is a problem with the inclusion of a section A without a section B in IV and V. Since the major sections are subdivisions of the thesis and the other sections are subdivisions of a section, an outline should never include an A without a B, a 1 without a 2, and so forth. *Fourth,* there is a problem with this outline in the overall lack of detail. None of the sections provide much information about the content of the argument, and it seems likely that the writer has not given sufficient thought to the content of the paper.

A better start to this outline might be the following:

```
Thesis: "The Open Boat" is a story that explores the
effects of a correspondent's confinement in a small
boat with three other men, all of whom must learn to
be cooperative and supportive in the face of danger.
The physical closeness, the fight for survival, and the
eventual encounter with land allow the correspondent
to develop and foster a sense of community in a hostile
world.

    I. Introduction and thesis

   II. The correspondent's sense of connection to the
       other men
```

    A. From their cooperation
    B. From the close physical proximity

III. The correspondent's feelings of threats
    A. From Nature as they struggle to get closer to shore
    B. From the lack of attention from other people
    C. From the eventual swamping of the boat as they near the land

IV. The correspondent's sense of connection to the larger world
    A. To the dying soldier in Algiers
    B. To the men on shore who rush to help
    C. To the larger world that needs to hear the correspondent's story

V. Conclusion

This new outline would prove much more helpful when it came time to write the paper. Notice that each Roman numeral section is a logical division of the thesis and that the lettered divisions are logical divisions of the Roman numeral sections. That logic in thought is reflected in the parallel structure of the subdivisions.

An outline like this could be shaped into an even more useful tool if the writer fleshed out the argument by providing specific examples from the text to support each point. Once you have listed your main point and your supporting ideas, develop this raw material by listing related supporting ideas and material under each of those main headings. From there, arrange the material in subsections and order the material logically.

For example, you might begin with another of the theses cited above: In *The Red Badge of Courage*, the young soldiers all want to be brave in battle, but the protagonist himself runs from the first skirmish. The novel ultimately argues that courage relies not on specific actions but on putting others' welfare above one's own. As noted above, this thesis already gives you the beginning of an organization: Start by supporting the notion that all the characters long to be seen as brave in battle and then explain how Crane presents this longing specifically through Henry's characterization and actions. You might begin your outline, then, with four topic headings: (1) Henry's early romantic notion of courage in warfare, (2) Henry's concern with courage and cowardice of the other young recruits, (3) Henry's display of his "red badge," and (4) Henry's actual courage in the final skirmish. Under each of those headings you could list ideas that support the particular point. Be sure to include references to parts of the text that help build your case.

An informal outline might look like this:

Thesis: In *The Red Badge of Courage*, the young soldiers all want to be brave in battle, but the protagonist himself runs from the first skirmish. The novel ultimately argues that courage relies not on specific actions but on putting others' welfare above one's own.

Introduction:
- Common idea of courage under fire or during battle
- Universal desire to be seen as brave common to all the recruits
- Thesis

1. Henry's early romantic notions of courage in warfare
   - Dreams of a Greek battle
     - Wants his mother to see his heroism
       - Disappointed that his mother is not impressed with his enlistment
       - Unhappy that she doesn't say anything about his returning with his shield or on it
     - Wants her to be proud of his part in the war

- Unhappy that she points out his small part in the whole war
- Annoyed that she worries about mundane issues such as clothing and food
- Unconcerned with her emphasis on the responsibility of doing what's right
  - Displays his new uniform as representation of courage
    - To his school mates
    - To crowds along the train journey to Washington

2. Henry's concern with the courage and/or cowardice of the other young recruits
   - Jim, the tall soldier
     - The seemingly courageous leader of the young recruits
     - The predictor of battle long before it occurs
     - The one killed in spite of seeming the most courageous of all
   - Wilson, the loud soldier
     - Who gives Henry a letter to be sent to his parents because he is afraid he will die
     - Who somewhat ashamedly asks for the letter back after the first skirmish
     - Who becomes concerned with taking care of Henry's wound

3. Henry's display of his "red badge"
   - Longs for a wound, a mark of his own courage
     - Needs an excuse for running away from his regiment

- ○ Sees that most other men retreating are wounded
- ○ Dreads going back to his own regiment
  - ■ Grabs another retreater to ask what has happened
  - ■ Encounters the tattered soldier, who tries to befriend him
    - ✧ Is mean to the tattered soldier who sympathizes with him
    - ✧ Abandons the tattered solder who is badly wounded and needs help
- Salvages his reputation by allowing Wilson to assume he has been shot in battle
  - ○ Wilson treats him like a hero
  - ○ Henry allows Wilson to take care of him
- Continues to be haunted by memories of abandoning the tattered soldier

4. Henry's display of true courage in the last battle of the book
   - Overhears the general and another officer discussing the fact that they will send their most expendable regiment into a battle they are convinced is not winnable: "They fight like a lot'a mule-drivers. I can spare them best of any" (Crane 101).
   - Goes into that battle willingly even though he knows the chances of being killed are great
   - Puts himself in the way of great harm by getting and carrying the regiment's flag after the color bearer is killed

Conclusion:
   - Final scene suggests Henry is truly courageous as he both achieves the appearance

of courage and risks his own safety to do
what is right for the regiment
- Novel strongly implies that courage demands
  that a person put the safety of others
  above self
- Novel also contrasts the reality of courage
  to the mere trappings of heroism

If you were asked to provide a formal outline for the above informal outline on *The Red Badge*, you would simply go back and substitute appropriate Roman numerals, letters, and numbers for the bullets and other symbols, making sure to maintain logical connections and subdivisions.

An example of a formal outline for a paper using another thesis, this time the earlier thesis about "The Open Boat," might look like this:

Thesis: "The Open Boat" is a story that explores the
effects of a correspondent's confinement in a small
boat with three other men, all of whom must learn to
be cooperative with one another and supportive in the
face of danger. The physical closeness, the fight for
survival and the eventual encounter with land allow
the correspondent to develop and foster a sense of
community in a hostile world.

   I. Introduction and thesis

  II. The correspondent's sense of connection to the
      men in the boat with him
      A. From the cooperation among the men
         1. The captain's continuing words of
           care
         2. The oiler's sharing of the rowing
           duties
         3. The cook's bailing out the water in
           the boat
      B. From the close physical proximity

III. The correspondent's feelings of threats from outside the boat
    A. Nature
        1. From the waves that threaten to swamp the boat
        2. From the shark that encircles the boat
    B. The tourists on land who are seemingly indifferent, simply waving at the shipwrecked men
    C. The landing itself
        1. Danger from the waves
        2. Danger of being hit by the boat
        3. Danger from fatigue

IV. The correspondent's sense of connection to the larger world
    A. To the dying soldier in Algiers
    B. To the men on shore who rush to help
    C. To the people in the larger world who need to hear the correspondent's story

V. Conclusion

As in the previous example outline, the thesis provided the seeds of a structure, and the writer was careful to arrange the supporting points in a logical manner, showing the relationships among the ideas in the paper.

Body Paragraphs

Once your outline is complete, you can begin drafting your paper. Paragraphs, units of related sentences, are the building blocks of a good paper, and as you draft you should keep in mind both the function and the qualities of good paragraphs. Paragraphs help you chart and control the shape and content of your essay, and they help the reader see your organization and your logic. You should begin a new paragraph whenever you move from one major point to another. In longer, more complex essays you might use a group of related paragraphs to support major points. Remember that in addition to being adequately developed, a good paragraph is both unified and coherent.

Unified Paragraphs

Each paragraph must be centered on one idea or point, and a unified paragraph carefully focuses on and develops this central idea without including extraneous ideas or tangents. For beginning writers, the best way to ensure that you are constructing unified paragraphs is to include a topic sentence in each paragraph. This topic sentence should convey the main point of the paragraph, and every sentence in the paragraph should relate to that topic sentence. Any sentence that strays from the central topic does not belong in the paragraph and needs to be revised or deleted. Consider the following paragraph about Henry's display of his fake "badge of courage" in *The Red Badge of Courage*. Notice how the paragraph veers away from the main point that the wound is a source of both pride and shame.

> After running from battle, Henry sees the many wounded and dead around him, and he wishes that he, too, had a wound, a badge of courage. Later he is wounded and that injury becomes a source of both pride and shame. Henry encounters the tattered soldier who is mortally wounded. The tattered man talks about Tom Jamison, his next-door neighbor at home, who had seen him shot. He talks about his children and how they are fun to play with. Because he believes Henry is wounded also, the man wants to help him. Henry responds by telling him not to bother him. Later Henry encounters a cheery soldier. The cheery soldier talks about Jack, a sergeant in his own unit who was killed that day. After the cheery soldier leads him back to his regiment, Henry sees that Wilson has survived the fight. Wilson has not been wounded, and he helps to take care of Henry's wound.

Although the paragraph begins solidly, and the second sentence provides the central idea of the paragraph, the author soon goes on a tangent. If the purpose of the paragraph is to demonstrate that Henry's superficial, accidental wound is the source of both pride and shame, the sentences about the tattered soldier and his next-door neighbor and children, about the cheery soldier and Jack, and about Wilson's lack of a wound are tangential here. They may find a place later in the paper, but they should be deleted from this paragraph.

Coherent Paragraphs

In addition to shaping unified paragraphs, you must also craft coherent paragraphs, paragraphs that develop their points logically with sentences that flow smoothly into one another. Coherence depends on the order of your sentences, but it is not strictly the order of the sentences that is important to paragraph coherence. You also need to craft your prose to help the reader see the relationship among the sentences.

Consider the following paragraph about the function of the "red badge," or wound, as a symbol of courage and shame in the novel. Notice how the writer uses the same ideas as the paragraph above yet fails to help the reader see the relationships among the points.

Henry's display of his "badge of courage" becomes finally a symbol of shame for him. Henry is happy to have an excuse for running away from his regiment. As he is fleeing, he encounters the tattered man, an older soldier whose wound will undoubtedly prove to be fatal. The tattered soldier is disoriented and hurting. He sympathizes with Henry and tries to help him. Henry is cruel to the badly wounded man. He will not accept the man's sympathy. Henry tells him twice not to bother him. He abandons the dying man, whom he could have tried to help. Henry walks away, leaving the man to die. Henry himself is wounded. He can pretend to be a victim of enemy fire. He allows the formerly loud soldier, Wilson, to treat him like an injured hero. Wilson dresses Henry's wound and lovingly cares for his friend. Henry continues to remember the tattered soldier, who was dying on the battlefield.

This paragraph demonstrates that unity alone does not guarantee paragraph effectiveness. The argument is hard to follow because the author fails both to show connections between the sentences and to indicate how they work to support the overall point.

A number of techniques are available to aid paragraph coherence. Careful use of transitional words and phrases is essential. You can use transitional flags to introduce an example or an illustration (*for example, for instance*), to amplify a point or add another phase of the same idea (*additionally, furthermore, next, similarly, finally, then*), to indicate a conclusion or result (*therefore, as a result, thus, in other words*), to signal a contrast or a qualification (*on the other hand, nevertheless, despite this, on the contrary, still, however, conversely*), to signal a comparison (*likewise, in comparison, similarly*), and to indicate a movement in time (*afterward, earlier, eventually, finally, later, subsequently, until*).

In addition to transitional flags, careful use of pronouns can aid coherence and flow. If you were writing about *The Wizard of Oz,* you would not want to keep repeating the phrase *the witch* or the name *Dorothy*. Careful substitution of the pronoun *she* in these instances can aid coherence. A word of warning, though: When you substitute pronouns for proper names, always be sure that your pronoun reference is clear. In a paragraph that discusses both Dorothy and the witch, substituting *she* could lead to confusion. Make sure that it is clear to whom the pronoun refers. Generally, the pronoun refers to the last proper noun you have used.

While repeating the same name over and over again can lead to awkward, boring prose, it is possible to use repetition to give your paragraph more coherence. Careful repetition of important words or phrases can lend coherence to your paragraph by reminding readers of your key points. Admittedly, it takes some practice to use this technique effectively. You may find that reading your prose aloud can help you develop an ear for effective use of repetition.

To see how helpful transitional aids are, compare the paragraph below to the preceding paragraph about the wound as a fake badge of courage. Notice how the author works with the same ideas and quotations but shapes them into a much more coherent paragraph whose point is clearer and easier to follow.

The later opportunity to display this "badge of courage" seems to be a way out of his predicament for Henry; however, it also becomes a source of shame for him. During his earlier flight from battle, he had encountered the tattered man, an older soldier whose wound will undoubtedly prove to be fatal. Even as the tattered soldier is disoriented and hurting, he sympathizes with the youth and tries to help him, although Henry at that point has no wound at all. Concerned that he will be seen as a coward if the tattered soldier learns that he is retreating for no reason, the young recruit is cruel to the badly wounded man, ignoring the man's sympathy and telling him twice not to bother him. Henry then abandons the dying soldier, whom he could have helped. Later when the youth sees the rest of the regiment running in defeat and tries to ask why they are retreating, a man whose arm he has grasped breaks free from his grip, swinging his rifle fiercely and knocking Henry to the ground. The young soldier then has a wound, but not one resulting from courage or fighting. Soon after, another soldier, one with a cheery voice, generously leads Henry back to his regiment, where the youth fears derision for his earlier flight from battle. Upon seeing Henry, however, Wilson attributes his friend's head wound to enemy fire and welcomes him. Relieved at the opportunity to avoid ridicule, Henry allows the formerly loud soldier, Wilson, to treat him as an injured hero. Wilson sees Henry's bloody head wound as a badge of courage: "Yer a good un, Henry. Most 'a men would a' been in th' hospital long ago. A shot in th' head ain't foolin' business" (Crane 79). As Wilson dresses the youth's wound and lovingly cares for him, Henry is still haunted by memories of abandoning the tattered soldier, whom he could have aided.

Similarly, the following paragraph from a paper on the cooperation of the four men in "The Open Boat" demonstrates both unity and coherence. In it, the author argues that Crane details the teamwork of the men to point to their sense of community in a hostile world.

> In "The Open Boat" Stephen Crane tells the story of four shipwrecked men in a small dinghy. The men work as a team as they fight to remain afloat and to get closer to shore. The injured captain gives directions and continues to assure the others that they will soon get to land, the cook bails water out of the boat, and the oiler and correspondent take turns rowing the small craft. As the men use their individual strengths to achieve safety, they feel warmed by the companionship of one another. The narrator points out the feeling of community by stating, "It would be difficult to describe the subtle brotherhood of men that was here established on the seas" (Crane 73). Although the men themselves never discuss their relationship, the correspondent thinks to himself at the time that it is "the best experience of his life" (73). The three men seal their friendship with a ritual of smoking, brought about by the correspondent's discovery that he has four dry cigars among the eight in his top coat pocket. After somebody else is able to find three dry matches, they puff contentedly and share the small amount of fresh water available. This ritualistic bonding brings the men even closer together in spirit.

Introductions

Introductions present particular challenges for writers. Generally, your introduction should do two things: capture your reader's attention and explain the main point of your essay. In other words, while your introduction should contain your thesis, it needs to do a bit more work than that. You are likely to find that starting that first paragraph is one of the most difficult parts of the paper. It is hard to face that blank page or screen, and as a result, many beginning writers, in desperation to start somewhere, start with overly broad, general statements. While it is often a good strategy to start with more general subject matter and then narrow your focus, do not begin with broad, sweeping statements such as "Everyone likes to be creative and feel understood." Such sentences are nothing but empty filler. They begin to fill the blank page, but they do nothing to advance your argument. Instead, you should try to gain your readers' interest. Some writers like to begin with a pertinent quotation or with a relevant question. Or, you might begin with an introduction of the topic you will discuss. If you are writing about Crane's presentation of the sense of community in "The Open Boat," for instance, you might begin by talking about how community is important even in a diverse population. Another common trap to avoid is depending on your title to introduce the author and the text you are writing about. *Always* include the work's author and title in your opening paragraph.

Compare the effectiveness of the following introductions.

1)

Throughout history, people have hated being without friends. Think how you feel when you are in a difficult situation with people you do not know: It makes you seem very alone, doesn't it? No one likes to think she has no friends. In this story, Crane shows the correspondent's growing sense of community by focusing on his thoughts, actions, and even cigars.

2)

Psychologists are well aware that companionship is an integral part of a healthy existence: Some studies have even revealed that babies who are deprived of human touch and caring do not thrive but eventually die. Human companionship is essential for a source of pleasure when we want to celebrate or a sense of well-being when we are in danger. Diverse people come together to celebrate weddings and birthdays, to mourn for a deceased loved one, or to aid victims of natural disasters, as each individual retains his separate identity. As Carl Jung has observed, a meaningful companionship thrives only when the individual does not lose his individuality to others. In "The Open Boat," Stephen Crane demonstrates the power of human

companionship for four very different individuals in the
face of immense danger. Crane shows the correspondent's
growing sense of community by focusing on his thoughts,
his actions, and even his ritual of sharing cigars with
the captain, the cook, and the oiler.

You should note that the first introduction begins with a vague, overly broad sentence; cites unclear, undeveloped examples; and then moves abruptly to the thesis. Notice, too, how a reader deprived of the paper's title does not know the title of the story that the paper will analyze. The second introduction works with the same material and thesis but provides more detail and is consequently much more interesting. It begins by discussing psychological understandings of the need for companionship, gives specific examples, and then speaks briefly about one psychologist's philosophy of the importance of human companionship. The paragraph ends with the thesis, which includes both the author and the title of the work to be discussed.

The paragraph below provides another example of an opening strategy. It begins by introducing the author and the text it will analyze, and then it moves on by briefly introducing relevant details of the story in order to set up its thesis.

When the four shipwrecked men in Stephen Crane's
story "The Open Boat" find themselves together in a
small dinghy, they have little in common. The ship's
captain, the cook, the oiler, and a news reporter, or
correspondent, huddle closely in the lifeboat, fighting
for survival as they are threatened by the waves, by the
shark encircling the boat, and by their growing fatigue
and hunger. In spite of having little in common with the
other men, the correspondent, from whose point of view
the story is told, soon views them as his own community.
As the risks become greater, the correspondent, who at
one point rows as the others sleep, notes that they are
even physically entwined. The feet of the three men are
touching, and the cook has his arm around the oiler's
shoulder, evoking an image of "babes of the sea" (Crane
83). This closeness reassures the correspondent, until a

shark circling the small dinghy heightens his fear and makes him long for his companions to be awake with him. Ultimately "The Open Boat" reveals the importance of community in a world filled with uncertainty. This story explores the effects of a correspondent's confinement in a small boat with three other men, all of whom must learn to be cooperative and supportive in the face of danger. The physical closeness, the fight for survival, and the eventual violent encounter with land encourage the correspondent to develop and foster a sense of community in a hostile world.

Conclusions

Conclusions present another series of challenges for writers. No doubt you have heard the adage about writing papers: "Tell us what you are going to say, say it, and then tell us what you've said." While this formula does not necessarily result in bad papers, it does not often result in good ones, either. It will almost certainly result in boring papers (especially boring conclusions). If you have done a good job establishing your points in the body of the paper, the reader already knows and understands your argument. Since there is no need to merely reiterate, do not just summarize your main points in your conclusion. Such a boring and mechanical conclusion does nothing to advance your argument or interest your reader. Consider the following ineffective conclusion to the paper about community in "The Open Boat."

In conclusion, Crane presents community as the only answer to life in a hostile universe. The correspondent realizes how much he wants the companionship of the other three men. His concern for the dead oiler at the end of the story indicates that, even when we are part of a community, we cannot always save others. I guess that is true for all of us.

Besides starting with a mechanical transitional device, this conclusion does little more than summarize the main points of the outline (and it does not even touch on all of them). It is incomplete and uninteresting (and a little too depressing).

Instead, your conclusion should add something to your paper. A good tactic is to build upon the points you have been arguing. Asking "why?" often helps you draw further conclusions. For example, in the paper on "The Open Boat," you might question how the correspondent's empathy speaks to what Crane is presenting as a human desire for true connections with other people. Scholars often discuss this story as a study of man in a hostile world, and your conclusion could discuss whether the story presents that hostility as the major point of the story. Another method for successfully concluding a paper is to speculate on other directions in which to take your topic by tying it into larger issues. You might do this by envisioning your paper as just one section of a larger paper. Having established your points in this paper, how would you build upon this argument? Where would you go next? In the following conclusion to the paper on "The Open Boat," the author reiterates some of the main points of the paper but does so in order to amplify the discussion of the story's central message and to connect it to other texts by Stephen Crane:

> In the end, the shipwrecked men are joined by the greater community on land, with a man on the beach stripping off his clothing and running to rescue them. As this rescuer is pulling the correspondent to shore, the oiler surfaces nearby with his face down in the shallows. The correspondent insists that his rescuer leave him to fend for himself and that he go help the oiler instead. In the end, the oiler still does not live, a result of the uncaring force of nature, which is described as "flatly indifferent" (Crane 88). Although this story emphasizes a hostile and unselective environment, it presents human fellowship and caring for one another as the solution to the human condition. Instead of questioning why he has been put at risk, the correspondent has learned empathy for his fellow man, and he is now in a position to spread that sense of community to the rest of mankind. Stephen Crane himself, the real-life counterpart of the correspondent, has written in numerous other works of the importance of community, beginning with the lack of

cooperative spirit in *Maggie: A Girl of the Streets* and the productive use of community during battle in *The Red Badge of Courage*. It is significant that at the end of "The Open Boat" the experience will allow the survivors to explain this importance of community to others: "they felt that they could then be interpreters" (Crane 93). As a correspondent, fiction writer, and poet, Crane continued to depict community, or the lack thereof, in other works following "The Open Boat," which deals most explicitly with the significance of human fellowship.

Similarly, in the following conclusion to a paper on courage in *The Red Badge of Courage,* the author draws a conclusion about what the novel has to say about friendship, or community, in a broader sense.

The final scene shows Henry as truly courageous when he both achieves the appearance of courage and risks his own safety to do what is right for his regiment. John J. McDermott states that "the fundamental thrust of his character has been set: he has discovered and developed within himself a capacity for a detached spirit of self sacrifice based on an imperfect but nonetheless profound self-knowledge" (331). Henry feels proud, and he tells himself that he has become a man, that he has approached the great death and has survived. Still a brief memory of the tattered man nags at his conscience, reminding the reader that Henry's mother had been more perceptive than Henry when she had told him that he was just a little part of the whole army and had urged him to do what is right at all times. Henry now sees his abandonment of the tattered soldier as a "sin," and in the end of the last chapter, he is still trying to deal with his action: "Yet gradually he mustered force to put the sin at a distance" (Crane 135). The novel then strongly implies that true courage requires that a person put the safety of others above the concern for

self. Ultimately, *The Red Badge of Courage* argues that
the appearance of courage can be superficial and that
the reality of courage demands unselfish action even
at the expense of personal safety.

Citations and Formatting

Using Primary Sources

As the examples included in this chapter indicate, strong papers on literary texts incorporate quotations from the text in order to support their points. It is not enough for you to assert your interpretation without providing support or evidence from the text. Without well-chosen quotations to support your argument, you are, in effect, saying to the reader, "Take my word for it." It is important to use quotations thoughtfully and selectively. Remember that the paper presents *your* argument, so choose quotations that support *your* assertions. Do not let the author's voice overwhelm your own. With that caution in mind, there are some guidelines you should follow to ensure that you use quotations clearly and effectively.

Integrate Quotations:

Quotations should always be integrated into your own prose. Do not just drop them into your paper without introduction or comment. Otherwise, it is unlikely that your reader will see their function. You can integrate textual support easily and clearly with identifying tags, short phrases that identify the speaker. For example:

> The narrator describes the men in the dinghy as "weirdly picturesque" if viewed from above at a distance.

While this tag appears before the quotation, you can also use tags after or in the middle of the quoted text, as the following examples demonstrate:

> "None of them knew the colour of the sky," states the narrator at the beginning of the story.

> "Funny," say the men several times, "they don't see us."

You can also use a colon to formally introduce a quotation:

> The sense of community is emphasized: "It would be
> difficult to describe the subtle brotherhood of men
> that was here established on the seas."

When you quote brief sections of poems (three lines or fewer), use slash marks to indicate the line breaks in the poem:

> As the poem about a truthful tongue ends, Crane explores
> the difficulty of relaying truth: "It will make no
> melody at will / But is dead in my mouth."

Longer quotations (more than four lines of prose or three lines of poetry) should be set off from the rest of your paper in a block quotation. Double-space before you begin the passage, indent it ten spaces from your left-hand margin, and double-space the passage itself. Because the indentation signals the inclusion of a quotation, do not use quotation marks around the cited passage. Use a colon to introduce the passage:

> The narrator implies the impossibility of ever being
> prepared for disasters such as shipwrecks:
>
>> Shipwrecks are apropos of nothing. If men could
>> only train for them and have them occur when
>> the men had reached pink condition, there would
>> be less drowning at sea. Of the four in the
>> dinghy none had slept any time worth mentioning
>> for two days and two nights previous to embarking
>> in the dinghy, and in the excitement of clambering
>> about the deck of a foundering ship they had also
>> forgotten to eat heartily.
>
> By now, the reader knows the men have not only the
> forces of the sea against them but also their own
> bodies weakened by lack of sleep and food.

The whole of Crane's poem speaks of relaying truth:

> Yes, I have a thousand tongues,
> And nine and ninety-nine lie.
> Though I strive to use the one,
> It will make no melody at will,
> But is dead in my mouth.

Clearly, he argues for the writer to strive to represent the truth even though such a representation proves virtually impossible.

After you introduce and use a quotation, it is also important to interpret it and explain how it helps to advance your point. You cannot assume that your reader will interpret the quotation the same way that you do.

Quote Accurately:

Always quote accurately. Anything within quotations marks must be the author's exact words. There are, however, some rules to follow if you need to modify the quotation to fit into the sentence structure of your prose.

1. Use brackets to indicate any material that might have been added to the author's exact wording. For example, if you need to add any words to the quotation or alter it grammatically to allow it to fit into your prose, indicate your changes in brackets:

   > Keeping the boat from swamping is difficult for the oiler and the correspondent who take turns rowing during the long night. The correspondent "wonder[s] ingenuously how in the name of all that [is] sane could there be people who [think] it amusing to row a boat."

2. Conversely, if you choose to omit any words from the quotation, use ellipses (three spaced periods) to indicate missing words or phrases:

> The men crowded in the small dinghy are tossed
> about by the rough waves: "A seat in . . .
> [the] boat was not unlike a seat on a bucking
> bronco, and by the same token a bronco is not
> much smaller."

3. If you delete a sentence or more, use the ellipses after a period:

> The narrator describes the dinghy seen from
> a distant point of view: "As the boat bounced
> from the top of each wave the wind tore through
> the hair of the hatless men, and as the craft
> plopped her stern down again the spray slashed
> past them. . . . It was probably splendid, it
> was probably glorious, this play of the free
> sea, wild with lights of emerald and white and
> amber.

4. If you omit a line or more of poetry, or more than one paragraph of prose, use a single line of spaced periods to indicate
   the omission:

> Yes, I have a thousand tongues,
> . . . .
> Though I strive to use the one,
> It will make no melody at will,
> But is dead in my mouth.

Punctuate Properly

Punctuation of quotations often causes more trouble than it should.
Once again, you just need to keep these simple rules in mind.

1. Periods and commas should be placed inside quotation marks,
   even if they are not part of the original quotation:

> Cooperation during the long night is clear in
> the division of duties: "The plan of the oiler

and the correspondent was for one to row until
he lost the ability, and then arouse the other."

The only exception to this rule is when the quotation is
followed by a parenthetical reference. In this case, the period
or comma goes after the citation (more on these later in this
chapter):

Cooperation during the long night is clear in
the division of duties: "The plan of the oiler
and the correspondent was for one to row until
he lost the ability, and then arouse the other"
(82).

2. Other marks of punctuation—colons, semicolons, question
marks, and exclamation points—go outside the quotation
marks unless they are part of the original quotation:

Why does the correspondent feel empathy for
"the soldier of the Legion who lay dying in
Algiers"?

The correspondent interrogates the captain, who
has seemed to be asleep: "Did you see that shark
playing around?"

Documenting Primary Sources

Unless you are instructed otherwise, you should provide sufficient information for your reader to locate material you quote. Generally, literature
papers follow the rules set forth by the Modern Language Association
(MLA). These can be found in the *MLA Handbook for Writers of Research
Papers* (7th edition). You should be able to find this book in the reference
section of your library. Additionally, its rules for citing both primary and
secondary sources are widely available from reputable online sources.
One of these is the Online Writing Lab (OWL) at Purdue University.
OWL's guide to MLA style is available at http://owl.english.purdue.edu/
owl/resource/557/01/. The Modern Language Association also offers

answers to frequently asked questions about MLA style on this helpful Web page: http://www.mla.org/style_faq. Generally, when you are citing from literary works in papers, you should keep a few guidelines in mind.

Parenthetical Citations:

MLA asks for parenthetical references in your text after quotations. When you are working with prose (short stories, novels, or essays) include page numbers in the parentheses:

> Cooperation during the long night is clear in the division of duties: "The plan of the oiler and the correspondent was for one to row until he lost the ability, and then arouse the other" (82).

When you are quoting poetry, include line numbers:

> Crane's speaker tells of the emotional cost of writing: "It was strange / To write in this red muck / Of things from my heart" (3-5).

Works Cited Page:

These parenthetical citations are linked to a separate works cited page at the end of the paper. The works cited page lists works alphabetically by the authors' last name. An entry for the above reference to Crane's "The Open Boat" would read:

> Crane, Stephen. "The Open Boat." *The Works of Stephen Crane: Tales of Adventure.* Ed. Fredson Bowers. Vol. 5. Charlottesville: UP of Virginia, 1970. 68-92.

The *MLA Handbook* includes a full listing of sample entries, as do many of the online explanations of MLA style.

Documenting Secondary Sources

To ensure that your paper is built entirely upon your own ideas and analysis, instructors often ask that you write interpretative papers without any outside research. If, on the other hand, your paper requires research, you must document any secondary sources you use. You need to document direct quotations, summaries or paraphrases of others' ideas, and factual information that is not common knowledge. When you use direct quotations from secondary sources, follow the guidelines above for quoting primary sources. Keep in mind that MLA style also includes specific guidelines for citing electronic sources. OWL's Web site provides a good summary: http://owl.english.purdue.edu/owl/resource/557/09/.

Parenthetical Citations:

As with the documentation of primary sources, described above, MLA guidelines require in-text parenthetical references to your secondary sources. Unlike the research papers you might write for a history class, literary research papers following MLA style do not use footnotes as a means of documenting sources. Instead, after a quotation, you should cite the author's last name and the page number:

> "The manuscript of 'The Open Boat' has not survived" (Jackson 78).

If you include the name of the author in your prose, then you would include only the page number in your citation. For example:

> David H. Jackson points out, "Although the passage in 'The Open Boat' in which four lines of verse 'mysteriously' enter the correspondent's head is widely considered to have central thematic importance, the textual questions raised by these misquoted lines from Carolyn Norton's 'Bingen on the Rhine' have never received adequate answers" (77).

If you are including more than one work by the same author, the parenthetical citation should include a shortened yet identifiable version of the title in order to indicate which of the author's works you cite. For example:

> William Randel tells of the real life ship on which Crane was shipwrecked: "On December 31, 1896, the

filibuster *Commodore* left Jacksonville with a cargo of
guns and ammunition for the insurgent army in Cuba"
("The Cook" 405).

Similarly, and just as important, if you summarize or paraphrase the
particular ideas of your source, you must provide documentation:

The *Commodore*, the actual ship that inspired Crane's
story "The Open Boat," was carrying guns and ammunition
to the insurgent army in Cuba (Randel, "The Cook" 405).

Works Cited Page:

Like the primary sources discussed above, the parenthetical references
to secondary sources are keyed to a separate works cited page at the end
of your paper. Here is an example of a works cited page that uses the
examples cited above. Note that when two or more works by the same
author are listed, you should use three hyphens followed by a period in
the subsequent entries. You can find a complete list of sample entries in
the *MLA Handbook* or from a reputable online summary of MLA style.

WORKS CITED

Jackson, David H. "Textual Questions Raised by Crane's
    'Soldier of the Legion.'" *American Literature* 55.1
    (1983): 77–80.
Randel, William. "The Cook in 'The Open Boat.'" *American
    Literature* 34.3 (1962): 405–11.
———. "From Slate to Emerald Green: More Light on Crane's
    Jacksonville Visit." *Nineteenth Century Fiction* 19.4
    (1965): 357–68.
Shulman, Robert. "Community, Perception, and the
    Development of Stephen Crane: From *The Red Badge*
    to 'The Open Boat.'" *American Literature* 50.3 (1978):
    441–60.

Plagiarism

Failure to document carefully and thoroughly can leave you open to
charges of stealing the ideas of others, which is known as plagiarism—a

very serious matter. Remember that it is important to include quotation marks when you use language from your source, even if you use just a few words. For example, if you wrote, The correspondent's misquoted lines from Carolyn Norton's 'Bingen on the Rhine' make the reader wonder about Crane's use of this poem, you would be guilty of plagiarism, since you used Jackson's distinct language without acknowledging him as the source. Instead, you should write: The correspondent's "misquoted lines from Carolyn Norton's 'Bingen on the Rhine'" make the reader wonder about Crane's use of this poem (Jackson 77). In this case, you have properly credited Jackson.

Similarly, neither summarizing the ideas of an author nor changing or omitting just a few words means that you can omit a citation. Robert Shulman's article on the theme of community in Crane's work contains the following passage about "The Open Boat":

> Crane waits until he has convincingly established the situation of the men in the open boat and then he has this recognition emerge from a representative context. In their exposed situation the men achieve a community that is their main resource against the natural forces and intellectual barriers that threaten them. Crane fully develops the correspondent's recognition and makes it a formal and philosophical organizing center for the story.

Below are two examples of plagiarism using the above passage:

> Crane shows the closeness of the men in the dinghy. Then he shows the correspondent recognizing how important community is in their fight against nature and their own prejudices. This idea of community is the organizing principle of the story.

> In "The Open Boat" Stephen Crane first establishes the situation of the men in the dinghy and then they

achieve a community. He develops the correspondent's recognition of that community and makes it a formal and philosophical organizing center of the story (Shulman 458).

While the first passage does not use Shulman's exact language, it does list the same ideas he proposes as the critical theme and the organizing force of the story without citing his work. Since this interpretation is Shulman's distinct idea, this use constitutes plagiarism. The second passage has shortened Shulman's passage, changed some wording, and included a citation, but some of the phrasing is his. The first passage could be fixed with a parenthetical citation. Because some of the wording in the second remains the same, though, it would require the use of quotation marks, in addition to a parenthetical citation. The passage below represents an honestly and adequately documented use of the original passage:

According to Robert Shulman, in "The Open Boat" Stephen Crane first establishes "the situation of the men in the open boat" and then shows how they achieve a community (458). He "develops the correspondent's recognition [of that community] and makes it a formal and philosophical organizing center of the story" (458).

This passage acknowledges that the interpretation is derived from Shulman while appropriately using quotations to indicate his precise language.

While it is not necessary to document well known facts, often referred to as common knowledge, any ideas or language that you take from someone else must be properly documented. Common knowledge generally includes the birth and death dates of authors or other well-documented facts of their lives. An often-cited guideline is that if you can find the information in three sources, it is common knowledge. Despite this guideline, it is often difficult to know if the facts you uncover are common knowledge or not. When in doubt, document your source.

Sample Essay

Gale Riley
Mr. Johnston
English II
February 5, 2011

MORE THAN A UNIFORM OR A WOUND:
DEPICTIONS OF HEROISM IN *THE RED BADGE OF COURAGE*:

Without ever having witnessed war himself, Stephen Crane wrote *The Red Badge of Courage* in 1895, three decades after the Civil War. This novel follows an enlistee, Henry Fleming, through only two days of battle. Although the site is never named, Lee Clark Mitchell asserts that "most certainly, the battle fought by Henry Fleming's New York regiment occurred on May 1 and 2, 1863, at Chancellorsville, Virginia" (16). Eager to prove his heroism, the young Union soldier soon confronts the reality of war as opposed to the romantic notions he has developed from hearing tales told by veterans and from reading heroic epics. In this novel, the untried soldiers all want to appear brave in battle, but the protagonist soon finds himself running from the first skirmish. The novel ultimately argues that courage relies not on specific actions but on putting others' welfare above one's own.

During a flashback in the first chapter, Crane reveals Henry's romantic notion of war as he recounts the incidence of Henry's decision to enlist. One night the boy has become excited by the ringing of church bells to announce a victorious battle, and he yearns to join the army before he is denied the chance of combat, about which he has read and fantasized: "He had read of marches, sieges, conflicts, and had longed to see it all. His busy mind had drawn for him large pictures extravagant in color, lurid with breathless deeds" (5). Henry perceives war as a glorious affair, one which will allow him to bring honor to himself, but his mother sees it differently. She first tries to discourage him from enlisting, and after he does, she scolds him. Her perception of war is quite different from her son's since she sees no glory in violence. James Nagel points out the significance of Henry's point of view: "No reading of *The Red Badge of Courage* can be complete . . . which does not deal with the significance of perception in the novel as both a methodological and thematic component" (53). Henry's viewpoint at the beginning is a romantic one, full of the desire to display his Greek-like courage to others, including his mother. To Henry's dismay, however, his mother says "nothing whatever about returning with his shield or on it" (6).

Henry's mother does not share her son's romanticized view of war or his desire for glory. His mother, in fact, deals with practical issues, such as supplying him with socks and shirts, and with what she deems more important philosophical issues, such as individual responsibility. She says, "If so be a time comes when yeh have to be kilt or do a mean thing, why, Henry, don't think of anything 'cept what's right" (7). Henry is irritated that her speech contains nothing about honor or glory but instead points out his small part in the war and his moral responsibility to do whatever is right. Her advice does not deter him, however, from seeking that coveted glory. When he gets his blue uniform, he first goes to the school to say goodbye to his classmates, and he revels in their attention, especially from one girl who has caught his eye. Later, as Henry and the other recruits ride the train from his hometown to Washington, the crowds at stations along the way make him feel like a character in one of his books: "The regiment was fed and caressed at station after station until the youth had believed that he must be a hero" (8). This sense of heroism has allowed Henry to continue to perceive war as glorious.

All the young recruits are eager to prove themselves in battle, but once the regiment gets into the field, they find the reality not glorious but boring. The waiting seems to go on forever. They find themselves with plenty of time to think about the ensuing melee, and they talk among themselves. Although Henry never voices his fears, he is afraid that he will look like a coward, and he questions his fellow soldiers. The three identified recruits—Jim Conklin, Wilson, and Henry Fleming—all talk about the idea of courage, or the opposite idea of cowardice, speculating on whether or not they might run from battle. None of them admits that possibility, but they all deal with it in different ways. Jim, often referred to as the tall soldier, philosophically replies that if everyone else stands and fights, he will probably fight also. Jim seems wise in his careful consideration. Jim also seems to be the one whom the other recruits most admire. He regales them with predictions of imminent fighting, but he is incorrect in heralding the beginning of battle, which seems to the eager recruits never to come. In spite of his seeming bravery, ironically, it is Jim who does not survive the first battle.

The second recruit, Wilson, at first called the loud soldier, will also not admit to his fear. When asked if he will do great things in battle, Wilson reports that he will probably do well:

> The loud soldier blew a thoughtful cloud of smoke from his pipe. "Oh, I don't know," he remarked with dignity. "I don't know. I s'pose I'll do as well as th' rest. I'm goin' t' try like thunder." He evidently complimented himself upon the modesty of this statement.
>
> "How do you know you won't run when the time comes?" asked the youth.

"Run?" said the loud one. "Run? Of course not." He laughed. (19)

In spite of this assertion of his own courage, later Wilson is so afraid he will die that he gives Henry a letter to send to his parents at his death: "'It's my first and last battle, old boy,' said [Wilson], with intense gloom. He was quite pale and his girlish lip was trembling" (28). Later, when Wilson comes through the fighting alive and after he has cared for Henry's wound, which he perceives as having been caused by enemy fire, he somewhat ashamedly asks for the letter back.

The third recruit of the group, Henry, who is usually called the youth, never reveals to the others his fear of running, but since the story is told from his point of view, the reader is well aware of Henry's anxieties. He fights automatically at first because he is part of a machine-like movement forward. At that point he declares to himself that he has been tried and found brave in battle. When the fighting resumes, however, the youth sees the strength of the opposing army and observes one, then two, then more of his comrades running in fear. He, too, retreats "like a proverbial chick" (41). After he does actually run, he is distraught, worrying about what others in his regiment will think of him now. As he comes upon badly wounded men, he longs for a wound himself so that he has an excuse for retreating. Later he takes advantage of a superficial injury accidently inflicted by the butt of a gun.

For Henry, this later opportunity to display his "badge of courage" seems to be a way out of his predicament; however, it also becomes a source of shame for him. During his earlier flight from battle, he had encountered the tattered man, an older soldier whose wound will undoubtedly prove to be fatal. Even as the tattered soldier is disoriented and hurting, he sympathizes with the youth and tries to help him, although Henry at that point has no wound at all. Concerned that he will be seen as a coward if the tattered soldier learns that he is retreating for no reason, the young recruit is cruel to the badly wounded man, ignoring the man's sympathy and telling him twice not to bother him. Henry then abandons the dying man, whom he could have helped. Later when the youth sees the rest of the regiment running in defeat and tries to ask why they are retreating, a man whose arm he has grasped breaks free from his grip, swinging his rifle fiercely and knocking Henry to the ground. The young soldier then has a wound, but not one resulting from courage or fighting. Soon after, another soldier, one with a cheery voice, generously leads Henry back to his regiment, where the youth fears derision for his earlier flight from battle. Upon seeing Henry, however, Wilson attributes his friend's head wound to enemy fire and welcomes him. Relieved at the opportunity to avoid ridicule, Henry allows the formerly loud soldier, Wilson, to treat him like an injured hero. Wilson sees Henry's bloody head wound as a badge of courage: "Yer a good un, Henry. Most 'a men would a' been in th' hospital long ago. A shot in th' head ain't foolin' business" (79). As Wilson dresses the youth's wound and lovingly cares for him, Henry is still haunted by memories of abandoning the tattered soldier, whom he could have aided.

At the point when Henry feels he has made his mark as a soldier, even though he knows that mark is fake, he has the opportunity to display true courage. He overhears the general and another officer discussing the fact that they will send their most expendable regiment into the next skirmish, which they already see as a lost cause: "They fight like a lot'a mule-drivers. I can spare them best of any" (101). In this situation, when Henry should be truly afraid and when his chances of survival are slim, he does not shirk his duty. Both he and Wilson go into the battle willingly, and they fight their hardest. When the regimental flag-bearer is struck down, Henry grabs the flag and risks his life by carrying it high enough to rally his own forces while making himself a more visible target for the enemy.

The final scene shows Henry as truly courageous when he both achieves the appearance of courage and risks his own safety to do what is right for his regiment. John J. McDermott states that "the fundamental thrust of his character has been set: he has discovered and developed within himself a capacity for a detached spirit of self sacrifice based on an imperfect but nonetheless profound self-knowledge" (331). Henry feels proud, and he tells himself that he has become a man, that he has approached the great death and has survived. Still a brief memory of the tattered man nags at his conscience, reminding the reader that Henry's mother had been more perceptive than Henry when she had told him that he was just a little part of the whole army and had urged him to do what is right at all times. Henry now sees his abandonment of the tattered soldier as a "sin," and in the end of the last chapter, he is still trying to deal with his earlier action: "Yet gradually he mustered force to put the sin at a distance" (135). This pronouncement strongly suggests that true courage requires a person to put the safety of others above the concern for self. Ultimately, *The Red Badge of Courage* argues that the appearance of courage can be superficial and that the reality of courage demands unselfish action even at the expense of personal safety.

WORKS CITED

Crane, Stephen. *The Works of Stephen Crane: The Red Badge of Courage.* Vol. 2. Ed. Fredson Bowers. Charlottesville: UP of Virginia, 1975.

McDermott, John J. "Symbolism and Psychological Realism in *The Red Badge of Courage*." *Nineteenth-Century Fiction* 23.3 (1968): 324–31.

Mitchell, Lee Clark. "Introduction." *New Essays on* The Red Badge of Courage. Ed. Lee Clark Mitchell. New York: Cambridge UP, 1986.

Nagel, James. *Stephen Crane and Literary Impressionism*. University Park: Pennsylvania State UP, 1980.

HOW TO WRITE ABOUT STEPHEN CRANE

Stephen Crane (November 1, 1871–June 5, 1900) enjoyed worldwide recognition during his short life of twenty-eight years, seven months, and four days. Although a few years after his death his work virtually disappeared from public recognition for some twenty years, critics were then able to revive interest, with Crane becoming an increasingly important figure in American literature. Stephen Crane was a prolific writer, producing five novels, two books of free verse, five collections of short stories, and a profusion of articles published in newspapers all over the United States and Great Britain. A rebel against the strict religious teachings of his father, a Methodist minister, and his mother, a temperance worker, Crane brought unwelcomed attention to himself by witnessing in court for Dora Clark, a prostitute in New York City. As a result of publicity in that case, Crane was never welcome again in that city, where Theodore Roosevelt was commissioner of police at the time. The negative publicity, his penchant for choosing to roam the Bowery and the less desirable areas of other cities, and his living in England with his common-law wife, who had been a proprietor of a brothel in Jacksonville, Florida, led to his reputation as a somewhat disreputable young man. When such facts came to light after his death, important men of letters such as Hamlin Garland and Joseph Conrad began to express less enthusiasm for his work.

In 1923 Thomas Beer stirred new interest in Crane's work in his biography *Stephen Crane: A Study in American Letters*, a publication that has proved to be both a blessing and a curse to Crane studies. Although the book revived interest in the rebellious, somewhat exotic writer whom Beer portrayed, it has greatly complicated writing about Crane. Anyone undertaking such a task must realize that this first biography of Crane has been proved to be fictionalized in places. In addition, any writer must realize that later biographies, such as those by John Berryman and R.W. Stallman, often incorporated what were supposedly Beer's findings, including letters that were nowhere substantiated and were probably fabricated. Although suspicions had earlier arisen about some of the facts and documents originating in Beer's book, it was not until 1990 that Stanley Wertheim and Paul Sorrentino revealed the errors in that biography in their article "Thomas Beer: The Clay Feet of Stephen Crane Biography." Unfortunately, all the work done on Crane and his art up until that time had already been corrupted by both inaccuracies and fictionalized letters and events that Beer himself had concocted and credited to Crane.

As a result of Beer's inaccuracies and fictionalization, it is most important to authenticate any biographical information that may impact writing about Crane or his work by verifying them in biographical texts written or compiled only *after* that revelation. For example, you can trust the biographical information in Wertheim and Sorrentino's books *The Correspondence of Stephen Crane* and *The Crane Log* and in Wertheim's *A Stephen Crane Encyclopedia*.

It is also important to realize that Beer was skillful in portraying Crane as an even more dashing and intriguing figure than perhaps he was. Stephen Crane in many ways reflected the values of his Methodist parents at the same time he broke rules that they had tried to impose. Crane was quite conventional in trying to protect his family from the knowledge that he and Cora had never actually married, and he went out of his way to help those in need, whether prostitutes falsely accused by the police or injured war reporters unable to file their own stories in a timely manner. At the same time he exhibited Christian ideals in his actions toward others, he did not abide by his father's admonitions that smoking, drinking, and reading novels were sinful activities to be avoided. Then, as today, the media were often responsible for the public's perception of

Crane. *The New York Times* and other newspapers were quick to report the Dora Clark affair, in which he went to court as a witness for a supposedly known prostitute, but they were equally quick to give him credit for bravery when the *Commodore,* a filibuster ship on which he was a passenger, sank in the Atlantic off the coast of Florida on its way to Cuba. To get a more accurate picture of Stephen Crane, you can read Wertheim and Sorrentino's collection of his letters and other accounts of his life by contemporaries, some of whom avoided hyperbole or distortion. Such accounts include Corwin Knapp Linson's remembrance in *My Stephen Crane* and other writings about Crane during and shortly after his own lifetime and now collected in Joyce Caldwell Smith and Harold Bloom's *Stephen Crane,* part of the series Bloom's Classic Critical Views.

A second problem in writing about Stephen Crane's works is a function of his particular type of writing; literary realism required that the narrator not intrude into the narrative, so the author includes no direct statements of judgment of his characters or their actions. For a better understanding of realism, you can find William Dean Howells's *Criticism and Fiction* (1891) at several online sources, including Open Book. Since the techniques of literary realism prevented Crane from using a narrator who tells the reader what to think or how to judge the content, sometimes it is easy to believe that Crane is the actual narrator of the text and that the text should be taken quite literally. Instead, Crane as the author uses other methods to allow the reader to form his or her own opinion about the characters and the events in the works. The reader must be on the lookout for such clues, especially uses of irony, for Crane's narrative voice is most often ironic. Seldom should his words be taken literally. Instead, a close reading is necessary to ascertain the tone of the work, as revealed in the author's choice of details or images.

Although Stephen Crane admired and agreed with Howells's definition of realism, Crane's style of realism differs from that practiced by Howells, his literary mentor and the man considered widely to be the "Dean of American Letters" at that time. In his own writing, Crane went beyond the techniques that Howells advocated, with his own techniques coming close to those of what would later be called modernism. To understand his advances beyond the typical realism of his age, you can read John Fagg's *On the Cusp: Stephen Crane, George Bellows, and Modernism.* Crane's work incorporates impressionist techniques and significant patterns of imagery, with the scenes often presented in an almost staccato sequence and including an accumulation of vivid details, much as scenes might be shown in a movie. As you are reading, you might imagine how you would see the characters and actions on a movie screen. In the movies, the hard work is done for you, but when you read, you must visualize for yourself. Crane's imagery lends itself readily to such visualization, and such a technique can help you to understand how he evokes emotions and presents tone. James Nagel's *Stephen Crane and Literary Impressionism* can give you some insight into the impressionistic nature of Crane's writing.

If you will keep these two problems in mind—the corruption of Crane's biography and the lack of direct narrative judgment in his works—you will soon learn to analyze Stephen Crane's work. Since much literary criticism has already been written about Crane's fiction and poetry, you should familiarize yourself with some of the works listed at the end of the chapter to see what others have already discovered. You should then, however, formulate your own argument about his writing. As you are reading a novel, a short story, or a poem closely and working to answer some of the questions posed throughout this book, you will make discoveries on your own that can be as valid as those of other critics. Never underestimate your own critical powers or tell yourself that everything has already been written. New essays appear constantly on writers who have been studied for much longer than Crane—Shakespeare, for example—and with a little investigation and inquiry you can present your own way to look at some aspect of Crane's writing. The key is to know as much as possible about what has been done and then to read the primary source, that is, Crane's own writing, as closely as possible.

Once you have read closely, formulated questions, and focused on one specific question, then you are ready to organize your evidence from the primary work, whichever Crane piece or pieces you have chosen, and to draft your own essay. You may then wonder what to do with the information you have gathered from your secondary sources. Most academic scholars cite in their introductory paragraphs any information that relevant sources have already presented on a given topic, and then they tell how their study builds on these previous ideas and how it differs from those earlier studies. Beware of putting your paper together by using too many quotes from secondary critical sources. Instead, formulate your own argument, showing how it differs, and then support it with significant details and quotes from the primary text.

READING TO WRITE TOPICS AND STRATEGIES

The rest of this chapter will present ideas to help you write your own essay on Stephen Crane. First, of course, you need to choose a particular novel, story, or poem on which to focus, or you may choose a combination of more than one work with the focus on a particular idea or topic. Be careful not to choose a topic that is too broad, since you cannot adequately discuss several works or several ideas in a few pages. For example, an ordinary class paper could not begin to make a strong argument about war in the novels, short stories, and poems of Stephen Crane; such a broad topic will result in an essay that does not go beyond the obvious, in other words, a weak essay and a poor grade. On the other hand, if you narrow that topic down to the role of female characters in war as depicted in *The Red Badge of Courage* and two short stories, "A Grey Sleeve" and "Three Miraculous Soldiers," you will be able to form an effective argument about this limited topic. As you plan to write about Stephen Crane, think about the assignment's length requirements, and realize that a clear, persuasive paper must provide in-depth support. Once you have narrowed your topic appropriately and have chosen a specific focus, you should provide a rationale for your selection, clarifying how your choice of topic and novel, story, or poem provides a persuasive thesis. An essay without a clear and compelling purpose in the introduction is likely to lose the reader before its end. The suggested topics given here should serve only as examples to get you to think about what in the text or texts really interests you. If you have good reasons for your choice, begin by conveying those reasons to your readers, and then support the major points of your thesis, and you will have the basis of a sound argument.

Themes

As typical of most writers, Stephen Crane explores similar themes in several different works. He clearly examines the theme of fear, for example, in several different works, from *The Red Badge of Courage* to the short stories of war and even to a story of the West, "The Blue Hotel." Other themes such as hypocrisy, community, and violence also appear in a variety of different works. When you choose to use a thematic approach, a wide assortment of choices become open. The sample topics given in this chapter are merely to suggest some themes in specific works, but they are only the beginning. You can include other works for a particular theme, or you can discover themes not suggested here.

The first step is selecting the work you are most interested in exploring and a theme that fits; then you need to reread that work very carefully, noting passages that fit your topic, analyzing those passages closely, and keeping notes with page number references. You might decide that you want to use a comparative approach to analyze the same theme in two or more works, or you may choose to take a theme that has been explored widely in one work, such as fear in *The Red Badge of Courage,* and write about it in a novel or story in which its presence has been somewhat neglected, such as fear in "The Blue Hotel." Once you select a theme and a work or works, you will need to reread and take notes. Then you will be ready to analyze your evidence to find a fresh thesis that is your own.

Sample Topics:

1. **Importance of community:** How does Stephen Crane show the importance of community and social interaction in his work?

   Begin by selecting novels or short stories that seem to say something about community, either the importance of it or its lack. You might consider "The Open Boat," "The Monster," *Maggie: A Girl of the Streets,* and/or *The Red Badge of Courage.* Both "The Monster" and *Maggie* portray communities that shun members who are suddenly deemed unfit. Would you say these communities are wrong in their exclusion of Pete Johnson or Maggie or the monster? Why or why not? Does the narrative seem to favor the communities or the expelled member? What is the evidence? Although "The Open Boat" and *The Red Badge of Courage* show cohesive communities, they both imply that the individual is still isolated within that structure. What seems to cause that isolation? What benefits are gained from the individual's embrace of other members of the community?

2. **Romantic illusions:** What does Crane's work have to say about romantic illusions versus reality?

For this essay, choose one or more Crane texts that feature a character caught up in romantic illusions. You might examine the Swede in "The Blue Hotel," a character whose idea of the West has been fostered by his reading of dime novels, analyzing particular elements of this story that are similar to the romanticized novels of the West. On the other hand, you might look at Maggie in the novel *Maggie: A Girl of the Streets,* whose romantic or idealized ideas of Pete are never realistic.

Besides "The Blue Hotel" and *Maggie,* you might also consider Henry in *The Red Badge of Courage.* What are the sources of Henry's romanticized ideas of war? What are his motives for volunteering to fight? In all these works, what does Crane imply about man's ability to deceive himself?

3. **Heroism:** How does Stephen Crane define heroism in his works? In other words, what constitutes a hero?

Crane treats the topic of heroism in several different works, including *The Red Badge of Courage,* "A Mystery of Heroism," and "The Veteran." All three of these works feature protagonists who can be seen as heroic. Would you say they all display the same type of heroism? Why or why not? What is different about the three men? What does this difference imply about heroism? What are the examples of true heroism as opposed to perceived heroism? How do the other characters regard heroism? Finally, how does Crane as a writer define heroism?

Characters

When you plan to write about a type of character in one or more texts, you need to identify a certain category of character, including specific traits you plan to analyze. In Stephen Crane's works, you might decide to write about soldiers, exploring what the various soldier characters have in common. Another possibility is to analyze characters who represent religions or religious philosophies. A third possibility is one on which very little work has been done: women or female characters. Whichever type of character you choose, you will need to reread the works in which they appear, taking careful notes as you complete your review. Reflect on the overall characteristics of the group so that you can develop an interesting and valid thesis about this particular collection of characters. Based on your study of several soldier characters or several religious characters or several female characters, what might you say about Crane's treatment of your chosen group? How does he represent soldiers? What is his typical characterization of religious figures? How does he portray women throughout his work?

Sample Topics:

1. **Crane's soldiers:** Soldiers figure prominently in Crane's novel of the Civil War and in many of his short stories. Looking at several different works, determine how the "soldier" is portrayed throughout Crane's writing.

   For this essay, you might compare Henry Fleming in *The Red Badge* to the older Henry Fleming in "The Veteran" or to other soldiers in Crane's short stories on war. Or you could compare Civil War soldiers to those in the Spanish-American War, keeping in mind that Crane wrote *The Red Badge of Courage* (1895), *The Little Regiment and Other Episodes of the American Civil War* (1896), and "An Episode of War" (written 1896, published 1899) before he had ever witnessed war firsthand. After he had seen the Greek-Turkish War in 1897, he wrote "Death and the Child," and after he had reported on the Spanish-American War in 1898, he wrote the stories collected in *Wounds in the Rain* (1900). After carefully studying and taking notes on each soldier character, consider these questions. What do the various soldiers have in common? How do they differ? What seem to be their major concerns? What generalizations can you reach about how Crane portrays soldiers?

2. **Women:** At first glance, there seem to be few women in Stephen Crane's work, but a careful study shows that there are actually several important women, the most obvious of whom is Maggie

in the novel of that title. How are the women, including Maggie, portrayed in Crane's writings?

You might want to begin your study by looking at secondary sources on Crane's women cited at the end of this chapter; for example, see specifically those by Carol Hurd Green, Marsha Orgeron, and Donald Vanouse. You can tell from the titles of these critical works that the analytical attention paid to Crane's women has generally centered on Maggie, or the so-called "fallen woman." Other types of women, however, play important but sometimes minor roles in other works: Henry Fleming's mother in *The Red Badge of Courage*, George's mother in *George's Mother*, various women scattered through-out the war stories, and several notable women in "The Monster." After carefully rereading the books or stories you choose to study, list the similarities and differences of the women. Do they seem to fall into types, such as the mother figures, the decadent women, the innocent women, the strong women, or any other specific categories? Which type is most important? How do they influence the people around them? How do they function in the story, especially when they are not central to the plot?

You might, for example, look particularly at Martha Goodwin in "The Monster," whose character seems particularly enigmatic.

> . . . she was a woman of great mind. She had adamantine opinions upon the situation in Armenia, the condition of women in China, the flirtation between Mrs. Minster of Niagara Avenue and young Griscom, the conflict in the Bible class of the Baptist Sunday-school, the duty of the United States toward the Cuban insurgents, and many other colossal matters. Her fullest experience of violence was gained on an occasion when she had seen a hound clubbed, but in the plan which she had made for the reform of the world she advocated drastic measures. For instance, she contended that all the Turks should be pushed into the sea and drowned, and that Mrs. Minster and

> young Griscom should be hanged side by side on twin gallows.
> In fact, this woman of peace, who had seen only peace, argued
> constantly for a creed of illimitable ferocity. (50)

What function does Martha serve in this story? How does she compare to other strong women characters in Crane's works? After looking at a variety of women in the novels and stories, what generalizations can you make about Crane's characterization of women? What argument can you make for his use of women in his fiction?

History and Context

At the end of the nineteenth century, when Stephen Crane lived and wrote, the country was undergoing changes on a great scale. Industrialization was in full swing, giving rise to more opportunities and greater possibilities of wealth while also virtually imprisoning the underclasses in factories for long hours each day. Railroads criss-crossed the country, allowing more ease of transportation and communication and opening up the nation to greater westward expansion, but there was also the feeling that the opportunities of the West had been somewhat exhausted. The country was still recuperating from the most devastating war in its history, with both a sense of nostalgia and a sense of loss of an older way of life. Although the Civil War had brought about the freeing of slaves some three decades earlier, racism was at its peak with newly enacted Jim Crow laws and record numbers of lynchings. At the same time that newspapers had become important means of communication, yellow journalism often exploited topics of public interest, not for the public good but to make money. While the United States had managed to avoid war for three decades, numerous small wars had erupted over the world with our country later becoming involved in the Spanish-American War near the end of the decade. As you can see, the atmosphere in which Stephen Crane wrote was rich with contradictions and with opportunities for exploring current problems and analyzing past events. An avid observer of humanity, Crane took advantage of the recent innovations and the richness of the culture to write and sell his newspaper reports, his fiction, and his poetry.

Sample Topics:

1. **The West:** What do Crane's works have to say about the American West, a favorite topic of dime novels and other sentimental fiction of that time?

   At the time Crane was writing, the West represented a newer, rougher, perhaps more honest way of life to many easterners. Crane in 1895 was sent by the Bacheller newspaper syndicate to travel in and write about Mexico and the West, areas of the old frontier long romanticized in popular fiction. Crane's trip resulted in two important short stories, "The Bride Comes to Yellow Sky" and "The Blue Hotel," and a number of lesser-known ones such as "One Dash—Horses," "A Man and Some Others," and "Twelve O'Clock." You might research so-called dime novels and read one or two to compare the activities and characters in this popular fiction to those in Crane's work. Which elements seem more up-to-date or more realistic in Crane's stories than in the popular fiction? What supports the idea that the West is very little different from the East as far as the ordinary person is concerned? How does Crane demythologize the West? Ultimately, what does he contribute to our knowledge of the West as a distinct section of the country?

2. **The author's life:** You might choose to explore the connection between Stephen Crane's own exploits and his fiction. How do reality and fiction intersect in his works?

   On many occasions Crane's own experiences are the basis for his fiction. For example, his being shipwrecked on the *Commodore* resulted in both a newspaper account of the experience and his most famous short story, "The Open Boat." His reporting in Greece led to his story "Death and the Child," and his reporting in Cuba resulted in stories in *Wounds in the Rain*. How do the fictional accounts reflect what is revealed in the reportorial essays? What does the fiction add that is missing in the factual accounts? How does the mythical town of Whilomville resemble Port Jervis, New York, where Crane spent his formative years? Finally, how does Crane as an author transform what happens in his actual life into fiction that transcends the ordinary?

Philosophy and Ideas

If you plan to write an essay on the philosophy and/or ideas in the works of Stephen Crane, you might trace his parents' Methodist beliefs as they are reflected or rejected in his work. You might consider how characters act according to their personal conceptions of right or wrong. You might also consider how the emerging field of psychology had an influence, though perhaps a subconscious one, on his writing. Sigmund Freud had not yet brought attention to the discipline of psychology during Stephen Crane's lifetime, but the field had already made its mark in America, with William James, brother of fellow writer Henry James, being perhaps the most prominent psychologist in this country. In addition to the emergence of a more systemized study of psychology and the subsequent influence on the public, Russian novelists such as Tolstoy and Dostoevsky had written fiction that explored the inner workings of men's minds. After reading old *Century Magazine* reports on the Civil War, Stephen Crane remarked, "I wonder that some of those fellows don't tell how they felt in those scraps. They spout enough of what they did, but they're as emotionless as rocks" (Knapp, *"Little Stories"* 19). Crane in his fiction seeks to remedy that omission he found so disheartening in the magazine reports. He again and again explores the psychological underpinnings of his characters.

Sample Topics:

1. **Concepts of right and wrong:** Determine Crane's concept of right and wrong as it is incorporated into both his life and his art.

   If you choose to write on this topic, you will want to explore the facts that are known of his life; for example, you might read Richard Harding Davis's article on Crane's devotion to duty and Edward Marshall's article on Crane's risking his own livelihood to deliver a wounded rival newspaper correspondent's dispatch. These real-life examples of doing what is right regardless of personal danger or discomfort can be examined along with the implied duty to do what is right in *The Red Badge of Courage,* "The Monster," "The Open Boat," and "The Blue Hotel."

2. **Psychological exploration of characters:** How does Crane use newly developed ideas of psychology to explore motivation in his work?

You might wish to read William James's *Principles of Psychology* (1890) to get an overview of the discipline of psychology at that time. Although Crane may or may have not read this volume, he became friends in England with Henry James, the brother of William, whose ideas of psychology had seeped into the public sphere. In addition to being aware of psychological interests of his time, Crane is often thought to have been influenced by Tolstoy, who explores the minds of his characters in his work. You might read one of Tolstoy's novels, *War and Peace* (1865–69) or *Anna Karenina* (1873–77), where the protagonist typically ponders what he or she should do in a given situation, or you might read his nonfiction book whose title is usually translated as *What to Do* or *What Is to Be Done* (1887). After doing some of this research on nineteenth-century ideas of psychological motivation for action, consider how Crane creates the psychological underpinnings of his characters: for example, Henry Fleming in *The Red Badge of Courage,* Jimmie in *Maggie: A Girl of the Streets,* the Swede in "The Blue Hotel," or the correspondent in "The Open Boat." What motivates these characters to do what they do? How do various characters' feelings of inferiority or superiority, shame, fear, or empathy function in the narrative? What do the works imply about humankind in general as far as psychological causes and effects?

Form and Genre

If you plan to write a paper considering form and genre, you will deal with how the literary work is constructed. Perhaps the most relevant aspect of Stephen Crane's fiction is the force of the literary realism movement of that time. Well aware of the promotion of realism by William

Dean Howells, the editor of several literary magazines and a major influence on other writers then, Crane stated that his own realistic aims were similar. Although the methods these two men used to incorporate realism into their writing differ significantly, all realistic fiction of the late nineteenth century shares certain traits:

- The characters are common people functioning in the present, as opposed to royalty or other highly ranked persons living in an idealized past.
- Plot is less important than characterization, with the often complicated ethics of a situation or decision most important.
- The language is ordinary speech, with the characters often using a specific, even lower-class, dialect.
- The narrator remains as objective as possible, never openly assessing a character or situation.
- The description of the locales and the characters often contain much specific detail, allowing the reader to make inferences about emotional conditions and motivations.

If you take into consideration all these characteristics, you can see how Crane's desire to write realistically obviously influenced how he presented his material.

Another consideration when looking at Stephen Crane's fiction is his conception of the short story as an episode in life. He even uses the word *episode* in the title of one of his collections, *The Little Regiment and Other Episodes of the American Civil War,* and in the short story "An Episode of War." This word choice indicates a single incident that somehow becomes significant enough to warrant a story. In "An Episode of War," a story in which a lieutenant is shot in the arm, Crane writes, "It was, for a wonder, precisely like an historical painting" (6: 91). The moment of the lieutenant's disengaging himself from the battle activity in order to have his wound tended allows him to see the scene from an emotional distance. This distance is then juxtaposed with his evident horror at realizing his arm will be amputated. What had seemed trivial soon becomes of utmost importance to the character, and it later is of great magnitude to his family when he arrives home with an empty sleeve. Crane's manipulation of the scene to move from emotional involvement to detachment serves to emphasize the importance of this "episode." Crane uses a similar technique in many of his short stories to give what appears to be a mere episode the dramatic importance that makes it into a compelling story.

In the genre of poetry, Crane is also innovative. Although his "lines," as he liked to call them, were ridiculed and parodied by literary friends and enemies alike when they were first published, it is now recognized that Crane led the way for later renowned imagists such as Ezra Pound, H.D., Amy Lowell, and William Carlos Williams. The later imagistic poems were usually written in free verse and centered on an important image that suggested rather than stated the message. Although this emphasis on the importance of things, to paraphrase Williams, continued to have great influence in modernist American poetry, Stephen Crane was among the first to incorporate such imagistic techniques.

Sample Topics:

1. **Crane's narration:** Choose one or two texts and examine the narration to determine its effects on your interpretation.

   Can you determine who the narrator is? Often in Crane's work the narrator appears to be outside the story and totally detached from the events; in these cases the narrator seems to be an implied version of the author himself. You might read Wayne Booth's *The Rhetoric of Fiction* (1961), for example, or Wolfgang Iser's *The Implied Reader* (1972) to learn more about this type of narrator. Ask yourself what kinds of information the narrator has and what seems to be his or her motivation in revealing the particular details he or she gives. In *The Red Badge of Courage,* for example, why does the narrator go into so much detail about the ants crawling on the face of the corpse Henry encounters in the woods? You can study the narration in any of Crane's works, but it will be especially productive in *The Red Badge, Maggie: A Girl of the Streets,* "The Monster," and the stories in *Wounds in the Rain.*

2. **Crane's short story:** Analyze one or more of Stephen Crane's short stories to identify the most important traits of his writing in this genre.

Edgar Allan Poe's essay "The Philosophy of Composition" (1846) refers specifically to his method of composing a poem, but as one of America's first great short story writers, Poe incorporated similar concerns into composing a story. Like other short story writers, he limited the length of the piece, focused on one or two main characters, developed one theme within the work, and often concluded with an unexpected twist. What techniques does Crane use in his short stories? What is his typical focus? What are the narrative strategies? How does he create interest and sustain it? Why is the term *episode* so appropriate for a story like "The Mystery of Heroism" or "The Lone Charge of William B. Perkins"?

Looking at how Crane's stories conclude, you might consider the end of "The Open Boat," for example. Why is the oiler's death unexpected? What does this conclusion contribute to the theme of the story? Do most of his stories end with this type of surprise? Given what you have deduced about Crane's short stories, in which genre would you place "The Monster," which some have termed a story and others view as a novella?

3. **Crane's poetry:** How does Stephen Crane both break with the tradition of American poetry and also foreshadow the later modernist poetry?

For this paper, you might pick a few of Crane's most well-known poems—"A man said to the universe," "A man saw a ball of gold in the sky," and "Black riders came from the sea," for example. How do these poems differ from the poetic expectations of the time? What makes them unique? What is the essential image in each? What message is suggested, and how does that message remain open-ended? Why do these poems still speak to us as readers today? Crane valued his poems as expressing his *philosophy of life*? What do you suppose he means by that term? How would you describe his philosophy after having read a wide selection of his poetry?

Symbols, Imagery, and Language

Symbols, imagery, and language can provide a fruitful way of examining a work of literature, but you must always be cautious to use the terms *symbol* and *imagery* in a meaningful sense. Because novice literary critics are particularly vulnerable to misusing the term *symbolism*, a clarification seems important here. A symbol functions on both a literal and a figurative, or symbolic, level, achieving an overall importance that is all-encompassing and cannot be summarized in a few words. Take, for example, a symbol familiar in everyday life—the American flag. The flag is literally a rectangle of cloth formed with red and white stripes and a smaller blue rectangle filled with white stars. Symbolically, however, this piece of cloth represents more than can be conveyed in a simple assessment. To many Americans, it represents a pride in country, a sense of patriotism, a feeling of love for liberty. For these people, the feelings associated with this piece of cloth are massive, so much so that pages of rules of etiquette govern how to display a flag and how to dispose of an old, worn flag. To other Americans, the flag may be a very different type of symbol. In the 1960s flag burning was not unusual for groups protesting our involvement in the Vietnam War or those bringing attention to racial or gender inequalities. To these protestors, the flag was a negative emblem. To other nations, the American flag involves many different emotional reactions; for some it is the insignia of an enemy and for others a friend. All of these attendant peripheral and emotional meanings blend together with the literal piece of cloth to make up the entire symbolic nature of the flag.

Probably the best-known and largest, both literally and figuratively, symbol in American literature is Moby Dick, the whale in Herman Melville's book of the same name. This fictional whale stands for much more than the literal creature; it has many different symbolic meanings for the different characters involved in its pursuit—knowledge or the limits of knowledge, the unknown, evil, exploitation, God, nature, vengeance, to name only some of the possibilities. Although big, overriding symbols occur frequently in the works of Melville, Edgar Allan Poe, and Nathaniel Hawthorne, such overriding emblems are less prevalent in later realistic works of fiction, including those of Stephen Crane. No matter which work of literature you are analyzing, you should never search for symbols like a child peeking behind each bush to find an Easter egg. If a book contains symbols, it usually has only one or two major ones, and these symbols achieve such importance that they cannot be easily overlooked and cannot be limited to a superficial explanation.

Of all the criticism of Stephen Crane's writing, few are directly concerned with the use of symbolism. Some critics such as Eric Solomon and Daniel Knapp, for example, have discussed religious symbols in Crane's work, but other critics have found that patterns of imagery are more important. Perhaps these images suggest a larger symbolic structure, but the images themselves almost never quite rise to the level of symbol. Since no one doubts that Crane's work does make extensive use of imagery, especially visual imagery, an analysis of imagistic patterns can be fruitful in all three genres of Crane's writing.

Finally, Stephen Crane's use of language is one of his strongest elements. From his effective use of dialect to his imaginative use of metaphors, the quality of Crane's language treatment is memorable, with specific lines or phrases lingering even after plot features have become vague. Consider the following: In *Maggie: A Girl of the Streets*, the preacher "composed his sermons of 'you's'" (1: 20). In *The Red Badge of Courage* the lieutenant's swearing is depicted: "Strings of expletives he swung lash-like over the backs of his men" (2: 120). In "The Blue Hotel" the Easterner explains, "This poor gambler isn't even a noun. He is kind of an adverb" (5: 170). Not only does Crane use language in unusual ways, but also he exhibits his knowledge of the subtlety of such uses by directly referring to language itself, as in these examples from his own fiction and poetry.

Sample Topics:

1. **Crane's use of religious imagery:** How does Crane use religious imagery to clarify theme in his work?

   You might wish to analyze *The Red Badge of Courage* and "The Monster" for this topic. Keep in mind that you will need to show how such imagery contributes to an overall theme of these works. Reread each of the works, noting particularly the use of names, such as Jim Conklin in *The Red Badge* and John Twelve in "The Monster." What have some critics found significant about these names? How do they tie in with the theme of religion and religious practices? What does this use of imagery indicate about religion and its influence on Crane's works as a whole?

2. **Imagery connected to knightly battles or trials:** How does Crane use the images of medieval literature or chivalry in his work?

Choose two or three different works, and trace the imagery of historical or medieval battle, looking particularly for words such as *knight* and *warrior.* In *Maggie: A Girl of the Streets* and "The Blue Hotel," the combatants in both verbal and physical battles are often described in terms of chivalric war imagery. What do these images indicate about each particular conflict? How do they suggest a larger conflict in his works as a whole? How were medieval or chivalric topics and characters used in romantic or popular fiction of the time? How does Crane's usage differ?

3. **Color imagery:** How does Crane use colors to indicate more than decorative embellishments in his work?

Notice first the titles that contain the names of colors—*red, blue, yellow,* for example. Then choose two or three works to analyze in terms of color usage. Why is the badge red, the hotel blue, and the sky yellow? What emotional tones are associated with the colors? What other actual objects are associated with the colors? What does the choice of color indicate in each individual work? When you consider his oeuvre, or work as a whole, how does Stephen Crane use color in a way unique to his own writing? You might research his friendship with several art students and their influence on his writing techniques.

Compare and Contrast Essays

When you write a compare and contrast essay, you must go beyond merely showing similarities and differences. If you stop at that point, you will have only a list, not a thesis or argument. To arrive at an authentic analysis, you must also explain why these relationships are important to an interpretation of the text. When you begin planning such an essay, you first must discover a compelling reason to make such comparisons. If, for example, you want to show how Crane demythologizes the idea of the Old West, you might decide to compare cowboys in several stories, such as "The Bride Comes to Yellow Sky," "The Blue Hotel," and "One Dash—Horses." You are not limited to comparing elements within Stephen Crane's own work; you can also make comparisons with works of other writers, in his own era, in an earlier time, or in a later period. You might, for example, want to compare his cowboys with those in popular fiction of the late nineteenth century or those in films of the twentieth century. If you with to show that Stephen Crane's depiction of prostitution is realistic, you could compare prostitutes and their fates in Crane's *Maggie: A Girl of the Streets* with those in another contemporary book such as Theodore Dreiser's *Sister Carrie* (1900), or you could show that he was perhaps more realistic than some later novels by comparing the character of Maggie to Belle Watling in Margaret Mitchell's *Gone with the Wind* (1936). If you decide to write a comparison essay, you must consider what is important about the similarities and differences of the two texts, and you must show how the comparison aids in interpretation.

Sample Topics:

1. **Comparing two Crane texts:** Compare and contrast a common theme, idea, or type of character in two different Crane works or across several of his works.

   You first should identify exactly what you want to compare and what that comparison will lend to an interpretation of the texts. For example, you might decide to compare the sheriff in "The Bride Comes to Yellow Sky" to Richardson in "One Dash—Horses." How do these two men deal with the potential violence with which they are confronted? What is the difference in the attitudes of the two men? What is similar? What is the difference or similarity of those actions? How does this comparison help to reveal theme in each of the stories? Finally, how is that theme important in an overall look at Crane's work?

Another fruitful comparison could be that of the young Henry Fleming of *The Red Badge of Courage* with the older one in "The Veteran." What do the similarities and differences reveal about Fleming's attitude toward courage? Does it remain the same or does it change? If it changes, what is the importance of these changes?

2. **Comparison of Crane's work with that of another author:** Compare and contrast Crane's work with that of an author who has influenced him, whom he has influenced, or whose work has similar elements.

You might, for example, want to compare and contrast Ernest Hemingway's *A Farewell to Arms* with Crane's *The Red Badge of Courage.* Hemingway was greatly influenced by Stephen Crane's writing, and Hemingway's life in many ways paralleled Crane's, with both being news reporters whose major literary interest was writing fiction. Since both these novels deal with war and reactions to war, you might want to compare the two protagonists, Henry Fleming and Frederick Henry. Noting even the similarities of their names, consider how the two men are alike in other ways. How are they different? How are these similarities and differences important? How do their characterizations contribute to a statement about war itself?

Bibliography and Online Resources

Ahnebrink, Lars. *The Beginnings of Naturalism in American Fiction: A Study of the Works of Hamlin Garland, Stephen Crane, and Frank Norris, with Special Reference to Some European Influences, 1891–1903.* Cambridge, MA: Harvard UP, 1950.

Bassan, Maurice, ed. *Stephen Crane: A Collection of Critical Essays.* Englewood Cliffs, NJ: Prentice-Hall, 1967.

Beer, Thomas. *Stephen Crane: A Study in American Letters.* New York: Knopf, 1923.

Benfey, Christopher. *The Double Life of Stephen Crane.* New York: Knopf, 1992.

Bergon, Frank. *Stephen Crane's Artistry.* New York: Columbia UP, 1975.

Berryman, John. *Stephen Crane.* 1950. Cleveland: World-Meridian, 1962.

Booth, Wayne. *The Rhetoric of Fiction.* Chicago: U of Chicago P, 1961.

Brown, Bill. *The Material Unconscious: American Amusement, Stephen Crane, and the Economies of Play.* Cambridge, MA: Harvard UP, 1996.

Cady, Edwin H. *Stephen Crane.* Rev. ed. Boston: G. K. Hall, 1980.

Cazemajou, Jean. *Stephen Crane.* Minneapolis: U of Minnesota P, 1969.

Colvert, James B. *Stephen Crane.* San Diego: Harcourt, 1984.

Crane, Stephen. *The Works of Stephen Crane.* Ed. Fredson Bowers. 10 vols. Charlottesville: UP of Virginia, 1969–76.

Davis, Linda H. *Badge of Courage: The Life of Stephen Crane.* Boston: Houghton Mifflin, 1998.

Davis, Richard Harding. "Our War Correspondents in Cuba and Puerto Rico." *Harper's New Monthly Magazine* May 1899: 938–48. Rpt. in *Stephen Crane: Bloom's Classic Critical Views.* Ed. Harold Bloom and Joyce Caldwell Smith. New York: Chelsea House, 2009. 11–12.

Dooley, Patrick K. *The Pluralistic Philosophy of Stephen Crane.* Urbana: U of Illinois P, 1992.

Esteve, Mary. "A 'Gorgeous Neutrality': Stephen Crane's Documentary Anaesthetics." *ELH* 62.3 (1995): 663–89.

Fagg, John. *On the Cusp: Stephen Crane, George Bellows, and Modernism.* Tuscaloosa: U of Alabama P, 2009.

Fried, Michael. *Realism, Writing, Disfiguration: On Thomas Eakins and Stephen Crane.* Chicago: U of Chicago P, 1987.

Gilkes, Lillian. *Cora Crane: A Biography of Mrs. Stephen Crane.* Bloomington: Indiana UP, 1960.

Green, Carol Hurd. "Crane's View of Women." *Readings on Stephen Crane.* Ed. Bonnie Szumski. San Diego: Greenhaven, 1998. 79–91.

———. "Stephen Crane and the Fallen Women." *American Novelists Revisited: Essays in Feminist Criticism.* Ed. Fritz Fleischmann. Boston: Hall, 1982. 225–42.

Gullason, Thomas A. *Stephen Crane's Career: Perspectives and Evaluations.* New York: New York UP, 1972.

——, ed. *Stephen Crane's Literary Family: A Garland of Writings*. Syracuse, NY: Syracuse UP, 2002.

Halliburton, David. *The Color of the Sky: A Study of Stephen Crane*. New York: Cambridge UP, 1989.

Holton, Milne. *Cylinder of Vision: The Fiction and Journalistic Writing of Stephen Crane*. Baton Rouge: Louisiana State UP, 1972.

Howells, W. D. *Criticism and Fiction*. New York: Harper and Brothers, 1891. http://www.gutenberg.org/ebooks/3377.

Iser, Wolfgang. *The Implied Reader: Patterns of Communication in Prose Fiction from Bunyan to Beckett*. Baltimore: Johns Hopkins UP, 1974.

James, William. *Principles of Psychology*, 1890. Ed. George A. Miller. Cambridge, MA: Harvard UP, 1983.

Knapp, Daniel. "Son of Thunder: Stephen Crane and the Fourth Evangelist." *Nineteenth-Century Fiction* 24.3 (1969): 253–91.

LaFrance, Marston. *A Reading of Stephen Crane*. Oxford: Clarendon, 1971.

Linson, Corwin Knapp. "Little Stories of 'Steve' Crane." *Saturday Evening Post* 11 April 1903: 19–20. Rpt. in *Stephen Crane: Bloom's Classic Critical Views*. Ed. Harold Bloom and Joyce Caldwell Smith. New York: Chelsea House, 2009. 37–43.

——. *My Stephen Crane*. Ed. Edwin Cady. Syracuse, NY: Syracuse UP, 1958.

Marshall, Edward. "Exciting Life Scenes of Stephen Crane, Journalist." *The San Francisco Call* 12 Aug. 1900: 12. Rpt in *Stephen Crane: Bloom's Classic Critical Views*. Ed. Harold Bloom and Joyce Caldwell Smith. New York: Chelsea House, 2009. 28–29.

Mitchell, Lee Clark. *New Essays on* The Red Badge of Courage. New York: Cambridge UP, 1986.

Monteiro, George. *Stephen Crane's Blue Badge of Courage*. Baton Rouge: Louisiana State UP, 2000.

Nagel, James. *Stephen Crane and Literary Impressionism*. University Park: Pennsylvania State UP, 1980.

Orgeron, Marsha. "The Road to Nowhere: Stephen Crane's *Maggie: A Girl of the Streets (a Story of New York)* (1893)." *Women in Literature: Reading through the Lens of Gender*. Ed. Jerilyn Silber Fisher, Ellen S. Sadker, and David Sadker. Westport, CT: Greenwood, 2003. 185–87.

Pizer, Donald. *Critical Essays on Stephen Crane's* The Red Badge of Courage. Boston: G. K. Hall, 1990.

Poe, Edgar Allan. "The Philosophy of Fiction," 1846. Rpt. in *Edgar Allan Poe: Critical Theory.* Ed. Stuart Levine and Susan F. Levine. Chicago: U of Illinois P, 55–76.

Pratt, Lyndon Upson. "The Formal Education of Stephen Crane." *American Literature* 10.4 (1939): 460–71

Smith, Joyce Caldwell, volume ed., and Harold Bloom, series ed. *Stephen Crane: Bloom's Classic Critical Views.* New York: Chelsea House, 2009.

Solomon, Eric. *Stephen Crane: From Parody to Realism.* Cambridge, MA: Harvard UP, 1966.

———. *Stephen Crane in England: A Portrait of the Artist.* Columbus: Ohio State UP, 1964.

Stallman, R. W. *Stephen Crane: A Biography.* Rev. ed. New York: Braziller, 1973.

Surfrin, Mark. *Stephen Crane.* New York: Atheneum, 1992.

Vanouse, Donald. "Women in the Writings of Stephen Crane: Madonnas of the Decadence." *Southern Humanities Review* 12 (1978): 141–48.

Weatherford, Richard M., ed. *Stephen Crane: The Critical Heritage.* London: Routledge & Kegan Paul, 1973.

Wertheim, Stanley. *A Stephen Crane Encyclopedia.* Westport, CT: Greenwood, 1997.

Wertheim, Stanley, and Paul Sorrentino. *The Crane Log: A Documentary Life of Stephen Crane 1871–1900.* New York: G. K. Hall, 1994.

———, eds. *The Correspondence of Stephen Crane.* New York: Columbia UP: 1988.

———, eds. *The Correspondence of Stephen Crane.* 2 vols. New York: Columbia UP, 1988.

———. *The Crane Log: A Documentary Life of Stephen Crane.* New York: G. K. Hall, 1994.

Wolford, Chester L. *The Anger of Stephen Crane: Fiction and the Epic Tradition.* Lincoln: U of Nebraska P, 1983.

THE RED BADGE OF COURAGE

READING TO WRITE

When Stephen Crane published *The Red Badge of Courage: An Episode of the Civil War* (1895), he was a young man of twenty-four who had never witnessed battle. First serialized in newspapers and then released as a book, the novel gained him almost instant international fame, with positive critical reviews both in the United States and in England. Although he had previously written numerous newspaper reports and had privately printed *Maggie, A Girl of the Streets,* he had received little acclaim until *Red Badge,* which remains his most popular work. This novel presents the story of Henry Fleming, a young American who volunteers to fight for the Union in the Civil War. Although the events of the novel take place over only a few days, Crane provides much insight into the psychology of the new recruit, who dreams of heroism in battle but who soon faces the grim reality of war. The story is told by a third-person narrator from the point of view of Henry, who is most often presented as "the youth." What Henry does and says is often at variance with his thoughts; as a result, paying close attention to the discrepancies between Henry's actions and his interior monologues can lead to a variety of topics suitable for essays.

The first technique anyone preparing to write an essay about literature should employ is close reading. Because any good piece of literature yields new insights with each rereading, you should read a passage multiple times, giving particular attention to the language and how it is used. You should ask yourself why Crane selected specific words and images and why he arranged them in the precise way that he did. Then ask how the sense of the passage would change with the replacement of key words with synonyms or with the rearrangement of sentences. Try the technique of close reading by choosing a passage of interest to you, perhaps the flashback in which Henry remembers contemplating going away to the war:

> He had burned several times to enlist. Tales of great movements shook the land. They might not be distinctly Homeric, but there seemed to be much glory in them. He had read of marches, sieges, conflicts, and he had longed to see it all. His busy mind had drawn for him large pictures, extravagant in color, lurid with breathless deeds.
>
> But his mother had discouraged him. She had affected to look with some contempt upon the quality of his war-ardor and patriotism. She could calmly seat herself and with no apparent difficulty give him many hundreds of reasons why he was of vastly more importance on the farm than on the field of battle. She had had certain ways of expression that told that her statements on the subject came from a deep conviction. Besides, on her side, was his belief that her ethical motive in the argument was impregnable (5–6).

The references in this passage to tales of great battles make it a particularly interesting one to analyze. When Henry has been thinking about enlisting, he has reflected on the glory of "marches, sieges, conflicts." As he has thought about such activities, he has even embroidered the events into more unrealistic word paintings, "extravagant in color, lurid with breathless deeds." Crane's use of "extravagant" and "lurid" serve to remind the reader that Henry is fantasizing about his own glory. What would be the difference if the text showed Henry's mind had drawn pictures "devoid of color, filled with breathless deeds"? Crane's words *extravagant* and *lurid* suggest many questions that you could address in an essay; for example, what does the novel have to say about the relationship of language to truth and reality? Does the author suggest that language can both disguise and reveal human behaviors as either noble or self-serving? Does language have other significant functions in the novel? The passage itself suggests that it does.

Even though he is disappointed with his mother's response to his enlistment, Henry understands as he muses over her reaction that his mother's position is more ethical, even "that her ethical motive in the argument was impregnable" (6). When he leaves the house, looking back at his mother with tears on her cheeks, he realizes his own faulty ethics: "He bowed his head and went on, feeling suddenly ashamed of his purposes" (8). These sentences suggest that his mother's convictions are superior to Henry's purposes, and they may also suggest that a novel should reveal war as it truly is, not as a vehicle for political or personal glory. Ask yourself if Henry ever seems to have a sense of duty to his country or to have a conviction that his fighting is for a greater cause, such as abolishing slavery.

Particularly explore not only the language of the novel but also the novel's references to literal language, both written and oral. Does the language suggest that war should be fought only for reasons that are noble? Does it suggest that enlistees are not always truthful about their motives? Reflecting on these questions, you might think about the letters written by Wilson, the loud soldier. Has Wilson written his letters because he wants to communicate with his family, or has he written them to ensure his glory will live on after he has been killed in battle, as he feels is surely going to happen once the fighting begins? Why do you think Henry keeps the letters as a weapon against Wilson's own perceived cowardice early in the novel? Does Crane suggest that some survivors of war feel a need to embellish their feats in order to validate their role in the fighting? Or does he suggest that fiction should not participate in glorifying what is a horrible and violent reality? Finally, how is it that language, in particular the derisive language used by the lieutenant and the colonel in describing Henry's regiment, causes both Henry and Wilson to fight harder than either has thought possible and to forget personal glory while ironically also attaining that glory? Based on the novel, is this type of glory something to be sought? What would be a more honorable motivation?

As you can see, reading a passage carefully and analyzing the specific language can generate possibilities for several essays. After you have examined a passage and produced a list of several questions and ideas, identify other passages that may be relevant in providing answers to your questions or helping you to refine your thoughts. When you have scrutinized several passages, try to identify common threads that will lead you to a claim or thesis that can be the basis of your essay.

TOPICS AND STRATEGIES

The following topics and essay ideas are merely suggestions that should help you to generate your own specific possibilities. Rather than limit or constrict you, they should spark your imagination. Do not look at these essay topics as a series of questions to be answered in sequence; instead, use them as springboards to your own ideas about a given topic. You might note, for example, the various wounds that the individual soldiers incur, and you might decide that the wounds themselves are emblematic of the characterization of the men. Once you have listed your ideas and analyzed several relevant passages in the novel, you will be ready to decide on your own claim and to use it as the basis for your essay. When you have established that claim, or thesis, you should then begin to collect specific evidence—words, phrases, images—from the text itself to support your claim. Finally you should organize that evidence effectively to form a persuasive essay.

Themes

To begin thinking about a novel's themes, ask yourself what main ideas or issues are addressed. Although many works will share the same themes, each deals with the themes differently. Your task in an essay will be to identify a primary theme and to show how this particular novel deals with it. *The Red Badge of Courage* deals, for example, with the themes of heroism, cowardice, maturity or coming of age, the role of nature, and perhaps even religion. Choose one of these or another theme and find the most significant passages pertaining to it. Carefully read and reread these passages, paying close attention to the language and how it is used. Once you have discovered specific patterns of language, you are ready to ask what the novel reveals about that particular theme. Then you can create a precise claim upon which to base your essay.

Sample Topics:

1. **Heroism:** What does the novel say about heroism? Is heroism an absolute or is it dependent on point of view?

As Henry waits for the fighting to begin, he contemplates the courage of his fellow recruits:

> In regard to his companions his mind wavered between two opinions, according to his mood. Sometimes he inclined to believing them all heroes. In fact, he usually admired in secret the superior development of the higher qualities in others. He could conceive of men going very insignificantly about the world bearing a load of courage unseen, and although he had known many of his comrades through boyhood, he began to fear that his judgment of them had been blind. Then, in other moments, he flouted these theories, and assured him that his fellows were all privately wondering and quaking. (14)

Henry finds that not only can he not gauge his own courage but that he is unsure of his companions as well.

What are Henry Fleming's ideas of heroism before he goes off to war? Where has he gotten these ideas? How does that concept of heroism change by the end of the novel, or does it? How does Henry's view of heroism contrast with his mother's?

2. **Cowardice:** What is the novel's message about cowardice in the context of war? Is it realistic to continue to fight in the face of insurmountable odds?

Analyze the scene where Henry Fleming runs from battle. Why does he run? How does he justify his retreat? Why is he glad to receive the blow that gives him a "red badge"? How does he use that wound to his advantage? Would you characterize Henry as a coward at this point? What effect does his running have on those around him?

3. **Coming of age:** According to the novel, what constitutes the state of manhood? Does the novel make the concept clear, or does it suggest that achieving maturity is more complicated than we might expect?

Crane gives us Henry's idea of being a man after he has been successful in battle: "He felt a quiet man-hood, non-assertive but of sturdy and strong blood. He knew that he would no more quail before his guides wherever they should point. He had been to touch the great death and found that, after all, it was but the great death. He was a man" (135). Should this passage be read literally, or is Crane being ironic? If so, in what way? Has Henry been completely transformed during only two days of fighting? Will he never again be afraid in the midst of battle? Are there other requirements for manhood than just proving oneself in battle? If so, what are they, and has Henry achieved any of those?

Character

Analyzing a novel's characters can provide important insights into the overall meaning of a work of fiction. In *The Red Badge of Courage,* we are presented with a number of characters who demand thorough investigation. Choose one of these characters who seems important and follow that person through the novel. Notice what he does and what he says. Is there a discrepancy between his thoughts and his actions? How does he interact with other characters? What is the motive for his specific actions? What are his values? What are his priorities? Is the character dynamic or static; that is, does he change over the course of the novel or does he stay the same? If he changes, what are the reasons? Is it a permanent change or just one that seems convenient at the time? You might focus on Henry, for example, using your analysis to determine how the novel ultimately presents him. Is he brave or cowardly? You might compare him to Wilson, the loud soldier, to discern similarities and differences in the two young recruits. Why is it significant that he is often referred to as "the youth"? You might also examine minor characters such as Henry's mother, who appears in only a few pages in a flashback. What are her greatest concerns about her son's going to war? Does Henry come to share any of those concerns? If so, how does that change the novel's emphasis on what is important? What is the function of other minor characters such as the tattered man or the cheery soldier?

Sample Topics:

1. **Henry Fleming:** Analyze the character of Henry Fleming, following him throughout the novel.

How does Henry develop during the course of the narrative? Is this development positive or negative or somewhere in between? The novel covers only a few days, but we learn much about Henry Fleming's feelings and actions during his first direct involvement with war. Although the novel is written in the third person, everything is filtered through Henry's point of view. We are privileged to know his thoughts and fears, his actions, and his reactions to other characters. As the protagonist of the novel, Henry Fleming presents us with much information: "The youth tried to observe everything" (23). He feels proud when he enlists and cowardly when he runs from battle, but at the end of the novel he thinks he has learned to distinguish between his earlier attitudes and his newfound maturity: "He found that he could look back upon the brass and bombast of his earlier gospels and see them truly. He was gleeful when he discovered that he now despised them" (135). Has he truly matured, or is he just considering some issues in a different light? Why does the tattered man still haunt him?

In analyzing Henry's character, you must deal with the fact that Henry's view is often distorted in one way or another, so his perception cannot always be trusted. Sergio Perosa states about Henry

Everything is related to his *vision*, to his *sense*-perception of incidents and details, to his *sense*-reactions rather than to his psychological impulses, to his confused sensations and individual impressions. Reality exists and can be artistically recreated in that it affects his eyes, his ears, his touch—his sensory, rather than mental, imagination. The battle field is to Henry Fleming colorful and exciting, new and phantasmagoric, mysterious and unforeseen. (88)

In your analysis, then, you must look at not only what Henry perceives but what may be distorted about his perception.

2. **Jim Conklin:** Analyze and evaluate the character of Jim.

Jim Conklin, one of the more intriguing characters in *The Red Badge of Courage,* has been written about by many critics of the novel. Try to decide what his function is and why he is called the "tall soldier." Begin by recording what you know about him. How do Henry and other characters react to him? Is he as knowledgeable and stoic as Henry sees him? When Jim forecasts what is going to happen next, he is repeating what he has heard about the possibility of movement, but he has "heard from a reliable friend who had heard it from a truthful cavalryman who had heard it from his trust-worthy brother, one of the orderlies at division head-quarters" (3). What does the path of the rumor say about Jim? How do the other young recruits react to him? Why? What eventually happens to Jim, and how does this affect Henry? Does the novel present Jim as a hero?

3. **Wilson:** Why is Wilson called the "loud soldier" and how is he characterized?

Analyze the introduction of Wilson in the first chapter. Presented simply as the loud soldier, Wilson makes several pronouncements in this chapter that fall quite short of sounding heroic: "Huh" or "Shucks" (11) or "Oh, you think you know—" (12). In addition, Wilson is described as giggling, not a particularly soldierly response. What does this language do to the reader's view of Wilson's character? Does Wilson change in any way during the course of the novel; in other words, is he a dynamic or a static character? If dynamic, how does he change from the opening chapter to the end of the novel?

4. **The tattered man:** Analyze and evaluate the novel's portrayal of the tattered man.

Look at the presentation of the tattered man in Chapters 8 and 10, paying particular attention to the conversations between him and Henry. How is the tattered man characterized? Why is he called the "tattered man" instead of the "tattered soldier"? Why does he appear before and after the presentation of Jim Conklin's death in Chapter 9? What is his major concern as he speaks with Henry? What are his positive and negative attributes? Why does he refer to Henry as "Tom Jamison" just before Henry abandons him? Why were the tattered man's questions "knife-thrusts" (62) to Henry?

5. **Henry's mother:** Analyze the function of Henry's mother in this novel.

Although she appears only briefly as Henry relives his decision to join the army, Henry's mother is an important character, for she provides the first contrast with the boy's conception of war and heroism. Look at the problems with which Henry's mother is most concerned. Henry sees her worries as inconsequential in Chapter 1. If he had contemplated these same concerns in the final chapter, would he see them somewhat differently? Do any of them account for his nagging concern with the tattered man?

History and Context

Although the war and the battle are never named, it is clear that Stephen Crane is writing about the American Civil War in *The Red Badge of Courage*. In spite of the fact that the novel's characters and actions are fictitious, Harold R. Hungerford has shown that the setting is the real-life Battle of Chancellorsville, a major historical conflict with thousands of casualties. Although Crane was born six years after the war had ended, the memory of it was still vivid for many citizens, with veterans continuing to retell the horrors of combat that had divided the country and killed more Americans than any other war. How does this chronological proximity to the war affect Crane's account of it, even though he was not even alive during the conflict? Does Crane's greater distance from the fighting make his account more realistic, or less?

Sample Topics:

1. **Using lofty aims to justify fighting:** What does the novel say about the motivation of many who fought in the Civil War or those who have fought in any other war?

Crane, according to most accounts, had read widely about the Civil War, especially the series "Battles and Leaders of the Civil War," which appeared in *Century Magazine* from November 1884 to November 1887. He apparently had also listened to many tales of veterans, including one of his teachers at Claverack College. After the publication of *The Red Badge*, one of the most negative comments about the book came from A. C. McClurg, himself a veteran of the Chickamauga and Chattanooga campaigns: "Nowhere are seen the quiet, manly, self-respecting, and patriotic men, influenced by the highest sense of duty, who in reality fought our battles. It can be said most confidently that no soldier who fought in our recent War ever saw any approach to the battle scenes in *this* book" (227, emphasis added). As a veteran of the Civil War, McClurg was convinced that the writing somehow contrived to make all veterans of the Union forces seem cowardly, yet later veterans of wars as recent as Vietnam have testified over and over to the psychological realism of Crane's account. Does McClurg have a case to say the book unfairly characterizes soldiers? Are all the soldiers portrayed as cowardly? Consider the difference in the young soldiers in Crane's narrative as compared to the older soldiers, especially the lieutenant and the colonel. How do their attitudes compare and differ?

2. **Critique of war:** What kind of commentary does the novel make about war in general?

After having written *The Red Badge of Courage*, Stephen Crane served as a news correspondent in two different wars: the Greek-Turkish War in Greece in 1897 and the Spanish-American War in Cuba in 1898. After his first war experience in Greece, he told Joseph Conrad that his war novel had been "all right" (Conrad). Other than revealing a recruit's unrealistic view of heroism, what points about war does Crane make in this novel? Which points are most important? Why? What does war do to the men who are fighting? What has it probably done to the families left at home?

Philosophy and Ideas

The Red Badge of Courage, like any other effective novel, incorporates philosophies and ideas that are important in the lives of the characters and in our own lives. These ideas range from questions about the ethics of war to the role of nature, or God, in our lives. Reread the novel with a philosophical or ethical issue in mind, searching for passages that reveal the world-view of a specific character. After analyzing a few characters and the passages you have identified, try to establish a claim to make in your essay. To discuss ethics in war, for example, you might look closely at Henry and his mother and study their different ideas about Henry's responsibility in battle. Or you might look at the lieutenant and the colonel and consider their ethics as they send Henry's unit to be sacrificed. Would it have been more ethical to send a stronger military unit? Why is Henry more concerned with his own small world than he is with the larger questions of why the war is being fought? How can a large-scale battle strategy seem perhaps more ethical than the individual philosophy of one untried soldier? After performing your analysis and considering these questions, you might arrive at a thesis such as the following: In The Red Badge of Courage, Stephen Crane demonstrates through the character of Henry that fears and self-interest often outweigh a sense of civic duty during war. On the other hand, a similar analysis might lead to the conclusion that soldiers such as Henry suffer psychological wounds that can continue to haunt them. Although Henry seems triumphant at the end of the novel, in reality he has barely begun to fight—many more days, weeks, and months of battle lie in store for him if he continues to survive. More excruciating events may await him to test both his courage and his ethics. Alternatively, your analysis might lead you to a different conclusion: Through the character of Henry, Crane demonstrates that an ethical code is just as necessary in wartime as it is in everyday life. When Henry abandons the tattered man, who is surely going to die, he abandons doing what his mother had told him: to do what is right. No amount of battle glory will obscure the fact that he has not been compassionate to one of his own comrades in need.

Sample Topics:

1. **Post-traumatic stress:** How does the novel suggest that interior wounds, or psychological wounds, are perhaps more important than physical wounds?

   The tattered man, on encountering Henry retreating on his own, believes the youth to be wounded: "Ye'd better take keer of yer hurt. It don't do t' let sech things go. It might be inside mostly, an' them plays thunder. Where is it located?" (61). At this point Henry has no physical wound at all; it is two chapters later that Henry acquires his mild head wound as a result of the flight of a fellow soldier, swinging his rifle to get Henry out of his path. The resulting wound is one that causes Henry little pain and provides the excuse he needs to explain why he has abandoned the rest of his unit during the last fighting. Analyze the novel's concentration on Henry's psychological pain more than on his physical pain, citing other instances of psychological trauma during the course of the novel.

   You might consider Henry's "wound" and that of the lieutenant in his company:

   > The lieutenant of the youth's company was shot in the hand. He began to swear so wondrously that a nervous laugh went along the regimental line. The officer's profanity sounded conventional. It relieved the tightened senses of the new men. It was as if he had hit his fingers with a tack-hammer at home.
   >
   > He held the wounded member carefully away from his side so that the blood would not drip upon his trousers (30).

   What are the major differences in the lieutenant's reactions to injury and Henry's? Why is that important? What does it reveal about Henry?

2. **Ethics in war:** What kind of commentary does the novel make about ethics during wartime?

How does Henry decide what is ethical? After he has been careful in concealing his own fear, he chooses to let Wilson continue to believe he has been honorably wounded. Is it ethical to allow Wilson to believe a lie? Can any other of Henry's actions be deemed unethical? What bothers him most at the end of the novel? Why? Do any other characters act in ways that might be considered unethical? Does the novel suggest there is a code of conduct even in the midst of battle?

3. **Nature as uncaring:** What kind of commentary does the novel make about the role of nature, or God, in human affairs such as war?

Review the "chapel scene" in Chapter 7. After Henry has fled, he eventually finds a landscape that gives him assurance. When he tosses a pine cone at a squirrel, the animal runs in fear, and Henry sees the squirrel's flight as a sign from nature that his own running is justified. Soon the youth reaches what seems to him a natural chapel in a peaceful setting, and he assumes that nature itself prefers peace, not war. When he enters the chapel formed by pine bows, however, he is confronted by reality: a corpse that stares back at him as ants run along its face.

> He was being looked at by a dead man who was seated with his back against a column-like tree. The corpse was now faded to a melancholy shade of green. The eyes, staring at the youth, had changed to the dull hue to be seen on the side of a dead fish. The mouth was opened. Its red had changed to an appalling yellow. Over the grey skin of the face ran little ants. One was trundling some sort of a bundle along the upper lip.
>
> The youth gave a shriek as he confronted the thing. He was, for moments, turned to stone before it. He remained staring into the liquid-looking eyes. The dead man and the living man exchanged a long look (47–48).

The horror of this scene propels Henry back toward the violence of battle. What does this encounter reveal about nature? What is the role of nature in the affairs of man, particularly in the case of war? How does Crane's presentation of Henry's encounter with nature differ from encounters with nature by earlier transcendentalist writers such as Henry David Thoreau or Ralph Waldo Emerson?

4. **Bravery in the face of certain defeat:** Analyze the actions of Henry and Wilson when they know they are expected to fail.

After hearing the lieutenant and the colonel talking about the upcoming fight and knowing that they plan to sacrifice Henry's regiment because it is the most expendable, both Henry and Wilson then fight their hardest, rallying their troops with the flag held high even though it makes them a bigger target. Analyze the courage of Henry and Wilson in this skirmish. Have they recovered from being afraid? Do they finally display valor? What do their actions in this scene seem to predict about their future behavior? Does anything in the text undercut the bravery of these two young soldiers?

Form and Genre

The way the author constructs a piece of literature is fertile ground for literary analysis. You may want to look at method of narration, point of view, and the organizational scheme of the novel. If you are looking at form, you should ask yourself why the author made the choices he did and how those choices affect the way you read the text. When analyzing *The Red Badge of Courage,* you might explore the twenty-four chapter structure of the novel, the same as the *Odyssey* and the *Iliad,* and connect this structure to the numerous allusions to ancient Greek mythology. You might, on the other hand, choose to examine why the story is told mostly from Henry's point of view. Another possibility is to analyze the almost photographic presentation of scenes. Why does Stephen Crane give us such detailed descriptions of the landscape and of specific events such as Henry's encounter with the corpse?

Sample Topics:

1. *The Red Badge* as realism: Analyze this novel as belonging to the genre of realistic fiction.

Literary critics place *The Red Badge of Courage* into the genre of realistic fiction. Your essay might be one that analyzes aspects of the novel that are realistic: the boredom of waiting for the first battle, the fear that Henry keeps to himself but tries to uncover in others, the need to justify his retreat, and the welcoming of an excuse for running. Stephen Crane uses realistic details, terse dialogue, and no overt sentimentality. Consider the description of the young recruits as they endure the early boredom of waiting for battle:

> The men had begun to count the miles upon their fingers. And they grew tired. "Sore feet an' damned short rations, that's all," said the loud soldier. There was perspiration and grumbling. After a time, they began to shed their knapsacks. Some tossed them unconcernedly down; others hid them carefully, asserting their plans to return for them at some convenient time. Men extricated themselves from thick shirts. Presently, few carried anything but their necessary clothing, blankets, haversacks, canteens, and arms and ammunition. "Yeh kin now eat, drink, sleep an' shoot," said the tall soldier to the youth. "That's all yeh need. What d' yeh want t' do—carry a hotel?" (21).

How does this passage reveal the reality of war? How does it contrast with the idealist vision of war the recruits had at first maintained? How does the organization of the passage, ending with the comic image of carrying a hotel, undercut that idealism?

2. **Organization:** What is significant about the organization of this novel as related to tales of classical warfare?

The Red Badge of Courage is organized into twenty-four chapters, and it begins in *media res,* that is, in the middle of the action, as did earlier epic depictions of war, such as the *Iliad.* This organization, along with myriad allusions to Homer and epic battle, suggests that the form is important to interpretation of the novel. Ask why Crane chose this particular organization, including a marked difference between the first twelve chapters and the last twelve. What does this epic organization have to do with Henry as the "hero" of *The Red Badge*? How does he compare to the typical epic hero? Are any other characters or actions typical of epics?

3. *The Red Badge of Courage* as impressionism: Analyze the novel as impressionistic in form.

Some painters, including some of Stephen Crane's artist friends, worked to create reality through a technique called impressionism. They sought to create the impression of reality by using the play of light and color on the individual paint strokes. How does Crane use a similar interplay of visual elements in his descriptions? How do these visual clips create a realistic impression of the horrors of war? Are there any other techniques of impressionism?

Language, Symbols, and Imagery

An effective way to analyze a piece of literature is to study the language, symbols, and imagery the author uses. Look for patterns of language or imagery, especially any that appear several times in the text. Highlight any passages that seem to have a special significance in relation to an important issue, an event, or a character or that seem to embellish or comment on language itself. Among the many symbols and images you might elect to focus on in *The Red Badge of Courage* are references to the soldiers as members of a unit, the red badge itself, and any humorous or incongruent images. Whatever language, symbol, or pattern of imagery you decide to analyze, you will want to demonstrate how that element shapes your reading of the novel. You might argue, for example, that through the use of humorous imagery, Crane encourages the reader to rethink the importance of certain actions or ideas. For example, the humor surrounding the various wounds the veterans experience causes us to examine their significance in light of both Henry's wound and the severe, even fatal wounds of others, such as Jim Conklin and the tattered man.

1. **Dialogue:** What does the language of the dialogue tell us about the novel's themes and meanings?

   Look again at the language Henry uses to conceal his own fear of cowardice when he asks Jim Conklin if he thinks any of the young recruits might run:

   > "How do you think the regiment'll do?"
   > "Oh, they'll fight all right, I guess, after they onct git inteh it," said the other with cold judgment. He made a fine use of the third person. "There's been heaps 'a fun poked at 'em b'cause they're new, 'a course, an' all that, but they'll fight all right, I guess.
   > "Think any of the boys 'll run?" persisted the youth. (11)

   In this passage Crane points out Jim's "fine use of the third person." How does his use of third person change the way the reader looks at this dialogue? Analyze the difference of a first person usage, that is, how is the meaning changed by having Jim say "Oh, *I'll* fight all right." What are the young soldiers hesitant to say? What do they realize about the attitudes of the veterans?

2. **The title:** What is the significance of the title *The Red Badge of Courage*?

   From the beginning of the novel, Henry's major concern is with the heroism that he craves and the fear that he will not achieve such heroism, in fact, the fear that he will behave as a coward. After he does actually retreat from the fighting, Henry is at his lowest point psychologically. He cannot figure out how he will handle his own cowardice when he must reunite with his regiment. While contemplating his predicament, he finds himself in the midst of a huge retreating throng of soldiers, grasping an older soldier by the arm to ask, "Why?" (70). As the man tries to free himself from Henry's grasp, he finally swings his rifle to rid himself of his encumbrance, wounding the youth's head. As Henry moves along in a dazed condition, a man with a cheery voice leads him back to his own regiment, where Henry's wound becomes a convenient means of garnering sympathy and admiration from his colleagues, who believe he has been grazed by a cannon ball. What is the irony of this "red badge"? How does Crane use that irony to reveal Henry's lack of ethics in this situation? How does it both connect Henry to his regiment and free him of his fear? How does this ironic term work more effectively than a more literal reference to the wound would have? How does having this "badge" as the title give it utmost importance?

3. **Religious imagery:** Analyze the biblical allusions in the novel.

Some critics have focused on Jim Conklin as perhaps a Christ figure and the "red sun . . . pasted in the sky like a wafer" at his death as a symbol of the rite of communion (58). Does Jim Conklin, the "tall soldier," actually function as a Christ figure? If so, in what ways? What other words or phrases seem to be biblical allusions? If this imagery does not mark Conklin as a religious martyr, what is its significance in the book? Early in the novel, Jim is described as "the fast-flying messenger of a mistake" (13); does this language undercut Jim's possible position as a Christ figure? How does Henry regard this friend? How do the other soldiers regard Jim? What is the relevance of his death?

4. **The color red:** How does Stephen Crane use the color red in the novel?

War is referred to as "the red animal, war, the blood-swollen god" (25, 69). How does this description function in the way the soldiers observe battle? Is it significant that the color red seems interspersed throughout the novel? How do these various references to red tie together aspects of the novel?

5. **The regiment as a unit:** Analyze the references to Henry's regiment as a unit. How are these important?

After the fighting begins, a variety of phrases are used to describe Henry as a small part of a great whole: "He was in a moving box" (23); "He became not a man but a member" (34). What is the difference in tone in the two previous sentences? Can you find other similar phrases? How do they reveal Henry's feelings about war? How do they reveal Crane's attitude to war? Is there a discrepancy between the two points of view? If so, what effect does that have on the story itself?

Compare and Contrast Essays

In *The Red Badge of Courage* Stephen Crane maintains an objective authorial viewpoint, allowing the reader to formulate opinions of Henry, his actions, and his comments. Because you have Henry's story from his own point of view, you must judge whether his comments or reactions are appropriate. Because you do not get any judgment calls via authorial intervention, you need help from the text itself to judge what Henry says and does. One way of clarifying your own judgment is to compare Henry to other characters in the novel. You might, for instance, compare and contrast Henry and Wilson to determine who the more compassionate soldier is, or you might compare Henry and Jim Conklin to see who has more courage. A different kind of intertextual comparison might involve looking at Henry in relation to soldiers outside this text; for example, you could compare Henry to Robert Jordan in Ernest Hemingway's *For Whom the Bell Tolls* or Frederick Henry in *Farewell to Arms*, or you might want to compare him to Tim O'Brien in the 1990 work *The Things They Carried*. When making comparisons between texts, it is especially important to show the relevance of your comparison. In other words, how does the comparison assist in an interpretation of the text?

Sample Topics:

1. **Henry and his mother:** Compare and contrast Henry Fleming and his mother.

What do you know about Henry's mother? How does she feel about her son going off to fight? What does she see as Henry's main obligation as he is fighting? What significant differences are there between her view of war and Henry's? Based on your analysis of the two characters, what generalizations can you make about the novel's depiction of duty?

2. **Henry and the cheery soldier:** Compare and contrast these two characters, particularly in regard to duty.

First, define what it means to do one's "duty" in the context of war. Then find and analyze those passages that reveal the actions of Henry and the cheery soldier. What do they have in common? In what ways are they different? How does each character view his duty to his fellow soldier? Based on their differing reactions to this duty, which of these two would you argue is more courageous?

3. **Henry and Stephen Crane's other Civil War soldiers:** Comparing Henry to soldiers in Stephen Crane's later stories about the Civil War, what can you say about the evolution of Crane's portrayal of courage?

Compare and contrast the young Henry in *The Red Badge of Courage* to soldiers in his story collection *The Little Regiment* (1897), especially to the older Henry in "The Veteran." What do the young Henry and the old Henry have in common? How are they different? Compare these two to the protagonist in "A Mystery of Heroism," also published in *The Little Regiment.* Considering all three characters, can you synthesize Crane's view of courage? Has his definition changed from *The Red Badge* to these later stories? If so, how? Why is the change or lack of it important?

4. **Nature at the beginning of the novel and at the end:** Stephen Crane uses an envelope structure to bracket the novel between

a beginning description of nature and an ending description. Compare and contrast these two descriptions.

When the novel opens, it depicts the cold passing reluctantly from the earth and the fog receding. This landscape of expectancy contrasts with the ending landscape where it rains and then a "golden ray of sun came through the hosts of leaden rain clouds" (135). What is similar about the air of expectancy in each? What is different in the tone of these two passages? What do these differences suggest about Henry's future as a soldier? Is this ending ironic? Why or why not?

5. *The Red Badge* and Tim O'Brien's *The Things They Carried:* Analyze the similarities and differences of the Civil War protagonist and the Vietnam War protagonist.

Just as Stephen Crane's book concentrates on Henry's psychological adjustments to war, so does Tim O'Brien's. Although their methods are very different, they both emphasize the emotional baggage of war. How is that baggage similar for the two protagonists? How is it different? Although methods of war differ with each generation, human nature remains much the same, so you will want to analyze how these two men react similarly and differently in war conditions.

Bibliography and Online Resources for *The Red Badge of Courage*

Anderson, Warren D. "Homer and Stephen Crane." *Nineteenth Century Fiction* 19.1 (1964): 77–86.

Beaver, Harold. "Stephen Crane: The Hero as Victim." *Yearbook of English Studies* 12 (1982): 186–93.

Beidler, Philip D. "Stephen Crane's *The Red Badge of Courage:* Henry Fleming's Courage in Its Contexts." *CLIO: A Journal of Literature, History, and the Philosophy of History* 20.3 (1991): 235–51.

Benfey, Christopher. "Badges of Courage and Cowardice: A Source for Crane's Title." *Stephen Crane Studies* 6.2 (1997): 2–5.

Berryman, John. "Stephen Crane, *The Red Badge of Courage.*" *The American Novel from James Fenimore Cooper to William Faulkner.* Ed. Wallace Stegner. New York: Basic, 1965. 86–96.

———. "*The Red Badge of Courage* Is America's First Modern Novel." Ed. Bonnie Szumski. *Readings on Stephen Crane.* San Diego: Greenhaven, 1998. 93–98.

Binder, Henry. "*The Red Badge of Courage* Nobody Knows." *Studies in the Novel* 10 (1978): 9–47.

Bonner, Thomas, Jr. "Experience and Imagination: Confluence in the War Fiction of Stephen Crane and Ambrose Bierce." *War, Literature, and the Arts: An International Journal of the Humanities* (1999): 48–56.

Boyer, Marilyn. "The Treatment of the Wound in Stephen Crane's *The Red Badge of Courage.*" *Stephen Crane Studies* 12.1 (2003): 4–17.

Cain, William E. "Sensations of Style: The Literary Realism of Stephen Crane." Ed. Robert Paul Lamb and G. R. Thompson. *A Companion to American Fiction, 1865–1914.* Malden, MA: Blackwell, 2005. 557–71.

Carlson, Eric W. "Crane's *The Red Badge of Courage.*" *Explicator* 16 (1958): 34.

Cazemajou, Jean. "*The Red Badge of Courage:* The 'Religion of Peace' and the War Archetype." Ed. James Dickey and Joseph Katz. *Stephen Crane in Transition: Centenary Essays.* DeKalb: Northern Illinois UP, 1972. 54–65.

Colvert, James B. "Crane, Hitchcock, and the Binder Edition of *The Red Badge of Courage.*" *Critical Essays on Stephen Crane's The Red Badge of Courage.* Ed. Donald Pizer. Boston: G. K. Hall, 1990. 238–63.

Conrad, Joseph. "*The Red Badge of Courage.* Crane's Realism Makes the Novel Great." Ed. Bonnie Szumski. *Readings on Stephen Crane.* San Diego: Greenhaven, 1998. 99–103.

Cox, James T. "The Imagery of *The Red Badge of Courage.*" *Modern Fiction Studies* 5 (1959): 209–19.

Crane, Stephen. *The Works of Stephen Crane: The Red Badge of Courage: An Episode of the Civil War.* Ed. Fredson Bowers. Vol. 2. Charlottesville: UP of Virginia, 1975.

Delbanco, Andrew. "The American Stephen Crane: The Context of *The Red Badge of Courage.*" *New Essays on The Red Badge of Courage.* Ed. Mitchell, Lee Clark. Cambridge, UK: Cambridge UP, 1986. 49–76.

Dillingham, William B. "Insensibility in *The Red Badge of Courage.*" *College English* 25 (1963): 194–98.

Dooley, Patrick K. "'A Wound Gives Strange Dignity to Him Who Bears It': Stephen Crane's Metaphysics of Experience." *War, Literature, and the Arts: An International Journal of the Humanities* Special Edition (1999): 116–27.

Eby, Cecil D., Jr. "Stephen Crane's 'Fierce Red Wafer.'" *English Language Notes* 1 (1963): 128–30.

Ellison, Ralph. "Crane's Fiction Depicts the Civil War in Everyday Life." Ed. Bonnie Szumski. *Readings on Stephen Crane*. San Diego: Greenhaven, 1998. 44–51.

French, Warren. "Stephen: Moment of Myth." *Prairie Schooner* 55 (1091): 155–67.

Fulwiler, Toby. "The Death of the Handsome Sailor: A Study of Billy Budd and *The Red Badge of Courage*." *Arizona Quarterly: A Journal of American Literature, Culture, and Theory* 26 (1970): 101–12.

Gibson, Donald B. *The Red Badge of Courage: Defining the Hero*. Boston: Twayne, 1988

Gullason, Thomas A. "New Sources for Stephen Crane's War Motif." *Modern Language Notes* 72.8 (1957): 572–75.

———. "Thematic Patterns in Stephen Crane's Early Novels." *Nineteenth-Century Fiction* 16.1 (1961): 59–67.

Habegger, Alfred. "Fighting Words: The Talk of Men at War in *The Red Badge of Courage*." *Critical Essays on Stephen Crane's The Red Badge of Courage*. Ed. Donald Pizer. Boston: G. K. Hall, 1990. 229–38.

Harkins, William E. "Battle Scenes in the Writing of Tolstoy and Stephen Crane." Ed. Robert L. Belknap. *Russianness: Studies on a Nation's Identity*. Ann Arbor, MI: Ardis, 1990. 173–84.

Hayes, Kevin J. "How Stephen Crane Shaped Henry Fleming." *Studies in the Novel* 22 (1990): 296–307.

Heilman, Patricia I. "Stephen Crane's Images of War in Fiction and Nonfiction." *War, Literature, and the Arts: An International Journal of the Humanities* Special Edition (1999): 236–49.

Hofmann, Bettina. "Gender in Stephen Crane's *The Red Badge of Courage*." *Krieg und Literatur/War and Literature: Internationales Jahrbuch zur Kriegs und Antikriegsliteraturforschung/International Yearbook on War and Anti-War Literature* 6 (2002): 5–12.

Hungerford, Harold R. "'That Was Chancellorsville': The Factual Framework of *The Red Badge of Courage*." *American Literature* 34 (1963): 520–31.

Kaplan, Amy. "*The Red Badge of Courage* Redefined the War Novel." Ed. Bonnie Szumski. *Readings on Stephen Crane.* San Diego: Greenhaven, 1998. 117–27.

Kent, Thomas L. "Epistemological Uncertainty in *The Red Badge of Courage.*" *Modern Fiction Studies* 27 (1981–82): 621–28.

Kotani, Koji. "Stephen Crane's Strategy of Irony in *The Red Badge of Courage.*" *Studies in English Language and Literature* 40 (1990): 45–79.

La France, Marston. "Stephen Crane's Private Fleming: His Various Battles." Ed. Marston LaFrance. *Patterns of Commitment in American Literature.* Toronto: U of Toronto P, 1967. 113–33.

Lawson, Andrew. "The Red Badge of Class: Stephen Crane and the Industrial Army." *Literature and History* 14.2 (2005): 53–68.

Lee, Robert A. "Stephen Crane's *The Red Badge of Courage:* The Novella as 'Moving Box.'" *The Modern American Novella.* Ed. Robert A. Lee. New York: St. Martin's, 1989. 30–47.

Marlowe, Jean. "Crane's Wafer Image: Reference to an Artillery Primer?" *American Literature* 43 (1972): 645–47.

McClurg, A. C. "The Red Badge of Hysteria." *Dial,* 16 April 1896: 227–28.

McDermott, John J. "Symbolism and Psychological Realism in *The Red Badge of Courage.*" *Nineteenth-Century Fiction* 23 (1968): 324–31.

Mitchell, Lee Clark, ed. *New Essays on* The Red Badge of Courage. Cambridge: Cambridge UP, 1986.

———. The Spectacle of War in Crane's *The Red Badge of Courage.*" *Determined Fictions: American Literary Naturalism.* New York: Columbia UP, 1989. 96–116.

Monteiro, George. *Stephen Crane's Blue Badge of Courage.* Baton Rouge: Louisiana State UP, 2000.

Nagel, James E. "Crane Is a Literary Impressionist." Ed. Bonnie Szumski. *Readings on Stephen Crane.* San Diego: Greenhaven, 1998. 63–72.

Nelson, Ronald J. "The Writing Styles of Two Correspondents: Stephen Crane and Ernie Pyle." *West Virginia University Philological Papers* 51 (2004): 36–42.

O'Brien, Tim. *The Things They Carried.* New York: Houghton-Mifflin, 1990.

O'Donnell, Thomas F. "DeForest, Van Petten, and Stephen Crane." *American Literature* 27 (1956): 578–80.

———. "John B. Van Petten: Stephen Crane's History Teacher." *American Literature:* 27.2 (1955): 196–202.

Osborn, Scott C. "Stephen Crane's Imagery: 'Pasted Like a Wafer.'" *American Literature* 23 (1951): 362.

Parker, Hershel. "*The Red Badge of Courage:* The Private History of a Campaign That—Succeeded?" *Flawed Texts and Verbal Icons: Literary Authority in American Fiction.* Evanston, IL: Northwestern UP, 1984.

Perosa, Sergio. "Naturalism and Impressionism in Stephen Crane's Fiction." *Stephen Crane: A Collection of Critical Essays.* Ed. Maurice Bassan. Englewood Cliffs, NJ: Prentice-Hall, 1967.

Pizer, Donald. "Henry Behind the Lines and the Concept of Manhood in *The Red Badge of Courage.*" *Stephen Crane Studies* 10.1 (2001): 2–7.

——, ed. *Critical Essays on Stephen Crane's* The Red Badge of Courage. Boston: Hall, 1990.

Pratt, Lyndon U. "A Possible Source of *The Red Badge of Courage.*" *American Literature* 11 (1939): 1–11.

Rechnitz, Robert M. "Depersonalization and the Dream in *The Red Badge of Courage.*" *Studies in the Novel* 6 (1974): 76–87.

Richardson, Mark. "Stephen Crane's *The Red Badge of Courage.*" *American Writers Classics, I.* Ed. Jay Parini. New York: Thomson Gale, 2003.

Schneider, Michael. "Monomyth Structure in *The Red Badge of Courage. American Literary Realism* 20 (1987): 45–55.

Shaw, Mary Neff. "Henry Fleming's Heroics in *The Red Badge of Courage.*" *Studies in the Novel* 22 (1990): 418–28.

Shulman, Robert. "Community, Perception, and the Development of Stephen Crane: From *The Red Badge* to 'The Open Boat.'" *American Literature* 50.3 (1978): 441–60.

Solomon, Eric. "Another Analogue for *The Red Badge of Courage.*" *Nineteenth-Century Fiction* 13 (1958): 63–67.

——. "The Structure of *The Red Badge of Courage.*" *Modern Fiction Studies* 5 (1959): 220–34.

Starr, Alvin Jerome. "The Concept of Fear in the Works of Stephen Crane and Richard Wright." *Studies in Black Literature* 6.2 (1975): 6–10.

The Stephen Crane Society. *Reviews of Crane's Works and Other Secondary Sites.* "The Red Badge of Courage: Critical Reception: Early Reviews." 4 August 2008. Web. 22 Feb. 2010.

Stowell, Robert. "Stephen Crane's Use of Colour in *The Red Badge of Courage.*" *Literary Criterion* 9.3 (1970): 36–39.

Tamke, Alexander R. "The Principal Source of Stephen Crane's *Red Badge of Courage.*" *Essays in Honor of Esmond Linworth Marilla.* Ed. Thomas A. Kirby, William J. Olive. Baton Rouge: Louisiana State UP, 1970.

Tavernier-Courbin, Jacqueline. "Humor and Insight Through Fallacy in Stephen Crane's *The Red Badge of Courage.*" *War, Literature, and the Arts: An International Journal of the Humanities* Special Edition (1999): 147–59.

Werner, William L. "Stephen Crane and *The Red Badge of Courage.*" *New York Times Book Review* 4 (1945).

Wertheim, Stanley. "*The Red Badge of Courage* and Personal Narratives of the Civil War." *American Literary Realism* 6 (1973): 62–65.

Westbrook, Max Roger. "The Progress of Henry Fleming: Stephen Crane's *The Red Badge of Courage.*" *CEA Critic* 61.2-3 (1999): 71–82.

Wogan, Claudia C. "Crane's Use of Color in *The Red Badge of Courage.*" *Modern Fiction Studies* 6 (1960): 168–72.

Wolford, Chester L. "*The Red Badge of Courage* Mocks the Greek Epic." Ed. Bonnie Szumski. *Readings on Stephen Crane.* San Diego: Greenhaven, 1998. 104–16.

Zhu, Weihong Julia. "The Absurdity of Henry's Courage." *Stephen Crane Studies* 10.2 (2001): 2–11.

MAGGIE: A GIRL OF THE STREETS

READING TO WRITE

When he was only twenty-one years old, Stephen Crane completed his short novel *Maggie: A Girl of the Streets (A Story of New York)*. Unable to interest publishers in the volume, Crane used some stock money inherited from his mother to have the book privately printed in 1893. Only after the writer achieved almost instant international fame with *The Red Badge of Courage* in 1895 was D. Appleton & Company interested in publishing *Maggie*. Even then Crane was forced to edit the original version, eliminating some of the profanity and refining the book to be deemed suitable for the public. Even with these revisions, the volume still seemed offensive to some reviewers, who were shocked at the violence and at the protagonist, a young woman forced into prostitution after being evicted from her mother's house.

This novel shows the hopes and the realities of life in a New York tenement of the late nineteenth century, revealing the poverty and violence inherent in such an existence. The opening scene exhibits the violence permeating the life of the children at a young age and pursuing them into adulthood.

A very little boy stood upon a heap of gravel for the honor of Rum Alley. He was throwing stones at howling urchins from Devil's Row, who were circling madly about the heap and pelting him.

His infantile countenance was livid with the fury of battle. His small body was writhing in the delivery of oaths.

"Run, Jimmie, run! Dey'll git yehs!" screamed a retreating Rum Alley child.

"Naw," responded Jimmie with a valiant roar, "dese mugs can't make me run."

Howls of renewed wrath went up from Devil's Row throats. Tattered gamins on the right made a furious assault on the gravel heap. On their small convulsed faces shone the grins of true assassins. As they charged, they threw stones and cursed in shrill chorus.

The little champion of Rum Alley stumbled precipitately down the other side. His coat had been torn to shreds in a scuffle and his hat was gone. He had bruises on twenty parts of his body, and blood was dripping from a cut in his head. His wan features looked like those of a tiny insane demon.

On the ground, children from Devil's Row closed in on their antagonist. He crooked his left arm defensively about his head and fought with madness. The little boys ran to and fro, dodging, hurling stones, and swearing in barbaric trebles.

From a window of an apartment house that uprose from amid squat ignorant stables there leaned a curious woman. Some laborers, unloading a scow at a dock at the river, paused for a moment and regarded the fight. The engineer of a passive tugboat hung lazily over a railing and watched. Over on the island a worm of yellow convicts came from the shadow of a gray ominous building and crawled slowly along the river's bank. (7)

These opening paragraphs, when closely scrutinized, reveal several important aspects of the Bowery environment in which these tenement children live.

A close reading of this opening scene provokes the reader to ask questions such as these: Why are the streets named Rum Alley and Devil's Row? Is this fight just a childish escapade, or is it a more significant event? Why don't the adult onlookers do something to break up the fracas?

A rereading of the passage soon reveals that the episode is filled with both actual and potential physical damage. The boys on the heap of gravel are not just scuffling; instead, they are throwing rocks capable of inflicting serious wounds. The resulting blood, the negative street names, and the narrative descriptions of the children all increase the nightmarish quality of the scene, one filled with comparisons of the boys to "true assassins" and "tiny demons," with sounds labeled "barbaric," and with actions such as "pelting" and "writhing." In more ordinary circumstances no adult would stand by and allow children to continue such an activity. Yet the laborers on the dock simply pause "for a moment" before continuing their unloading of a scow. The woman in the apartment house continues to lean out the window to watch, and an engineer of a tugboat merely observes them as he continues on his way. None of these adults interfere or even show concern. Finally, the intimation is that the boys' futures will be much like the lives of the convicted criminals who crawl "slowly along the river's bank."

After reading these few paragraphs carefully, you may also notice that the boy is referred to as a *champion* and that he exhibits the *fury of battle*. These terms indicate that more is involved than a simple battle for turf, even if the turf is only a few heaps of gravel. For these boys, such fighting seems to be a way of life, and the reader can infer from the grandiose imagery inflating the childish fight to epic proportions that not only is the Bowery filled with similar violence on a daily basis but also that the inhabitants encourage such behavior.

TOPICS AND STRATEGIES

This section of the chapter includes discussions of various possible topics for essays on *Maggie*. These suggestions should serve as a starting point for you to generate and refine your own topics. Whether you choose one of the topics here or formulate your own, you will still need to go through the usual processes of brainstorming, organizing, and finalizing your approach to the topic.

After you have considered the questions listed with each topic and have analyzed other passages from the novel, you can begin to generate questions of your own. These questions should lead you to even more passages to clarify points you have raised. Eventually you must settle on one particular question that interests you, and you can then begin to search for an answer to that question. The search will ultimately allow you to reach a conclusion that will become your thesis. Once you have a thesis with which you are satisfied, the next step is to select evidence to support it. The final planning step is to arrange that evidence in a logical order to organize your own argument about a major feature of the book, such as theme, characterization, or philosophy.

Themes

A novel's themes are the major ideas explored within the text. Although many novels share similar themes or "big questions" of society, each novel treats each theme differently, in its own way. *Maggie* deals with several major themes, or concepts, that organize the action of the novel. The section above briefly contained several of these: violence, ineffective adult authority, the hellish existence of the tenement environment, and the promise of a gloomy future. The novel also deals with other themes such as hypocrisy, skewed values, the romantic versus the realistic, and the role of women in the tenements. Writers approaching any book can begin by identifying a central theme they see as important and then deciding what that novel is saying about that theme.

To identify a theme, you would look for ideas or even words that suggest a particular idea; for example, in the initial discussion, violence appears as a central concern and a further search for violent behaviors in other passages will confirm that it is an important theme. The next step is deciding what the book *Maggie* is saying about the theme of violence. Similarly, you can choose other themes, choosing one to pursue and considering how the novel deals with that theme. As you study the language relating to your chosen theme, you will begin to formulate an argument that can develop into a specific thesis.

Sample Topics:

1. **Violence:** How does the novel represent and evaluate the use of violence? How does it judge the violent behaviors?

   To write an essay on this theme, you can begin by identifying passages where the novel either represents or discusses violence. Then you should look at what kinds of judgments characters offer and what kinds of reactions these moments produce both in the novel and in the reader. Are there ever any positive results? Is anyone *not* involved in violent activity? How does that violence make you as a reader feel?

During the opening scene above, one adult does interfere—
Jimmie's father. He is upset with his son for fighting, and he
stops the fracas:

> "Here, you Jim, get up, now, while I belt yer life out, yeh damned
> disorderly brat."
>
> He began to kick into the chaotic mass on the ground. The
> boy Billie felt a heavy boot strike his head. He made a furi-
> ous effort and disentangled himself from Jimmie. He tottered
> away, damning.
>
> Jimmie arose painfully from the ground and confronting
> his father, began to curse him. His parent kicked him. "Come
> home, now," he cried, "an' stop yer jawin', er I'll lam the ever-
> lasting head off yehs." (10)

What does this exchange tell you about violence in Jimmie's
own family? What type of reception do you expect when Jimmie gets home? What actually happens? Has Jimmie learned
anything about avoiding violence?

2. **Poverty:** What is the nature or function of economic status in
the novel?

How does the novel represent the poverty of the Johnson family? Who works and what type of work is done? You might look
at the different types of jobs and think about how successful
the workers are. What are their attitudes toward their work?
Is the poverty more than economic; in other words, is there a
poverty of spirit or outlook?

Until his father dies, Jimmie stands on street corners watching passersby with no occupation, nothing to take up his time.
Then he becomes a truck driver. His biggest satisfaction is
looking down from his vehicle, pulled by a pair of horses, and
feeling superior to those around him. Is he as important as he
likes to believe? Does his work seem successful or rewarding?
What sort of future can Jimmie expect?

Maggie goes to work in a collar and cuff factory, sewing during the long work days. What other jobs are open to her? How does she feel about Pete's employment in relation to her own situation? Why does she see the bar he works in as "elegant"? Do Jimmie and Maggie have any hopes of moving beyond the tenement? Why or why not?

3. **Hypocrisy:** Many characters in the book seem to be insincere in their concern for their fellow humans. Identify some of these characters and analyze their actions and motivations.

Of the several religious figures appearing in the book, are any truly helpful to Maggie or other characters when they are in need? What is Jimmie's experience at the mission church where he goes for a bowl of soup?

Is there a discrepancy between the characters' spoken ideas of "respectability" and their actions? Although he looks down on most people, Jimmie "achieved a respect for a fire engine" (23). On what is that respect based? Jimmie is upset that his sister has been "ruined," but he chooses not to think about the girls he himself has seduced over the years. Does he care more about Maggie or his own sense of power in the tenement? How does Mary Johnson react to her daughter's death? Do her reactions seem sincere?

4. **Values:** What are the primary values of residents in the slum? How have those values been formed?

What type of entertainment do Maggie and Pete attend? How do they view it? Identify each of the passages that detail their social outings. As you look at the progression of the types of places to which they go for entertainment, you might ask how the nature and sophistication of these places change over time. What other activities might be more meaningful or uplifting for these two young people?

The family and society tend to be the social structures that inculcate, or instill, appropriate values in the young. How do the Johnson family and the other Bowery inhabitants function as role models for the children? Do any of them provide appropriate guidance or care? What do Jimmie, Pete, and Maggie value in their lives? How have Maggie's mother and father contributed to her value formation? How has the society around her contributed? Do Maggie's values seem different from those of the other characters? If so, in what way are they different?

Character

An examination of a character in a novel can often result in valuable insights into meaning or theme. Papers dealing with characterization can examine character development, which includes details that distinguish a specific character, such as Maggie's concern for her brother Jimmie when he comes home after fighting; her concern for her baby brother, Tommie; and her attempts to make the squalid flat more livable. Other papers can examine means of characterization, such as the way the reader learns about Mary, beginning with observing her reactions of extreme anger at Jimmie for his fighting and hearing her words to him, reading the narrator's descriptive phrases, such as "massive shoulders" (12) and "chieftain-like stride" (13), and seeing the reactions of others to her—her husband when he tires of her anger, the judge during her numerous court appearances, and the neighbor who asks Maggie, "[W]hat is it dis time?" (15). Still other papers can analyze changes in a particular character as the novel proceeds, such as how Pete goes from being the older boy who breaks up the opening fight, to seeming a "knight" who gives promise of a better life for Maggie, to being a barroom brawler, and finally to becoming a derelict looked down on even by the prostitute Nell.

If you decide to analyze a character, you should determine whether that character is dynamic or static, that is, whether she changes or stays the same during the course of the novel. You should determine how you react to the character and how those reactions are provoked by the narrator or other characters. Finally, you should make a connection of the characterization to the meaning of the novel. In other words, why is it important that you have seen a character in a particular way? What does that characterization lend to an interpretation of the book?

Sample Topics:

1. **Maggie:** Analyze the characterization of this young girl of the slums.

   How does Maggie manage to maintain a sense of respectability throughout the novel? Why is she portrayed as a static character? Consider this passage:

   > The girl, Maggie, blossomed in a mud puddle. She grew to be a most rare and wonderful production of a tenement district, a pretty girl.
   >   None of the dirt of Rum Alley seemed to be in her veins. The philosophers up stairs, down stairs and on the same floor, puzzled over it. (24)

   Does the narrator here indicate more than physical beauty? How is Maggie an attractive girl in other ways? How does her attractiveness become almost a negative attribute in the Bowery District?
     Eventually Maggie becomes a prostitute. Do you feel sympathetic to her or disdainful of her? Why? How does she compare to the prostitute Nell? How can you explain the difference in the two women? What is Maggie's biggest weakness? Whose fault is that weakness? What does her eventual demise indicate about life in the tenements?

2. **Jimmie:** Analyze how this character functions in the novel.

   How does Jimmie's character differ from that of his sister? What is the significance of the differences? Jimmie seems to see himself as tough and important. He wants to be the best fighter on the street corner, he wants to look down on the other vehicles from his truck seat, and he does not want the other slum dwellers to see him as the brother of a fallen woman. In the following passage, we can see Jimmie's life summarized:

> When Jimmie was a little boy, he began to be arrested. Before he reached a great age, he had a fair record.
>
> He developed too great a tendency to climb down from his truck and fight with other drivers. He had been in quite a number of miscellaneous fights, and in some general barroom rows that had become known to the police. Once he had been arrested for assaulting a Chinaman. Two women in different parts of the city, and entirely unknown to each other, caused him considerable annoyance by breaking forth, simultaneously, at fateful intervals, into wailings about marriage and support and infants.
>
> Nevertheless, he had on a certain starlit evening, said wonderingly and quite reverently: "D' moon looks like hell, don't it?" (23)

Jimmie is a troublemaker, a philanderer, and a man who does not care about the problems he has caused for others. The last sentence in this passage, however, suggests that somewhere deep inside Jimmie might exist the possibility of his being a better person. What is the significance of his pronouncement that the moon looks like "hell"? What word or words would you have used instead of that one? How does his treatment of Maggie compare to his treatment of the women whom he has seduced and abandoned? What has caused him to become the person he is?

3. **Mary:** Examine Mary's role in the book. What kind of mother is Mary? Why does she act as she does?

When the reader first encounters Mary, she is angry that Jimmie has been fighting, and she begins hitting at him. When she sees that he has torn his clothes in the fight, she becomes even more enraged and hits him even more. This violence is only the beginning of her completely inappropriate reaction to her children. What do the neighbors think of Mary? How do you know? How does the judicial system treat Mary? How does she contribute to Maggie's demise? How does she react to

Maggie's eventual death? What can the reader surmise at her last words: "Oh, yes, I'll forgive her! I'll forgive her!" (77)

4. **Pete:** Analyze the characterization of the bartender Pete.

Maggie sees Pete as a way out of the chaotic and dismal life she has led with her family. She sees him as an "ideal man" (26), a hero to rescue her from the squalid flat where violence is the norm:

> He [Pete] walked to and fro in the small room, which seemed then to grow even smaller and unfit to hold his dignity, the attribute of a supreme warrior. That swing of the shoulders which had frozen the timid when he was but a lad had increased with his growth and education at the ratio of ten to one. It, combined with the sneer upon his mouth, told mankind that there was nothing in space which could appall him. Maggie marveled at him and surrounded him with greatness. She vaguely tried to calculate the altitude of the pinnacle from which he must have looked down upon her. (27)

Although Maggie idealizes Pete, Crane's depiction of this young bartender undercuts this idealism from the beginning, with a close reading revealing that Pete is not nearly so superior as Maggie thinks. He dresses better than Jimmie, works in a bar that Maggie sees as "elegant" (25), and exudes an air of confidence, but he dismisses the concepts of religion and philosophy with a one-word response: "Rats!" (25). What does this emphatic pronouncement reveal about Pete? How does Pete compare to Jimmie? How do these two characters differ? How are they similar?

History and Context

Another productive approach to this novel is through history and context. In the 1890s, the influx of immigrants into New York was immense, with the city's population having risen from 600,000 in 1860 to more than 3 million in 1900. The new arrivals were generally poor and uneducated, and most wound up living in the crowded tenements of New York

City. Although westward expansion was at its height and transportation by rail had opened up the country for travel, the immigrants usually did not have the financial means to leave the city. As a result, families were crowded into tiny rooms with intolerable sanitary conditions.

Stephen Crane was not the first to write about tenement conditions. Other fictional literature on this topic typically fell into one of two categories: a melodramatic tale of a boy or girl who rises from rags to riches, such as Edward Townsend's *A Daughter of the Tenements* (1895), or an equally melodramatic story of girls or women who had been seduced, such as Edgar Fawcett's *The Evil That Men Do* (1889). The second group always ended appropriately with the death of the female protagonist and included much moralizing about the results of her sordid way of life. A third type of writing about tenement conditions was the nonfictional exposé designed to garner sympathy from readers, such as Jacob Riis's *How the Other Half Lives* (1890). *Maggie* follows the life of a prostitute in New York City's tenements, but Stephen Crane omits the melodrama and moralizing of both the contemporary fiction and nonfiction. The result is a more realistic and, in many ways, more sympathetic treatment of the girl, Maggie.

Sample Topics:

1. **Immigrants in New York in the 1880s and 1890s:** Analyze how the problems of immigrants in the slums inform Stephen Crane's novel.

   To understand the extreme conditions endured by Bowery inhabitants of the late nineteenth century, you may want to examine Jacob Riis's journalistic writing, complete with photographs and diagrams, or you may want to read historical accounts of immigrants of that time period, especially the Irish.

   You can access Jacob Riis's *How the Other Half Lives* online to see some facts about immigrant girls working in New York City. In Chapter 20 he writes:

   > Sixty cents is put as the average day's earnings of the 150,000, but into this computation enters the stylish "cashier's" two dollars a day, as well as the thirty cents of the poor little girl who

pulls threads in an East Side factory, and, if anything, the average is probably too high. Such as it is, however, it represents board, rent, clothing, and "pleasure" to this army of workers. Here is the case of a woman employed in the manufacturing department of a Broadway house. It stands for a hundred like her own. She averages three dollars a week. Pays $1.50 for her room; for breakfast she has a cup of coffee; lunch she cannot afford. One meal a day is her allowance. This woman is young, she is pretty. She has "the world before her." Is it anything less than a miracle if she is guilty of nothing worse than the "early and improvident marriage," against which moralists exclaim as one of the prolific causes of the distress of the poor?

Consider the economic options that Maggie has in Crane's novel. What alternatives does this young girl have? In your analysis of the book, explain how Crane represents the economic problems of the tenements, including both the Johnson family and their neighbors.

2. **The temperance movement in America:** Examine the role of alcohol in this novel of the Bowery.

Stephen Crane's mother was a lecturer who lobbied against alcohol, even demonstrating what happened when an egg was submerged into a glass of liquor. His father, the Reverend Jonathan Townley Crane, also an advocate of temperance, published the religious tract titled *The Arts of Intoxication: The Aim and the Results.* As you trace the use of alcohol in the novel *Maggie,* consider its impact. What argument can you make about Crane's depiction of alcohol? Is it a major contributing factor to Maggie's demise, or is it simply part of the scene?

3. **Prejudice against the Irish:** Stephen Crane has been said to show prejudice in his depiction of the Irish. Read, for example, Stanley Wertheim's article "Unraveling the Humanist: Stephen

Crane and Ethnic Minorities." What evidence can you find that shows prejudice against the Irish? Agree or disagree that there is prejudice in the presentation.

Philosophy and Ideas

At the end of the nineteenth century, many new scientific and philosophical ideas had entered the American culture. Charles Darwin's biological determinism had been adopted and adapted by social scientists, who used it in their own fields, with a major example being Karl Marx's economic determinism. The idea is that if biology determines who survives, then the environment itself is important, with economic status and other social conditions shaping the fate of humanity. Such philosophical thinking resulted in a literary movement referred to as naturalism and included writers such as Frank Norris, Jack London, and Theodore Dreiser. Often associated with this movement, Stephen Crane's writing is not as clearly naturalistic as some of his peers, but in *Maggie* he does reveal the importance of environmental influences.

Another idea that evolved at this time was the importance of philanthropy, a result of the massive accumulation of wealth by such people as the Vanderbilts, the Rockefellers, and the Carnegies. With their newly acquired riches, these men built huge mansions, entertained lavishly, and enjoyed the good life, but they also felt the need to be philanthropic. Cornelius Vanderbilt used his money to provide for a new university in Nashville, Tennessee, that still bears his name, and both John D. Rockefeller and Andrew Carnegie established foundations to funnel money to numerous projects for the less fortunate.

You might choose to write on either of these two ideas—naturalism or philanthropy—to form an argument about the novel *Maggie*. As you think about these two philosophies or ideas, you may generate others, such as gender discrimination, religious responsibility, or the importance of family.

Sample Topics:

1. **Naturalism:** *Maggie* depicts the fate of the title character in such a way that the environment seems to determine the girl's fate. Analyze aspects of the novel that seem deterministic.

An essay on the question of determinism will consider the ability of the characters to respond to events, to learn from them, and to change future outcomes of similar events. Do the characters in the novel learn from their experience? How can they change their method of dealing with problems? Such an essay might also look at how the environment is portrayed. How are the tenement buildings themselves described? For example, we are told that "from a careening building a dozen gruesome doorways gave loads of babies to the street and the gutter" (11). Look for other descriptions of the buildings in the Bowery. Do the buildings themselves seem to be capable of action in a way that the characters are not? How does this power infuse the naturalistic focus of the novel?

2. **Philanthropy:** During the time the actions of *Maggie* occur, philanthropy had become an important part of being prosperous. What does Crane indicate about philanthropy in this novel?

This is another large question, one that is difficult to answer. Although many people at the time were aware of slum conditions, little was being done to bring about real reform. What evidence is there in *Maggie* that philanthropy is virtually absent? What services or actions might have saved Tommie and Maggie from their early deaths?

3. **Ethics and responsibility:** Examine the question of ethics and responsibility as it is repeatedly raised in this novel.

This question is related to the idea of determinism but focuses instead on how to evaluate the characters' personal responsibility for actions that appear to be predetermined. Is Maggie only a pawn? Is she morally responsible for her "fall" or does responsibility lie elsewhere?

What is the nature of the Johnson family's responsibility to one another? What is Pete's responsibility to Maggie? How does the novel represent ethical/unethical behavior?

Form and Genre

Form and genre are important elements of any constructed writing, especially fiction and especially in the latter part of the nineteenth century when a reaction against Romanticism in literature resulted in a new movement: Realism. Championed and practiced by the eminent man of letters William Dean Howells, realism aimed to present life as it really is, a depiction that Howells termed "verisimilitude." This effort of realistic writers to recreate in fiction the average man in the current time, not some idealized version set in the past, resulted in several changes in form. The previous emphasis on plot changed to an emphasis on characterization and on the ethical choices that the characters face in their lives. In addition, the narrator in this type of writing works to remain largely objective, with the reader having to judge whether the characters' choices are ethical or not. Because of this narrative objectivity, the use of irony became an important stylistic device, forcing the reader to reach conclusions not overtly stated in the text. Finally, realistic novels and stories used the language of the common man, often with the inclusion of dialect or slang appropriate for the specific characters and circumstances.

Sample Topics:

1. **Realism:** Analyze *Maggie* as an example of literary realism.

Stephen Crane spent a great deal of time in the Bowery to learn about its inhabitants and their way of life. He would have been familiar with the published sermons on the evils of the slums, the nonfictional essays highlighting the conditions in the tenements, and the melodramatic fictional treatments of slum life. How does Crane avoid the sermonizing and the melodrama of these other media? In other words, how does he make this novel realistic?

This kind of essay would need to focus on the ways that the novel represents poverty, both economic poverty and intellectual and spiritual poverty. What is realistic about the characters and the events? You should look especially at specific details of daily life, for example, the description of the surface glamour of the bar where Pete works and the dirty dishes there.

2. **Irony:** Analyze Crane's employment of irony in this novel.

Consider, for example, this passage:

> Down the avenue came boastfully sauntering a lad of sixteen years, although the chronic sneer of an ideal manhood already sat upon his lips. His hat was tipped over his eye with an air of challenge. Between his teeth, a cigar stump was tilted at the angle of defiance. He walked with a certain swing of the shoulders which appalled the timid. (8)

This topic asks the writer to consider whether to take the narrator's words literally. Does the author really want us to believe that Pete represents "ideal manhood," or does he want to suggest the opposite, that Pete is insecure in spite of his swaggering gait?

Language, Symbols, and Imagery

The language in *Maggie* is perhaps more significant than that in other treatments of life in the slums of New York. Ranging from vivid descriptions, to dialect, and to important imagery, all the language techniques enable the reader both to envision what is happening and to judge the significance of each event. When the boys are daring each other to fight, they speak in the language of the streets: slang punctuated with "hell" and "damn." Although D. Appleton & Company insisted that Crane remove some of the profanity, he still kept enough to portray accurately the poverty of language for these downtrodden slum dwellers. When they cannot adequately portray their feelings, they use profanity or a pronouncement such as "Rats!" to express their emotions.

In addition to the meaningful dialect, the images permeating the narrative convey the squalid existence of these slum dwellers. Although seldom do any of the images rise to the level of being symbolic, the patterns of imagery themselves establish the simulated bravery of Jimmie and undercut his desire to gain power by means of fighting and carousing. Although he puffs himself up as some type of hero, he is actually just hiding his cowardice under a façade. By tracing various patterns of imagery, you will begin to see how they provide insight into larger issues in the novel.

Sample Topics:

1. **Pattern of chivalric imagery:** Analyze images related to knights or warriors.

   Typically these are exaggerations of events, which in themselves may seem trivial but which Crane's imagery elevates to almost epic status. For example, Mary is referred to as a "gladiator" and a "chieftain" (40). What effect do these images have on the reader? How do they help to interpret the characters and the actions?

2. **The moon:** Analyze references to the moon or to another aspect of nature.

   In Chapter 3, for example, when the parents have passed out after much drinking, the children try to comfort each other. Crane then presents the exterior moon: "Out at the window a florid moon was peering over dark roofs, and in the distances the waters of a river glimmered pallidly" (19). What is the significance of this and the other references to the moon? How does the juxtaposition of natural elements and the unceasing violence lend more understanding of the children's position within society?

3. **Cartoonlike actions:** Analyze imagery that indicates exaggerated machine-like actions of the various characters.

   In Chapter 4, Jimmie perceives that he is powerful as he drives his cart through the traffic: "he and his team had the unalienable right to stand in the proper path of the sun chariot, and if they so minded, obstruct its mission or take a wheel off" (22). How does the absurdity of this action—defying the mythical chariot of the sun god, Apollo—exemplify Jimmie's self-perception? What other images seem more appropriate for cartoons than for a realistic novel? How do they aid in the interpretation of the novel?

Compare and Contrast Essays

Often elements of a novel are set up in juxtaposition to each other, enabling the reader to draw conclusions about the two elements—events, characters, or settings. You might look for such juxtapositions, such as the characterizations of the two prostitutes Maggie and Nell, and try to evaluate the similarities and differences of the two, deciding why this comparison is important or how it allows you more insight into the work. You should avoid simply listing the similarities and differences and stopping there. The crucial step is interpreting the importance of these similarities and differences.

In addition to looking within the novel itself, you may also want to look outside the novel to other works dealing with similar topics, such as slum life or prostitution. You might also look at published sermons dealing with tenement problems, the various nonfictional treatments of the slum, or even other novels of the time that have female protagonists who become prostitutes.

Sample Topics:

1. **Chapter 1 and Chapter 17:** Compare the opening chapter and the last chapter of the novel.

   The opening chapter about the fight for the honor of Rum Alley and Devil's Row ends with a walk home for Jimmie and his father. The final chapter in which Maggie appears ends with her walk to her final destiny: "She hurried forward through the crowd as if intent upon reaching a distant home" (68–69). What is the result of each walk? How are they alike? How are they different? What do these similarities and differences mean in terms of understanding the novel? Does the idea of "home" seem important?

2. **Crane's two versions of a tenement existence:** Compare Stephen Crane's essay "Experiment in Misery" with this novel.

How is this nonfiction account of a night Crane spent in a tenement similar to *Maggie*? How does it differ? What is the importance of these similarities and differences? Pay particular attention to tone as you consider the two works. This kind of essay will examine Crane's purposes in writing the two works. You may also want to think in terms of audience and purpose for each piece. You may conclude that the purpose of each is similar in some ways and different in others. What is the importance of these similarities and differences?

3. *Maggie* and Edgar Fawcett's *The Evil That Men Do* (1889): Compare these two fictional treatments of prostitution.

This topic asks the reader to look at the presentation of the slums of New York and the position of a prostitute at that time. Important elements of each presentation include dialect or lack of dialect, tone, imagery as opposed to more literal language, characterization, and the consequences of prostitution. Like Maggie, Fawcett's heroine, Cora, finds no happy ending. What else is alike about these two stories of a prostitute? What is different? Why are these similarities and differences important in a better understanding of Crane's novel? Which do you prefer? Why?

Bibliography and Online Resources for *Maggie: A Girl of the Streets*

Bassan, Maurice, ed. *Stephen Crane's Maggie: Text and Context.* Belmont, CA: Wadsworth, 1966.

Begiebing, Robert J. "Stephen Crane's Maggie: The Death of the Self." *American Imago: A Psychoanalytic Journal for Culture, Science, and the Arts* 34 (1977): 50–71.

Church, Joseph. "'Excellent People': Naturalism, Egotism, and the Teaching of Crane's Maggie." *ALN: The American Literary Naturalism Newsletter* 1.2 (2006): 10–15.

Crane, Stephen. *The Works of Stephen Crane: Maggie.* Ed. Fredson Bowers. Vol. 1. Charlottesville: UP of Virginia, 1969.

Cunliffe, Marcus. "Stephen Crane and the American Background of Maggie." *American Quarterly* 7 (1955): 31–44.

Dingledine, Don. "'It could have been any Street': Ann Petry, Stephen Crane, and the Fate of Naturalism." *Studies in American Fiction* 34.1 (2006): 87–106.

Dooley, Patrick K. "Stephen Crane's Distilled Style (and the Art of Fine Swearing)." *Stephen Crane Studies* 15.1 (2006): 28–31.

Dowling Robert, M. "Stephen Crane and the Transformation of the Bowery." *Twisted from the Ordinary: Essays on American Literary Naturalism.* Ed. Mary E. Papke. Knoxville: U of Tennessee P, 2003. 45–62.

———, and Donald Pizer. "A Cold Case File Reopened: Was Crane's Maggie Murdered or a Suicide?" *American Literary Realism* 42.1 (2009): 36–53.

Fitelson, David. *"Maggie: A Girl of the Streets* Portrays a 'Survival of the Fittest' World." *Readings on Stephen Crane.* Ed. Bonnie Szumski. San Diego: Greenhaven, 1998. 168–79.

———. "Stephen Crane's *Maggie* and Darwinism." *American Quarterly* 16 (1964): 182–94.

Fudge, Keith. "Sisterhood Born from Seduction: Susanna Rowson's Charlotte Temple, and Stephen Crane's Maggie Johnson." *Journal of American Culture* 19.1 (1996): 43–50.

Gandal, Keith Leland. "Stephen Crane's 'Maggie' and the Modern Soul." *ELH* 60.3 (1993): 759–85.

———. *The Virtues of the Vicious: Jacob Riis, Stephen Crane, and the Spectacle of the Slum.* Oxford, UK: Oxford UP, 1997.

Graham, Kevin. "Outcasts and Social Exclusion in Stephen Crane's Maggie: A Girl of the Streets." *Interactions: Aegean Journal of English and American Studies/Ege Ingiliz ve Amerikan Incelemeleri Dergisi* 16.1 (2007): 63–74.

Gullason, Thomas A. "The Prophetic City in Stephen Crane's 1893 Maggie." *Modern Fiction Studies* 24 (1978): 129–37.

Gullason, Thomas Arthur. "The Sources of Stephen Crane's *Maggie.*" *Philological Quarterly* 38 (1959): 497–502. *MLA*

Kahn, Sholom J. "Stephen Crane and Whitman: A Possible Source for *Maggie.*" *Walt Whitman Review* 7 (1961): 71–77.

Karlen, Arno. "Stylistic Weakness in *Maggie.*" *Readings on Stephen Crane.* Ed. Bonnie Szumski. San Diego: Greenhaven, 1998. 180–84.

Kuga, Shunji. "'Feminine Domesticity and the Feral City: Stephen Crane's *George's Mother, Maggie,* and 'A Detail.'" *Stephen Crane Studies* 13.2 (2004): 21–31.

LaFrance, Marston. *"George's Mother* and the Other Half of *Maggie." Stephen Crane in Transition: Centenary Essays.* Ed. Joseph Katz and James Dickey. DeKalb: Northern Illinois UP, 1972. 35–53.

Lawson, Andrew. "Class Mimicry in Stephen Crane's City." *American Literary History* 16.4 (2004): 596–618.

Nagel, James. "Donald Pizer, American Naturalism, and Stephen Crane." *Studies in American Naturalism* 1 (2006): 30–35.

———. "Limitations of Perspective in the Fiction of Stephen Crane." *Stephen Crane Studies* 15.1 (2006): 9–12.

Orgeron, Marsha. "The Road to Nowhere: Stephen Crane's *Maggie: A Girl of the Streets (a Story of New York)* (1893)." *Women in Literature: Reading through the Lens of Gender.* Ed. Jerilyn Fisher, Ellen S. Silber, and David Sadker. Westport, CT: Greenwood, 2003. 185–87.

Pittenger, Mark. "A World of Difference: Constructing the 'Underclass' in Progressive America." *American Quarterly* 49 (1997): 26–65.

Riis, Jacob. *How the Other Half Lives.* New York: Charles Scribner's Sons, 1890. *Bartleby.com: Great Books Online.* http://www.bartleby.com/208/

Salemi, Joseph S. "Down a Steep Place into the Sea: Suicide in Stephen Crane's *Maggie." ANQ: A Quarterly Journal of Short Articles, Notes, and Reviews* 1.2 (1988): 58–61.

Slotkin, Alan R. "You as a Multileveled Dictional Device in Stephen Crane's Representation of Bowery Dialect in *Maggie: A Girl of the Streets." South Central Review* 7.2 (1990): 40–53.

Stasi, Paul. "Joycean Constellations: 'Eveline' and the Critique of Naturalist Totality." *James Joyce Quarterly* 46.1 (2008): 39–53.

Stein, William Bysshe. "Crane's use of Biblical Parables in *Maggie." Readings on Stephen Crane.* Ed. Bonnie Szumski. San Diego: Greenhaven, 1998. 185–90.

Sweeney, Gerard M. "The Syphilitic World of Stephen Crane's *Maggie." American Literary Realism* 24.1 (1991): 79–85.

Weatherford, Richard M., ed. *Stephen Crane: The Critical Heritage.* London: Routledge & Kegan Paul. 1973.

Wertheim, Stanley. "Unraveling the Humanist: Stephen Crane and Ethnic Minorities." *American Literary Realism* 30. 3 (1998): 65–75.

Wilson, Christopher P. "Stephen Crane and the Police." *American Quarterly* 48.2 (1996): 273–315.

THE BLACK RIDERS AND OTHER LINES

READING TO WRITE

When Stephen Crane published *The Black Riders and Other Lines* in 1895, he was not prepared for the reception of this first volume of his poetry. Because of its somewhat irreverent stance on God and religion and because of its unconventional form, the poetry was discussed widely and parodied often. In an 1897 letter to John Northern Hilliard, Crane insisted that he liked his poetry better than the popular *Red Badge* because the poems contained his philosophical ideas, rather than relating a "mere episode," as he claimed his fiction had done. Crane's "lines," as he preferred to call his poems, were printed in all capital letters, each situated at the top of its own page followed by a large blank space and identified by only a Roman numeral. Both the appearance and the contents of the book seemed too unconventional for most of the reviewers, who found little merit in the volume. A notable exception is Elbert Hubbard, who in a March 1896 *Lotus* review of *Black Riders* praised the poetry highly.

Although readers of the current time have become accustomed to free verse of all types, Crane's individual poems and the book as a whole still present a challenge. To propose a valid interpretation of this work and to see how it fits into the genre of poetry, you must read each of the poems in Crane's *Black Riders*, getting a feel for the language and the content and looking for common themes or images. You will notice that many of the poems present a vivid visual image, and you should ask yourself how that image functions in that particular poem. You should also notice the tone, and determine if it is humorous, satiric, or solemn. Then you might consider the narrator and his possible identity and stance. Finally, you might consider which specific words are particularly striking or important.

Try a close reading of the following poem:

> XLVI
> Many red devils ran from my heart
> And out upon the page,
> They were so tiny
> The pen could mash them.
> And many struggled in the ink.
> It was strange
> To write in this red muck
> Of things from my heart. (1–8)

The first image that jumps out is that of the tiny red devils. What, you might ask yourself, does this image suggest? Is the implied evil truly malevolent in this poem? If not, what keeps it from seeming evil? Perhaps it is the fact that the devils are red, a bright color that suggests not evil so much as the imaginative representation of something unconventional. The fact too that the devils are so tiny makes them seem more victims than victimizers. Then they are said to have "struggled in the ink." Sympathy, not fear or loathing, seems to be in order for these tiny, struggling organisms capable of being mashed by a pen.

A rereading of the poem may cause you to wonder how it is or why it is that these tiny red devils are running from the narrator's heart and out onto the page. Who is the narrator? What type of person is he or she? Is the narrator's tone serious or playful, scornful or mocking? How is a pen involved in this whole ordeal? You might decide that the narrator is a writer, since he or she is obviously holding a pen and finds it "strange / To write in this red muck / Of things from my heart." Why is it strange? What does this phrase imply about the narrator's ability as a writer? Why is the narrator writing in "red muck"? The word *muck* suggests dirt, manure, sewage, or mess. Which of these synonyms seems best to represent the type of muck that Crane's narrator is using as a referent?

After you have considered all the questions posed above, what meaning do you think the poem overall is trying to convey? What does it have to say about the act of writing? Is writing a poem an easy activity? How is it connected to the writer's heart? And why does he use the image of devils? This is not the only poem in *Black Riders* that refers to the act of writing. You might want to choose another poem or two to show how Crane represents the practice of writing in this volume.

As you can see from all the questions generated by this one short poem, you could produce a whole series of questions about each poem in the text. When you have analyzed several poems that seem to have qualities or ideas in common, you can then try to find common threads that will lead you to an argument or thesis to become the starting point of an essay.

TOPICS AND STRATEGIES

As you read through the following topics and essay ideas, remember that you must make the argument your own. These are only suggestions to help you generate your own unique thesis. These suggestions should lead to other questions and ideas. Once you have made a list of the questions or points that interest you, try to group the poems which have similarities. After you have analyzed several poems within a specific group, such as poems about the act of writing or poems about religion, you will be ready to make your claim and to gather relevant evidence from that group of poems to support it. Then you can begin to organize and expand that evidence into an effective essay.

Themes

When you have placed the poems into several groups, ask yourself what main ideas or issues are addressed in each of the groups. Although much poetry will share some themes, each poem will deal with a specific theme differently. Your job will be to identify a major theme and show how some specific poems represent and use that theme. Several poems in *Black Riders* are especially concerned with the theme of perception, that is, how a particular event or person is perceived and how the perception changes with a change in position. Other poems deal with God or religion, with the act of writing, with tradition and its importance, and with the act judging other people. Choose one of these themes or some other one and decide which specific poems seem to convey that idea. Then carefully read and reread each of the chosen poems, paying particular attention to the central images and the specific language. When you have discovered similar patterns or important variations of patterns, you will be ready to formulate a claim about what these poems reveal on that theme.

Sample Topics:

1. **Perception or point of view:** Analyze what the poems have to say about the difficulty of perceiving correctly or clearly, considering whether a change in position clarifies perception.

   See especially poems XXVI with a long climb up a hill, XXXV with its golden ball, LVI with its assassin and victim, and LVIII with its sage and pupil. In the first two of these poems, how does a change in physical location effect a change in what is being seen? What do the poems suggest about the person who has changed locations and who still does not see what he thought he would see? What do these two poems say about human nature? What do the objects observed from afar—the "gardens / Lying at impossible distances" (6–7) and the "ball of gold in the sky" (1)—suggest about idealism, perfection, or desirable items? What do the poems suggest about the attainability of such goals?

   In the last two poems the characters are paired—the assassin and the victim in poem LVI and the sage and the pupils in poem XXVIII, and the opposite members of each pairing are set against each other. What is the implied difference between the assassin and the victim? Who is wiser, the sage or the pupils? What do these two poems say about point of view? What do they say about human nature?

2. **Truth:** Analyze what the poems have to say about the concept of truth.

   See especially poems IV with a thousand tongues, VII with a mystic shadow, and XXVIII with its varied definitions of truth. In these three poems, each first person narrator views truth somewhat differently. What is that difference? Why is truth in poem VII "bitter as eaten fire" (5)? What are the various characteristics of truth in poem XXVIII? Is absolute truth attainable? Why or why not? Taken altogether, what do these three poems indicate about truth?

3. **God:** What do the poems have to say about God? Do the poems totally reject the idea of God, or do they prefer one type of God over another?

God is depicted or alluded to in a variety of poems, including VI with God as a shipmaker, XII with its punitive god, XIX with a god who beats a man, XXXIV with its differing patterns of God, XXXIX with God whispering, LI with a strange god, LXVI with nothing where God should be, LXVII with God dead, and LXVIII with man in what at first appears to be a fruitless search for God. Because Stephen Crane's father and grandfather were ministers and his mother a devoted temperance worker in the church, he was exposed to all aspects of religion, at least in the Methodist Church at the time. His writing, including his poetry, often emphasizes the problems of hypocrisy at the same time it upholds values such as empathy, aiding others, and providing understanding.

Looking at the poems listed above, decide how each depicts God differently. What do the poems have in common? Which image of God is most positive? Why? Which is most negative? Why? Would you call Crane an atheist? Why or why not?

Character

Although character is a clear concept in Stephen Crane's fiction, it becomes a bit more difficult in the poetry where few true characters emerge. One that is not always clearly labeled is the "little man," a man who faces the rest of the world, a place which to him always seems somewhat daunting. Another type of character is the sinner, or at least one who is identified as a sinner or whom others recognize as having sinned. A third possibility is that of the youth, or of other young people, such as the pupils in poem XXVIII. Choose one of these types of characters and

follow them through several poems. What does Crane seem to be imply-
ing about each? How does that character or type of character interact
with others? What do the poems seem to imply about specific character
types?

Sample Topics:

1. **The little man:** Analyze the character of the little man, arriving
   at a conclusion about his function in the poems.

   In poem XXII, for example, the little man seems very small
   indeed when compared to the natural landscape:

   > XXII
   > Once I saw mountains angry,
   > And ranged in battle-front.
   > Against them stood a little man;
   > Aye, he was no bigger than my finger.
   > I laughed, and spoke to one near me,
   > "Will he prevail?"
   > "Surely," replied this other;
   > "His grandfathers beat them many times."
   > Then did I see much virtue in grandfathers—
   > At least, for the little man
   > Who stood against the mountains. (1–11)

   What is the significance of the little man's size as compared to
   that of the angry mountains? Why are the mountains said to be
   angry? What is the difference in his position as opposed to that
   of his "grandfathers"? What does the poem convey about the
   possibilities for this little man? For humanity in general?
   Comparing the man in the above poem to the one in poem
   XXIV who questions the reason for war, ask yourself how they
   are similar, even though the second man is not labeled as "little." What do these two poems together indicate about man
   and nature? About man's goals and desires? Are there other
   poems that feature a similar specimen of humanity?

2. **Sinners:** Several of Crane's poems feature characters that are either labeled as sinners or could be labeled as sinners because of their actions or someone else's perceptions. Analyze this type of character to see what the poems convey about the concept of sin.

See especially poems IX with many devils recognizing fellow sinners as brothers, XVIII with the humble blades of grass, XXX with the sinful blood, and XXXIII with sins being the only wares of the poor soul. What are the primary character- istics of the sinner characters? How are they alike? How are they different? What overall implications do the poems make about people who sin? What is the tone in each of these poems? Think, for instance, of how and why the carousing devils in poem IX refer to the narrator as "comrade" and "brother" (6). Are they happy to see him? Why? What does their attitude infer about the narrator? About humanity in general?

Philosophy and Ideas

Stephen Crane's upbringing in the Methodist Church gave him a strong background in the Bible and in church doctrine. In his writing, however, Crane seems to reject the more restrictive teachings of the church and to move toward his own philosophy, one which coincides much more with the loving God pictured in the New Testament, and to reject the vengeful God portrayed in the Old Testament. His poems in *Black Riders* reflect his own set of values, as opposed to those of either his parents or his grandparents. Both in his life and his writing he exhibited a concern for his fellow human beings, and he generally rejected judgmental attitudes in others. With either of these two ideas in mind or with another of your own choosing, reread the poems to look for examples that support that specific philosophy of life. Why, for example, does the narrator seem to align himself or herself with groups known as "sinners"? What does that alignment reveal about Crane's philosophy in the poems?

Sample Topics:

1. **Rejection of the Old Testament view of God:** How do Crane's poems show a rejection of the strict, punitive father figure as portrayed in that portion of the Bible?

Look, for example, at poem LI, which clearly delineates two different views of God. What are the major differences? Which seems preferable? How does "the man" (8) who confronts these two Gods react to each? After carefully analyzing this poem, look at several more poems featuring God or religion to find a pattern. Then construct a thesis to argue about that pattern.

2. **Rejection of the organized church:** How do several of Crane's poems express a negative view of the church or members of the church?

See this poem, for example:

> LVII
> With eye and with gesture
> You say you are holy.
> I say you lie;
>
> For I did see you
> Draw away your coats
> From the sin upon the hands
> Of a little child.
> Liar! (1–8)

What does the narrator feel about the person who claims to be holy? For what action does the narrator scold the person? Why does the person's lie seem to be so important? Find other poems that reject or rebuke people who claim to be "holy." Analyze them as representatives of the church or the church's constituency.

3. **God as creator but not as caretaker:** As you have perhaps observed, Crane characterizes a God in his poetry, but it is not the God about whom some preachers preached. Analyze the characteristics of Crane's God.

You might begin with poem VI to formulate what you think is Crane's characterization of God in his poetry.

VI

God fashioned the ship of the world carefully.
With the infinite skill of an All-Master
Made He the hull and the sails,
Held He the rudder
Ready for adjustment.
Erect stood He, scanning His work proudly.
Then—at fateful time—a wrong called,
And God turned, heeding.
Lo, the ship, at this opportunity,
slipped slyly,
Making cunning noiseless travel down the ways.
So that, forever rudderless, it went upon the seas
Going ridiculous voyages,
Making quaint progress,
Turning as with serious purpose
Before stupid winds.
And there were many in the sky
Who laughed at this thing. (1–17)

With what religious philosophy would you connect this characterization? Do other poems present a consistent philosophy of this particular type of God or do they differ?

Form and Genre

Although it may seem unclear as to why the title poem and the book itself contain *black riders,* the history of that term is important. First, it is a biblical allusion to the book of Revelation. Of the four horsemen of the apocalypse, the third horseman rides a black horse and carries a pair of balances or weighing scales. The scales themselves may represent the weighing of wheat for bread during the time of famine or they may retain the traditional idea of the scales of justice. In addition to this allusion, the term *black riders* probably refers to actual print itself. Jerome J. McGann explains this allusion in his book, pointing out that Crane was quite forward-thinking in bringing attention to the materiality of the text as it gallops across the page:

I
Black riders came from the sea.
There was clang and clang of spear and shield,
And clash and clash of hoof and heel,
Wild shouts and the wave of hair
In the rush upon the wind:
Thus the ride of sin. (1–6)

If you consider the text of this title poem, you can imagine that Crane here seems to revel in being iconoclastic, opposing traditional views of God and sin in his slim volume of poems. His own black riders relish the noise and excitement generated by their appearance on the literary scene.

Sample Topics:

1. **Crane's poetry as breaking with the tradition:** Analyze Crane's poems in light of traditional poetry of the late nineteenth century.

Although Emily Dickinson's heavily edited but nontraditional poems, first published in book form in 1890, sold well, the public was still accustomed to the more traditional poetry of Thomas Bailey Aldrich, James Whitcomb Riley, John Greenleaf Whittier, and Joaquin Miller, whose poem "Columbus" was widely known and often memorized and recited by schoolchildren. Although his poetry is no longer a part of the curriculum, Miller is remembered today, among other reasons, for one of his poems, "Burns and Byron":

In men whom men condemn as ill
I find so much of goodness still.
In men whom men pronounce divine
I find so much of sin and blot
I do not dare to draw a line
Between the two, where God has not. (150–55)

In this poem Miller deals with the subject of sin, but his treatment is not like Crane's. How is the subject matter similar and/

or different? In its form, how does this much-recited poem differ from Crane's poetry on sin? Consider rhyme, rhythm, and use of language as well as attitude.

2. **Crane as forerunner to modernist poets:** How does Stephen Crane project some of the values and styles of later modernist poets, including the imagists, in the presentation of his "lines"?

You might do some research on imagism and modernist American poets, learning about poets such as Amy Lowell, Ezra Pound, Wallace Stevens, and William Carlos Williams. You will find that modernist poetry is typically brief and puzzle-like, leaving the reader to arrive at his or her own interpretation, that it defies tradition, subverting conventional images and symbols to arrive at very different interpretations, and that it is often itself about the act of writing poetry. Consider William Carlos Williams's famous statement about "no ideas / but in things" (9–10) and his use of objects to relay information and ideas in his poetry. How does Crane present "things" in a similar manner? Consider all these characteristics if you wish to argue that Crane paves the way for later modernism in poetry.

Language, Imagery, and Sound

Language in poetry becomes even more important than in prose since each word carries a heavy burden of presentation and subsequent interpretation, so it is essential to make yourself aware of the word choices—both their meaning and their sound. Going back to the title poem, think about the sounds and how they affect your analysis:

> I
> Black riders came from the sea.
> There was clang and clang of spear and shield,
> And clash and clash of hoof and heel,
> Wild shouts and the wave of hair
> In the rush upon the wind:
> Thus the ride of sin. (1–6)

The onomatopoeic words *clang, clash,* and *shout* combine to create a jarring rush of sound—these riders are not entering quietly. Instead, they are loudly and violently coming on the scene. How does this aggressive entry work to clarify meaning? What does it suggest about the nature of the poems within the volume? If we equate the riders with the four horsemen of the apocalypse, should we suspect the end of an era and/or the beginning of a new one? If it is a new one, how does this poem fit into the revolution? How do others in the collection fit?

Continuing to look at this same poem, what specific words seem to have greatest importance? Why? Why does Crane have all the riders black, since the ones in the Book of Revelations are white, red, black, and pale green? How does the black connect more firmly with the final word in the poem? You might conclude that "the black riders" as an image is quite powerful, but with the addition of the sound imagery and the connection to sin at the end, the language makes an even more potent statement about the poem itself and the following poems in this volume.

Sample Topics:

1. **Sound as important in Crane's poems:** Choose several poems in which the sound itself seems particularly significant. Analyze the sound patterns as they contribute to meaning.

   See, for example, poems XXVIII with its allusions to breath and wind, LIII with its noises and curses, and LXVIII with its moans and groans. Try reading the poems out loud to get the full effect. You might notice that the sound is soft and pleasant in some poems but bold and abrasive in others. Observe sound devices such as alliteration, assonance, and onomatopoeia, noting for example words like *blustering* (1), *blasting* (9), and *braggart* (10) in poem LIII. Then notice how the sound fits the tone and the message, leading to a greater understanding of the poem.

2. **Visual images:** Analyze the most compelling visual images in a few poems.

One of the most memorable images is in poem III, that of a "creature, naked, bestial" (2) eating its own heart. Some others are the "ball of gold" (XXXV, 1) in the sky, a "man pursuing the horizon" (XXIV, 1) and "three little birds in a row" (II, 1). You might choose these and/or other images to show how Crane uses striking visual imagery to make a poetic statement.

Compare and Contrast Essays

In a comparison-contrast essay, you can look at similarities and differences in two or more Stephen Crane poems or you can look at similarities and differences in specific poems by Crane and another poet. That poet could be of the same time period if you wish to show, for example, attitudes toward God. Or the poet could be of an earlier or a later time if you wish to show changes in how God is portrayed. One way of clarifying Crane's innovations in poetry is to compare one of his poems on a specific subject, such as war, to a poem of one of his more traditional contemporaries on the same topic. Whatever comparisons you make, you need to remember that just pointing out similarities and differences is not sufficient. You need to demonstrate how the comparison assists in the interpretation of the Crane poetry.

Sample Topics:

1. **The first and the last poem:** Compare and contrast poems I with its noisy riders of sin and LXVIII with God lying dead in heaven.

   Stephen Crane was meticulous about arranging the poems in this volume, especially the beginning and the concluding poems. The first begins with the rushing in of the black riders and the last ends with the atheist being struck dead. Read these two poems together, paying close attention to the tone and the messages. What does this comparison reveal about the overall theme or idea of the poetry?

2. **The poems about writing:** Compare and contrast poems II, XLVI, and LXV with the idea that they may be about the act of imagination and writing poetry.

The first of these poems has three birds laughing at a man singing, the second has the red devils in the ink, and the last has the songs of birds, with the birds flying away "Until they were as sand / Thrown between me and the sky" (10–11). What do these poems have in common? How do they differ? How do they comment on the act of singing or writing, especially perhaps the act of writing poetry? What are the good and bad aspects of that act?

Bibliography and Online Resources for *The Black Riders and Other Lines*

Basye, Robert C. "Color Imagery in Stephen Crane's Poetry." *American Literary Realism* 13 (1980): 122–31.

Campbell, Donna. "Reflections on Stephen Crane." *Stephen Crane Studies* 15.1 (2006): 13–16.

Cavitch, Max. "Stephen Crane's Refrain." *ESQ: A Journal of the American Renaissance* 54. 1–4 (2008): 33–54.

Colvert, James B. "Fred Holland Day, Louise Imogen Guiney, and the Text of Stephen Crane's *The Black Riders*." *American Literary Realism* 28.2 (1996): 18–24.

Cox, James M. "The Pilgrim's Progress as Source for Stephen Crane's *The Black Riders*." *American Literature* 28.4 (1957): 478–87.

Crane, Stephen. *The Works of Stephen Crane: Poems and Literary Remains*. Ed. Fredson Bowers. Vol. 10. Charlottesville: UP of Virginia, 1975.

Dooley, Patrick K. *The Pluralistic Philosophy of Stephen Crane*. Urbana: U of Illinois P, 1993.

Gandal, Keith. "A Spiritual Autopsy of Stephen Crane." *Nineteenth-Century Literature* 51.4 (1997): 500–30.

———. "Stephen Crane's 'Mystic Places.'" *Arizona Quarterly: A Journal of American Literature, Culture, and Theory* 55.1 (1999): 97–126.

Gillis, E. A. "A Glance at Stephen Crane's Poetry." *Prairie Schooner* 28 (1954): 73–79.

Hoffman, Daniel G. *The Poetry of Stephen Crane*. New York: Columbia UP, 1957.

Huang, Jiaxiu. "Stephen Crane's Poetry of the Absurd." *Re-Reading America: Changes and Challenges*. Ed. Weihe Zhong and Rui Han. Cheltenham, England: Reardon, 2004. 131–35.

Katz, Joseph. "Toward a Descriptive Bibliography of Stephen Crane's *The Black Riders*." *Papers of the Bibliographical Society of America* 59 (1965): 150–57.

Kuga, Shunji. "Momentous Sounds and Silences in Stephen Crane." *Stephen Crane Studies* 15.1 (2006): 17–19.

McGann, Jerome J. *Black Riders: The Visible Language of Modernism.* Princeton, NJ: Princeton UP, 1993.

Paschke-Johannes, J. Edwin. "Existential Moments in Stephen Crane's Poems." *Stephen Crane Studies* 15.1 (2006): 32–36.

Pastore, Stephen R. "The Aesthetics of Stephen Crane's *The Black Riders and Other Lines:* A Bibliographical Study." *Stephen Crane Studies* 6.2 (1997): 6–14.

Saunders, Judith P. "Stephen Crane: American Poetry at a Crossroads." *Teaching Nineteenth-Century American Poetry.* Ed. Paula Bernat Bennett, Karen L. Kilcup, and Philipp Schweighauser. New York: Modern Language Association of America, 2007. 185–99.

Sutton, Walter. "The Modernity of Stephen Crane's Poetry: A Centennial Tribute." *Courier: Syracuse University Library Associates* 9.1 (1971): 3–7.

Vanouse, Donald. "Hobby-Horses, Horseplay, and Stephen Crane's 'Black Riders.'" *Courier: Syracuse University Library Associates* 13.3-4 (1976): 28–31.

———. "The First Editions of Stephen Crane's *The Black Riders and Other Lines* and *War is Kind.*" *Syracuse University Library Associates Courier* 29 (1994): 107–25.

Westbrook, Max. "Recognizing the Two Voices in Crane's Poetry." *Readings on Stephen Crane.* Ed. Bonnie Szumski. San Diego: Greenhaven, 1998. 191–96.

———. "Stephen Crane's Poetry: Perspective and Arrogance." *Bucknell Review* 11.4 (1963): 24–34.

Williams, William Carlos. "A Sort of Song." *The Collected Poems of William Carlos Williams.* Vol. 2. New York: New Directions, 1988. 55.

GEORGE'S MOTHER

READING TO WRITE

After Stephen Crane completed *Maggie: A Girl of the Streets,* his first novel of the Bowery, he began a second one, perhaps in response to the criticism of Hamlin Garland, who wrote that *Maggie* "is typical only of the worst elements of the alley. The author should delineate the families living on the next street, who live lives of heroic purity and hopeless hardship" (103). Although Crane seems to have heeded Garland's advice, he did not complete *George's Mother* until after the publication of *The Red Badge of Courage,* which brought him enough fame to make publishers interested in what had become his third novel. The main characters in the later book are indeed what the average reader might deem more "normal," although they live in the same tenement house as the Johnsons. George's mother, Mrs. Kelcey, unlike the violent Mrs. Johnson, is a pious woman, truly caring about her son and always wanting what is best for him. Although some critics agree that this novel lacks the power of the earlier Bowery study, the characters may be more relatable to the average reader. One advantage of writing about this novel is that little criticism has been written, so you may find more topics that are quite original.

As you read the novel, you need especially to consider the typical concerns: point of view, specific language, and patterns of imagery. You might start with the very first paragraph:

> In the swirling rain that came at dusk the broad avenue glistened with that deep bluish tint which is so widely condemned when it is put into pictures. There were long rows of shops, whose fronts shone with full,

golden light. Here and there, from druggists' windows, or from the red street-lamps that indicated the positions of fire-alarm boxes, a flare of uncertain, wavering crimson was thrown upon the wet pavement. (115)

From what point of view does this description seem to be? Why would the particular shade of blue mentioned be "widely condemned" in artists' paintings? Visualize the scene in your head—is it pleasant, unpleasant, puzzling? Which words seem particularly important?

Those questions should lead to others. As is often the case in Stephen Crane's writing, color seems important. The picture with its "swirling" rain, its "bluish" tint, and its "full, golden light" seems to suggest a pleasant street. But amid that glistening rain and the shining storefronts, the final focus is on "druggists' windows" and "red street-lamps" that signal fire-alarm box locations. Somehow that last sentence undercuts all the romanticism of the first glimpse. When we connect the druggists with medicine or even addiction and the fire alarms with potential destruction, we see the possibilities of impending problems. In fact, in the paragraph after the one quoted above, which can be seen as generally positive, the lights become responsible for shadows, suggesting that the scene is growing more ominous. Carefully reading this novel's first chapter should cause you to ask more questions. What brings about the growing sense of gloom so early in the story? After considering this effect, you might conclude then that this passage suggests that what appears to be pleasant may be just a façade, masking the reality of a situation.

Continue to choose other passages that seem particularly interesting and look closely at the language. You might even consider Crane's original proposed title for the book: *A Woman Without Weapons*. How does the tone of this title differ from the final chosen title: *George's Mother*? What *are* the mother's weapons? You can see the woman attacking the dirt and grime with brooms and clothes, but does she have psychological weapons as well as these physical weapons? At whom are her psychological weapons aimed? Why? Is she winning any of her battles?

As you can see, your close attention to the details of the various passages raises all sorts of questions you might not have considered during just a quick reading of the novel. Continue this close reading technique until you find a topic that seems important and that holds your interest.

TOPICS AND STRATEGIES

Remember that the following are only a few of the possible topics on this second book of life in the slums. Use the questions to help you generate a topic in which you are interested. Ask yourself what question you can pose to which you would like to find an answer. Once you have a specific question, then begin collecting evidence to answer the question you have raised. When you have answered that question to your own satisfaction and gathered sufficient evidence, then you are ready to decide on the most effective organization of that evidence. At that point, you will be ready to begin a preliminary draft of your essay.

Themes

What are the main ideas with which this novel seems to deal? Although many works deal with family interaction or friction, which is one possible theme, *George's Mother* deals with the mother-son relationship in a different way from other books. If you choose this theme, you must think about how that relationship works in this novel, and then you should decide on what Crane reveals about this particular association. *George's Mother* also deals with other themes—slum living, the dangers of alcohol, the difficulty of perception, maturity or coming of age, and even the role of religion. Choose one of these themes or another one and begin to look for passages that help to support your choice. Continue to look for other passages, paying particular attention to the language used, until you have a good idea of what you think the novel reveals about your particular theme. Then you can refine your thesis so that you have a persuasive argument.

Sample Topics:

1. **Drinking alcohol:** What does the novel say about the problems of drinking alcohol?

   What is Mrs. Kelcey's stand on the use of alcohol? How does she react to George's drinking? How does she react to others who drink? What problems does alcohol cause for George? For others in the book? What stand does the novel itself seem to promote on the use of alcohol? What support is there for that conclusion?

2. **Maturity or coming of age:** Argue that George does or does not mature in the course of this book.

At the end of the book, the women of the slums and the clergyman gather around the dying mother. George is there too, and he is described as follows:

> Kelcey began to stare at the wall-paper. The pattern was clusters of brown roses. He felt them like hideous crabs crawling upon his brain.
>
> Through the door-way he saw the oil-cloth covering of the table catching a glimmer from the warm afternoon sun. The window disclosed a fair, soft sky, like blue enamel, and a fringe of chimneys and roofs, resplendent here and there. An endless roar, the eternal trample of the marching city, came mingled with vague cries. At intervals the woman out by the stove moved restlessly and coughed. (178)

The book ends with the line: "The little old woman was dead" (178). How do you think George feels about his mother's death? What changes have occurred in him during the book? What changes do you anticipate after his mother has died? Has he learned anything about himself or about life? How do you know?

3. **Making appropriate choices:** Analyze the choices George makes.

Although little is made of the relationship, early in the book the reader learns that the Kelceys live near the Johnsons and that Maggie Johnson rejected a relationship with George for one with Pete. You might analyze this choice on her part and George's choice of companions. What motivates either of the young people to make the choices they make? What is each looking for in companionship? Imagine a marriage between Maggie and George and decide if it would have been a more appropriate arrangement than the events as recounted in the novel.

Character

An analysis of a specific character in a work can often provide meaningful input into understanding that novel. In *George's Mother*, the two main characters are George and his mother, Mrs. Kelcey. You might choose either one to analyze and then follow that one through the novel. As you concentrate on the character, be aware of what he or she does and says. Is there a discrepancy between words and actions? How do other characters interact with the character you have chosen? What motivates the character to perform specific actions? What are the character's values? What are his or her priorities? Does the character change in the course of the novel? If so, why does he change? If you choose to focus on George, for example, you need to look at the novel's overall presentation of his character. Is he independent or dependent? You might compare him to Jones or Bleecker. What are the similarities and differences? You might also choose one of the minor characters to analyze—Jones, Bleecker, or the clergyman, for example. What do their roles contribute to an understanding of the novel?

Sample Topics:

1. **George Kelcey:** Analyze the character of George Kelcey, following him from the beginning of the novel to the end.

   How does George develop during the course of the story? Is this development positive, negative, or somewhere in between these two extremes? The book covers only a few weeks, during which we see George as he interacts with his acquaintances and with his mother. You might ask yourself if he has any friends at the time he met Jones. We never really get much of George's own point of view, mostly the point of view of an objective narrator, so the reader must judge him by his words, his actions, and the actions of others.

2. **George's mother:** Analyze the character of George's mother.

   It is especially important to think of Mrs. Kelcey as a "woman without weapons," since that is the title proposed to his editor by Stephen Crane. What are her weapons? List as many as you can think of, both physical and psychological. Then consider the following two sentences about Mrs. Kelcey: "She had paused for a moment, but she now hurled herself fiercely at the stove that lurked in the gloom, red-eyed, like a dragon. It hissed, and there was renewed clangor of blows. The little old woman dashed to and fro" (121). Later, we are told, "She resembled a limited funeral procession" (125). In the first sentence, what is the mother battling with her weapons? Is she successful? In the second sentence, why does she resemble a funeral procession? Of what is she afraid? Why did Crane propose the title *A Woman Without Weapons*? What is the irony in that title?

Also, consider the rest of the family. What do you know about George's father? His siblings? What effect does their absence have on George? On George's mother?

3. **Jones and Bleecker:** Analyze the function of these two minor characters.

First, consider their relationship with George. How close in friendship are they? How do these relationships change when George loses his job? How are these men like George? How are they different? What does Mrs. Kelcey say of them? What would she think of their actions if she could see them? What solution would she propose to reform their ways? Would it likely be helpful? Why or why not?

History and Context

The action of this novel takes place in the New York Bowery in the 1890s. Stephen Crane himself explored the Bowery area, interviewing its inhabitants and even spending a night in a homeless shelter to observe homelessness and to see how it felt to be homeless. When he wrote *Maggie* and when he first started this novel, he himself had little money, sharing a small apartment with a group of artists and often sleeping in shifts to make the best of the living quarters, yet he never reached the depths of slum living in his own home.

In addition to understanding poverty, Stephen Crane knew that the use of alcohol was seen to be a growing problem in the late nineteenth century, as the Woman's Christian Temperance Union (1874) and the Anti-Saloon League (1895) worked to curb the use of alcohol by using arguments about morality. Crane's own mother worked industriously as a temperance writer and speaker, and his father wrote religious tracts against alcohol. Crane himself drank, although there is no evidence to show he drank excessively. These facts make his writing in this novel, which has been said to be based partly on his own mother's character, even more interesting from the point of view of the historical context. How does his own background contribute to his literary characterization of George's mother and George himself? How does his concern with poverty and Bowery life account for his writing in this novel?

Sample Topics:

1. **The fight to abolish alcohol abuse:** What does this novel indicate about the methods of the temperance workers to abolish alcohol abuse?

   You could choose a book about alcohol during the 1890s, such as Eric Burns's *The Spirits of America: A Social History of Alcohol,* which will give historical facts about the use of alcohol in this country. On the other hand, you could choose a biography of Carrie Nation, who at various times spelled her first name differently, as in Fran Grace's *Carry A. Nation: Retelling the Life,* which chronicles Nation's zeal to eradicate the evils of alcohol. Stephen Crane was quite aware of the social pressures involved with the issue of temperance, and he was aware of the problems of alcohol as well. Consider the presentation of alcohol in *George's Mother.* What does the novel have to say about both the problems of abuse and the problems of confronting that abuse? How does Crane use the cultural biases at that time in the novel? Does he adequately present both sides? If so, how? If not, why not?

2. **Bowery life:** Analyze how this novel presents the life of the Bowery.

Find a nonfictional expose of Bowery life in the 1890s designed to garner sympathy from readers, such as Jacob Riis's *How the Other Half Lives* (1890). How does it inform Crane's presentation of the Bowery in *George's Mother*. Does Crane work to arouse sympathy in a similar way to Riis's work? Why or why not? How does Crane work to avoid melodrama in his work? Or does he?

Philosophy and Ideas

During Stephen Crane's lifetime, he rebelled against the Methodist upbringing to which he had been subjected, often in subtle ways. At the same time he greatly valued the admonition to love his neighbors as himself, often putting himself into great jeopardy to help out his fellow human beings, he did not appreciate the more punitive or restrictive aspects of the religion he had been taught. His insistence that he had been interviewing Dora Clark and his later court testimony is one example of his reaching out to help someone while putting himself in an undesirable position. Afterward he found himself harassed by the police in New York City.

On the other hand, he was well aware of the disapproval that the church and his family would have shown him had they known of his living with Cora without the ritual of marriage, so much so that he kept the relationship a secret until Cora herself revealed it. His own father's religious tracts denouncing smoking, drinking, and reading novels must have made his own smoking, drinking, and writing novels conscious acts of rebellion. Although both his parents died before he ever published his work, he probably still resisted the disapproval he knew they might have had. That nagging conscience more than likely resurfaced from time to time when he broke rules they had championed.

Sample Topics:

1. **The church:** Analyze the role of religion in this novel.

   Consider the following passage describing George's attendance at a prayer meeting:

   > When Kelcey entered with his mother he felt a sudden quaking. His knees shook. It was an awesome place to him. There

was a menace in the red padded carpet and the leather doors, studded with little brass tacks that penetrated his soul with their pitiless glances. As for his mother, she had acquired such a new air that he would have been afraid to address her. He felt completely alone and isolated at this formidable time.

There was a man in the vestibule who looked at them blandly. From within came the sound of singing. To Kelcey there was a million voices. He dreaded the terrible moment when the doors should swing back. He wished to recoil, but at that instant the bland man pushed the doors aside and he followed his mother up the centre aisle of the little chapel. To him there was a riot of lights that made him transparent. The multitudinous pairs of eyes that turned toward him were implacable in their cool valuations. (156)

How is the church characterized? Why does Mrs. Kelcey attend church so regularly? Why does she acquire "a new air"? Why does she want George to go to church with her? Why does he not want to go? How does he feel as he enters the church? What does the book indicate is the main problem that George has with the church?

2. **The mother-son relationship:** Analyze the relationship between George and his mother.

Brenda Murphy sees this book as Stephen Crane's assault against the religion in which he grew up. She states:

> *George's Mother* is not Crane's most virulent attack on the fanatic Methodism he had seen in his youth, but it is, in the end, perhaps the most affecting. The irony of Crane's original title, *A Woman without Weapons,* is rife. Mrs. Kelcey is dead. She has used her last weapon. But there is no doubt about the identity of the victor in this scene. George's mother has succeeded in wresting her son from the forces of sin. It matters little to her "moral victory" that she may have destroyed both of them in the process. (92)

How do you see the relationship between George and his mother? Is it healthy or unhealthy for the two people? Are they actually both destroyed in the process, as Murphy declares? Does the relationship create more problems for George's psyche or does he just use it as a convenient excuse for not going home?

Language, Symbols, and Imagery

As already discussed, Stephen Crane made great use of imagery in his writing, and *George's Mother* is no exception. Although some of the images in this novel seem to serve more as decoration than as integral parts of the story, some become quite important. At the beginning of the second chapter, for example, two images are juxtaposed in a meaningful pattern: As George's mother is cleaning "with the flurry of a battle" (120), the man in the opposing tenement "put forth his head from a window and cursed violently. He flung a bottle high across two backyards at a window of the opposite tenement" (119). These two images set up the preeminent conflict in the novel: the mother's constant battle against the evils of alcohol. As the mother remains oblivious to the flung bottle, she fights unrelentingly against dirt and disorder. Many other images throughout the book help to clarify her position in her fight to keep her house, her son, and the world free of dirt and alcohol. You might reread sections of the novel to find other prominent images, with that of the saloon perhaps reaching the level of symbolism.

Sample Topics:

1. **The brewery and the saloon:** What do the brewery and the saloon represent in this novel? Do they function symbolically or are they just major images?

Consider the backdrop when the mother is cleaning and the man across the way is flinging beer bottles at her apartment:

> In the distance an enormous brewery towered over the other buildings. Great gilt letters advertised a brand of beer. Thick smoke came from funnels and spread near it like vast and powerful wings. The structure seemed a great bird, flying. The

letters of the sign made a chain of gold hanging from its neck. The little old woman looked at the brewery. It vaguely interested her, for a moment, as a stupendous affair, a machine of mighty strength. (120)

Why is this structure depicted as a "great bird"? The edifice's strength is made evident with the word *towered*. Why is its strength important to this woman? Find depictions of the saloon, and decide if they are similar to that of the brewery. Then decide how these images function to illuminate understanding of the novel.

2. **Importance of the title:** Discuss why this book is titled *George's Mother* when it is largely about George himself?

Throughout the novel, the reader follows George as he goes about his way to the saloon and to Bleecker's flat and to his own home. Occasionally, the mother is the focus of the novel, but most often George is center stage. Why does Crane call the novel by this title? What is the function of the mother? What does she represent in George's life? When the novel concludes, for whom do we have the most empathy? Why?

3. **Images of the church:** Find any images connected to religion or the church, and analyze how they function in the novel.

When George gives in to his mother's begging him to go to prayer meeting, the mother does "a little antique caper," as George himself envisions "dreary blackness arranged in solemn rows" (124). Find other similar images and assess their function and importance. Then ask why this mother and son have totally different visions of religion and its roles in their lives.

Compare and Contrast Essays

In *George's Mother,* the reader is given a third-person objective narrator, one who does not make judgments about the characters, but one who leaves the reader that role. The narration does, however, include descriptions of the characters and the scenes, the characters' words, and the interaction of the various forces to allow the reader to form an opinion. One device that Stephen Crane makes much use of is the juxtaposition of various characters, scenes, and actions, leaving the reader the freedom to compare and contrast the novel's important elements. Because of this juxtaposition, the reader can readily use comparison and contrast essays to arrive at an understanding of the text's main ideas. The most obvious characters to compare are, of course, George and his mother, but many other possibilities exist. Other elements that may be productively compared are the church and the saloon, George and Bleecker, George and Jones, and the beginning paragraphs and the concluding paragraphs.

Sample Topics:

1. **George and his mother:** Compare and contrast George and his mother in their ideas of duty and pleasure. Why are their ideas of these elements so different?

   Remember that George is the only one left of "all that mob 'a tow-headed kids" (117). What does this pronouncement by Jones tell the reader about George's probable relationship with his mother? What does the mother want for her son? What does George want for himself? Why do they see people and events so differently?

2. **George and Bleecker:** Compare and contrast George and Bleecker in their attitudes toward life and each other.

   When George is introduced to Bleecker for the first time, we are told: "He admired Bleecker immensely" (127). What does George find admirable about this new acquaintance? What is Bleecker's attitude toward George at this point? Does either character have a change in attitude over the course of the novel? Why or why not? What is significant about the similarities in these two men? What is significant about the differences? How does this comparison help to interpret the novel?

3. **George's attitude at the beginning of the novel and at the end:** Analyze the first few paragraphs and the conclusion of the book to compare and contrast George's attitude at the start of the book and at the conclusion.

Consider this description at the novel's beginning:

> A brown young man went along the avenue. He held a tin lunch-pail under his arm in a manner that was evidently uncomfortable. He was puffing at a corn-cob pipe. His shoulders had a self-reliant poise, and the hang of his arms and the raised veins of his hands showed him to be a man who worked with his muscles. (109)

Now reread the last two chapters of the book and consider the changes that you see in George. Account for those changes and show how they help to construct meaning in the text.

Bibliography and Online Resources for *George's Mother*

Burns, Eric. *The Spirits of America: A Social History of Alcohol.* Philadelphia: Temple UP, 2004.

Crane, Stephen. *The Works of Stephen Crane: Bowery Tales: Maggie, George's Mother.* Ed. Fredson Bowers. Vol. 1. Charlottesville: UP of Virginia, 1969.

Dowling Robert, M. "Stephen Crane and the Transformation of the Bowery." *Twisted from the Ordinary: Essays on American Literary Naturalism.* Ed. Mary E. Papke. Knoxville: U of Tennessee P, 2003. 45–62.

Edelstein, Arthur. *Three Great Novels by Stephen Crane: Maggie, George's Mother, the Red Badge of Courage.* New York: Fawcett, 1970.

Garland, Hamlin. "An Ambitious French Novel and a Modest American Story," *Arena* (June 1893): 11–12. Rpt. in *Stephen Crane: Bloom's Classic Critical Views.* Eds. Harold Bloom and Joyce Caldwell Smith. New York: Chelsea House, 2009. 103–04.

Grace, Fran. *Carry A. Nation: Retelling the Life.* Bloomington: Indiana UP, 2001.

Jackson, Agnes M. "Stephen Crane's Imagery of Conflict in *George's Mother.*" *Arizona Quarterly* 25 (1969): 313–18.

Knapp, Daniel. "Son of Thunder: Stephen Crane and the Fourth Evangelist."
    Nineteenth-Century Fiction 24.3 (1969): 253–91.

Kuga, Shunji. "'Feminine Domesticity and the Feral City: Stephen Crane's
    George's Mother, Maggie, and 'A Detail.'" *Stephen Crane Studies* 13.2 (2004):
    21–31.

LaFrance, Marston. *"George's Mother* and the Other Half of *Maggie." Stephen
    Crane in Transition: Centenary Essays.* Ed. Joseph Katz and James Dickey.
    DeKalb: Northern Illinois UP, 1972. 35–53.

Monteiro, George. "The Drunkard's Progress: Bowery Plot, Social Paradigm in
    Stephen Crane's *George's Mother." Dionysos: The Literature and Addiction
    TriQuarterly* 9.1 (1999): 5–16.

Murphy, Brenda. "A Woman with Weapons: The Victor in Stephen Crane's
    George's Mother." Modern Language Studies 11.2 (1981): 88–93.

Pizer, Donald. "From a Home to the World: Stephen Crane's *George's Mother."
    Papers on Language and Literature: A Journal for Scholars and Critics of
    Language and Literature* 32.3 (1996): 277–90.

Riis, Jacob. *How the Other Half Lives.* New York: Charles Scribner's Sons, 1890.
    Bartleby.com: Great Books Online. http://www.bartleby.com/208/

Simoneaux, Katherine G. "Color Imagery in Crane's *George's Mother." College
    Language Association Journal* 14 (1971): 410–19.

"THE OPEN BOAT"

READING TO WRITE

On December 31, 1896, Stephen Crane boarded the *Commodore* in Jacksonville, Florida, with the intention of going to Cuba to cover the Spanish-American War. Instead the *Commodore* soon sank, probably as a result of sabotage, and Crane, the captain, and two others left the ship in the final lifeboat. The four men struggled for some thirty hours, striving to reach shore without capsizing the small dinghy. After finally reaching land, Crane filed a newspaper account of the episode, with his story appearing in major newspapers all over the country. More importantly, he later wrote a fictionalized version that many critics consider his finest short story, "The Open Boat." This story is told from the point of view of the correspondent, Crane's fictionalized counterpart, as he works through a fearful night in the dinghy with the captain, the oiler, and the cook.

Because this story is presented by a third-person narrator who knows the mind of the correspondent, you must read closely to judge the character's thoughts and to evaluate what they add to the story. As always, you should look carefully at the specific examples, details, and word selections and ask why they were chosen, remembering that the correspondent's view is limited, although he occasionally supposes what another view might be. In the following passage, for example, look closely at word choice as you read and reread, asking yourself about the significance of the language chosen.

> As the boat bounced from the top of each wave, the wind tore through
> the hair of the hatless men, and as the craft plopped her stern down again

the spray slashed past them. The crest of each of these waves was a hill, from the top of which the men surveyed, for a moment, a broad tumultuous expanse, shining and wind-driven. It was probably splendid. It was probably glorious, the play of the free sea, wild with lights of emerald and white and amber. (70)

Because this passage only tells what "probably" should have been "splendid" and "glorious," the reader must ask how the scene actually seemed to the four men in the dinghy. Was it splendid for them? Or was it terrifying? Why is the word *plopped* used? The craft itself seems more able to complete effective movement than the men at whom the spray seems to slash. Notice the difference in tone in "plopped" and "slashed." The first word is lighthearted, almost playful in contrast to the violence of the second. You can deduce from this analysis of the word choice that the contrast indicates two or more points of view, not just that of the men but of other unknowns, even nature or someone for whom the sight might have been glorious.

TOPICS AND STRATEGIES

As you look at the following ideas for papers, remember that this story has withstood the test of time, seemingly as relevant today as when it was written in 1897. The following topics will help you to think of other ways to look at the text and to discover that relevancy. When you decide on a topic, such as the theme of "community," carefully look for passages that reveal cooperation, mutual respect, and sharing. If the topic claims your interest, begin to analyze these passages, looking for specific evidence to support your thesis. After you have collected enough evidence concerning cooperation and sharing, you will want to consider organization. Typically you will organize from the least convincing evidence to the most convincing, but other types of organization may be suitable for your thesis—chronological or comparative-contrasting, for example.

Themes

You might begin by asking yourself what are some other major ideas in the story. Then you should determine how the story deals with those ideas. For analyzing theme in "The Open Boat," you can consider not only the importance of community but also the indifference of the natural world and the random nature of survival in that world. If you choose one of these or another theme, you are ready to look for relevant passages.

Sample Topics:

1. **Community:** Although the four men in "The Open Boat" have little in common except for their current situation, they develop a strong sense of community. How does Crane use the importance of community in this story?

   Start, perhaps, with the narrator's statement, "It would be difficult to describe the subtle brotherhood of men that was here established on the seas" (73). Besides this direct statement, what other evidence is given that these men genuinely care for one another? Robert Shulman points out,

   > The correspondent's concern and affection for his companions emerge not only in the famous explicit passages but pervasively in his gestures and responses. He is as skillful, controlled, and humane as any of the four, a point worth calling attention to, not to detract from the oiler or the captain, for example, but to emphasize that their achievement is carefully presented as a communal one. The men share equally and Crane deliberately avoids setting up a hierarchy of merit. (459)

   How is this sharing and caring projected even beyond the bounds of the small dinghy? Consider what each character does as well as what each says, looking for close physical proximity as well as a spirit of concern for one another. In a time when mechanization, immigration, and urbanization created divisions in American society, what is the message of this story about the importance of community?

2. **Nature:** As the men are combating the dangers of the sea, they must fight against nature itself. How does Crane characterize nature and its forces in "The Open Boat"?

First, make a list of all the dangers they encounter as the four men struggle to keep the dinghy afloat. It is not just the waves, but numerous other forces such as sharks and seagulls. Notice that even the seaweed seems to mock them as they are separated from the land that is their goal. Then look for terms that are used to describe these various threatening aspects of nature, with the waves being "barbarously abrupt and tall" (68), "snarling" (69), "formidable" (77), and "sinister" (81) as they bombard the boat and intimidate the men. Although nature can sometimes be seen as serene, in this story it is either "flatly indifferent" (88) or outright dangerous. Finally, try to articulate the relationship between nature and these four men.

3. **Survival:** We typically talk about survival of the fittest, echoing Darwin's theory of evolution. How does Crane's representation of the mystery of survival differ from this perhaps simplistic view?

In the story there is a "house of refuge just north of the Mosquito Inlet" (70), yet it is of absolutely no help to these four victims of the shipwreck. Instead, what do they see there? Why is that sight significant? Notice that one refrain is repeated three times in three different places in the story: "If I am going to be drowned—if I am going to be drowned—if I am going to be drowned . . ." (81, 84, 87). What tone does this almost excessive repetition evoke? How does it work to represent and reinforce the struggle of the men in the dinghy? At the end of the story, what do you believe is the message about survival? Ask yourself who survives and who dies and why in each case. The correspondent feels that he has almost a mission at that point. What is that mission? What is its connection, if any, with survival?

Character

Of the four men in the boat, none is similar to any of the others; each is distinctly his own person. Reread the story, paying particular attention to one character, such as the captain, all the way through. Then reread, paying attention to another character, such as the oiler. Each time make a list of the character's physical traits, his actions, and his words. Think about how each man interacts with the others. In a short story, characters, with the possible exception of the main one, are usually static; that is, they stay the same throughout the story. In this story, is the correspondent, the major character or protagonist, static or dynamic? If he changes, how are those changes manifested? There are a few very minor characters, such as the man on the shore who strips to rush into the sea. You might want to focus on him and his role in the story along with the vacationers who merely wave. Could the story be told as well without them? Why or why not?

Sample Topics:

1. **The correspondent:** Analyze the character of the correspondent, first deciding whether or not he is static or dynamic and then showing how the event in the dinghy does or does not change him.

   What are the physical and emotional characteristics of the correspondent? The story occupies only thirty hours, yet this newspaper correspondent reveals many of his thoughts and emotions as he battles the sea. What does he learn about himself? What does he learn about his fellow sailors? What is the significance of the verse he remembers from school? At the end of the story, he feels that the survivors can "then be interpreters" (92). How can the correspondent be an "interpreter"? What will he interpret?

2. **The captain:** Analyze the character of the captain.

   The ship's captain is himself injured, unable to take part in the physical labor necessary to keep the small lifeboat afloat, yet he is quite important to the survival of his three companions. What does he contribute to the other men? Look at his actions and his words. How do the other men react to him? What keeps the injured captain from drowning once the dinghy is swamped?

3. **The oiler:** Analyze the character of the oiler, paying particular attention to his fate at the end of the story.

Describe the physical attributes of the oiler. Then tell about his actions. Look particularly at this passage:

> In the meantime the oiler and the correspondent rowed. And also they rowed.
>   They sat together in the same seat, and each rowed an oar. Then the oiler took both oars; then the correspondent took both oars; then the oiler; then the correspondent. They rowed and they rowed. (75)

What does this passage reveal about the oiler? Why is he paired here with the correspondent? How does he compare to the correspondent in physical strength and build? How would you characterize him as a companion? What are the other two men doing as these two are rowing? Once the four men try to make their way toward the shore from the swamped dinghy, the oiler is ahead of the other three men. What is the significance of his position? Why do you suppose he is the only of the four men whom Crane names—"Billie," or once "Willie"?

History and Context

This story takes place as the rebellion in Cuba is becoming more violent, with the actual event of the sinking of the filibustering *Commodore* on December 31, 1896. After the events memorialized in this story, Stephen Crane did not sail to Cuba; instead, he soon went to Greece to report on the Greek-Turkish War being fought there. Although neither the war in Cuba nor the war in Greece directly affected the United States at this point, you may wish to research these two conflicts to ascertain exactly what was happening worldwide at the time Crane wrote this story. The only mention of war in the story is in the verse about the soldier of Algiers, yet this poem does somehow seem to connect with the violence with which men must contend whether at war or at sea. After being rescued from the ocean, Crane, always the conscientious news reporter, filed his story, which appeared as "Stephen Crane's Own Story" on January 7 in the *New York Press.*

Sample Topics:

1. **War and "The Open Boat":** Although there is no war in this short story, the growing war in Cuba against Spain does supply a tension that may be manifested in this story. Make a case that war is an important background in this piece.

   Start with the verse that is quoted in the story, thinking about its influence and its connection to the correspondent's plight. Then research how and why Stephen Crane chose to enroll as a crew member on the *Commodore,* using an assumed name. Although he never reached the battle on this particular trip, Crane was assuming a tremendous risk just going to Cuba on a filibustering ship whose goal was to smuggle arms to the troops there. Do these facts seem to have any relation to the story? Is another type of war going on in the dinghy? Does the idea of war help to explain how the verse on the soldier in Algiers is perhaps more relevant than is at first apparent?

2. **Stephen Crane's own story:** After reading this factual account of the four men in the dinghy, you might show how actual experience informed and enhanced Crane's fictional account.

   Consider how and why Crane planned to go to Cuba and report on the war. What were the dangers he might have faced in that situation? Since Crane had become an internationally known figure after the publication of *The Red Badge of Courage,* the *New York Times* and other newspapers in New York and elsewhere were reporting on January 2, 1897, his being lost at sea. After the rescue the following day, they reported his bravery. How does the actual experience provide a great depth of feeling to the story?

Philosophy and Ideas

In much of Stephen Crane's writing, he shows man as dependent upon himself to make meaning in the world of an uncaring nature or God. "The Open Boat" is no exception. This story shows the four men adrift in a dinghy that could at any moment be overturned by waves, leaving them vulnerable not only to the sea itself but to all the creatures there, including sharks. They question why they should be in such a predicament and why they have come so far in the dinghy only to face probable death. Although the four men form a community and they act kindly to each other, each is also very much alone, a situation made clear as the correspondent rows in the night while the shark circles the small boat. The predicament of men in such a hostile universe is much clearer to the men than perhaps it had ever been previously. As you reread the story with the idea of philosophy in mind, look for the world-views of the characters.

Sample Topics:

1. **Christian ethics:** Analyze the Christian ethics the four men practice in "The Open Boat."

   Although "The Open Boat" never suggests any belief in God to comfort the men in their plight, they behave toward one another very much as Christianity and other religions teach. As you reread the story, look for passages that show the way the men treat one another. You might also look at the way the remembered school verse causes the correspondent to have empathy for his fellow beings.

2. **Existentialism:** Research this term in a good encyclopedia or other reference work and argue that many passages in the book are examples of existentialistic philosophy.

   Look, for example, at the following passage, which concludes a long dialogue among the men as they watch a man on shore whom they see at first as a rescuer:

   > "Well, I wish I could make something out of those signals. What do you suppose he means?"
   >
   > "He don't mean anything. He's just playing."
   >
   > "Well, if he'd just signal us to try the surf again, or to go to sea and wait, or go north, or go south, or go to hell—there would be some reason in it. But look at him. He just stands there and keeps his coat revolving like a wheel. The ass!"
   >
   > "There come more people."

"Now there's quite a mob. Look! Isn't that a boat?"

"Where? Oh, I see where you mean. No, that's no boat."

"That fellow is still waving his coat."

"He must think we like to see him do that. Why don't he quit it. It don't mean anything." (80)

The difficulty of finding meaning in a universe that seems meaningless is here underscored by the desperation of the men to be saved from the sea and in the repetition of the word *mean* in the passage. The men strive to make meaning or find meaning in the whole episode. Look at other passages in the story where one or all of the men search for meaning in individual events or in their existence as a whole. Does the story eventually conclude with meaning or does it continue to defy meaning?

Form and Genre

Although "The Open Boat" retells a real event, the story itself is quite impressionistic, with the point of view shifting from the correspondent to all the men in the boat to an exterior vantage point. This use of literary impressionism puts the reader into the scene with the characters, beginning with the story's first sentence, "No one knew the color of the sky." Like the characters, the reader too is lost at sea, wondering what is to happen next. As you read the story, think of the varying impressions that the characters have, the impressions they impart to the reader, and the impressions Crane sets up to make the reader feel a part of the story. Then notice that the narrator occasionally backs away and suggests that the scene might be picturesque if viewed from afar or from another perspective.

Another choice of topics on form might be to examine the irony in the story, with the biggest irony being the death of the oiler, the physically strongest man in the dinghy. You could continue to look for other ironies—for example, the irony of the correspondent's feeling totally alone because he thinks all the other men are asleep, only to discover later that the captain had been awake and had also been aware of the shark.

Sample Topics:

1. **Point of view:** Analyze the point of view in "The Open Boat."

Reread the story, marking when the point of view changes. You will likely conclude that much is from the correspondent's point of view, but you need to identify when that point of view shifts, when it becomes more of a group point of view, or when it becomes the narrator's objective point of view. After you have completed this task, then form a thesis that takes into consideration how that shifting point of view is important in the story.

2. **Irony:** Analyze the irony in the story, showing its importance.

The man most physically equipped to have survived the whole shipwreck experience is the one who dies. What other important ironies are included in the story? How do they function? Do they contribute to the realism of the piece? If so, in what way?

Language, Symbols, and Imagery

As you have come to realize, the study of specific language usage, symbols, and imagery can lead to a better understanding of any piece of literature. In a short story, language patterns are especially important because a short piece must be very tightly constructed. Rereading "The Open Boat," look for specific patterns, where words or phrases appear several times. Highlight any passages or word patterns that seem significant, beginning with the title itself. Why, for example, is it called an open boat? In the story, why are several passages repeated, sometimes with variations? You might note the references to safety, for example. The lighthouse is meant to be a refuge, a place of safety. What other possible refuges are there? You might also look at the many references to drowning. Are all of these references to the physical act of drowning, or can they also be metaphorical?

Sample Topics:

1. **The boat as a symbol:** Although the boat is a physical thing, it can also be seen as a symbol. Analyze the boat as symbolic of man's position in the universe or in life itself.

Think about the fact that the boat is open, that it seems to give very little protection to the men within it. Although it is a lifeboat designed to move to safety, it gives very little comfort as they struggle to keep it afloat. How does their position in the boat seem similar to a human's journey through life? How does the boat itself become a danger? What must the men do to get through the experience alive? What must humans do to get through life with the dangers and discomforts to be endured?

2. **The cigars:** Analyze the function of the cigars in the story.

The correspondent discovers he still has four dry cigars among the eight in the top pocket of his coat. Although the cigars seem to be somewhat unimportant in the struggle for survival, they function metaphorically here as an important part of the story. With which real-life rituals can you connect the sharing of the cigars? How are these cigars more important than such objects would ordinarily be? What do they do for the men's attitudes? How can the cigars be compared to the situation of the men themselves?

3. **Color imagery:** Analyze the function of the color imagery in the story.

As in many of Stephen Crane's works, color seems to play an important role. In "The Open Boat" you will find many uses of the colors black, white, and gray. How do they function in the story? Are other colors also included? If so, how do they function?

Look, for example, at the following passage: "It was probably splendid. It was probably glorious, this play of the free sea, wild with lights of emerald and white and amber" (70). Think of other colors you associate with the sea and the way they differ from the black, white, and grays in the story. How does Crane's use of colors add to the meaning of the story?

Compare and Contrast Essays

Stephen Crane wrote a variety of short stories, many dealing with war, some with other dangerous situations, and several with children as the main characters in a mundane everyday setting. You might read some of the other stories to see the variety of subject matter and treatment. Then you can compare two that have significant similarities or significant differences. You might, on the other hand, decide to compare this story to another important short story by a different author. The short story genre is rather recent in the history of literature, with the early famous short story writers including Guy du Maupassant, a French writer; Anton Chekhov, a Russian writer; and Edgar Allan Poe, an American.

Sample Topics:

1. **Poe and Crane:** Write an essay that compares and contrasts "The Open Boat" with the famous Edgar Allan Poe short story "A Descent into the Maelström."

   Poe's stories fall into two categories—detective stories and so-called ideal short stories, those with events that are built on a predetermined "effect." The protagonist in Poe's story, like the correspondent, is shipwrecked, but during his adventure he finds a whirlpool, or maelstrom, to be a beautiful and awesome creation. Afterward, he manages to cling to a wooden barrel and fight his way to safety. As you read this particular ideal Poe story, make a list of the similarities and the differences between it and Crane's story. Finally, decide what this comparison shows that helps to interpret or better understand "The Open Boat." Keep in mind that Stephen Crane wrote several decades after Poe and that he likely was familiar with most of Poe's writing.

2. **Crane's newspaper story and "The Open Boat":** Compare and contrast the two pieces, showing how the genre of the short story allowed Crane to include important ideas not appropriate in the newspaper account.

   After you have read the newspaper account, make a list of what is included in the short story that is not in the news report. Then determine what appears in the newspaper account that is omitted from the story. What is the significance of the differences?

Bibliography and Online Resources for "The Open Boat"

Bender, Bert. "'The Open Boat' Is a Traditional Sea Story." *Readings on Stephen Crane*. Ed. Bonnie Szumski. San Diego: Greenhaven, 1998. 141–49.

Bergon, Frank. "'The Open Boat' Is a Story of Revelation." *Readings on Stephen Crane*. Ed. Bonnie Szumski. San Diego: Greenhaven, 1998. 150–59.

Claviez, Thomas. "'Declining' the (American) Sublime: Stephen Crane's 'The Open Boat.'" *Amerikastudien/American Studies* 53.2 (2008): 137–51.

Colvert, James B. "Style and Meaning in Stephen Crane: 'The Open Boat.'" *Texas Studies in English* 37 (1958): 34–45.

Crane, Stephen. "The Open Boat." *The Works of Stephen Crane: Tales of Adventure*. Ed. Fredson Bowers. Vol. 5. Charlottesville: UP of Virginia, 1970. 68–92.

———. "Stephen Crane's Own Story." *The Works of Stephen Crane: Reports of War: Dispatches. Great Battles of the World*. Ed. Fredson Bowers. Vol. 9. Charlottesville: UP of Virginia, 1971. 85–94.

De Benedictis, Michel. "The Open Boat: Fiction vs. Reportage in the Work of Stephen Crane and Mark Twain." *Florida Studies: Proceedings of the 2005 Annual Meeting of the Florida College English Association*. Ed. Steve Glassman, Karen Tolchin, and Steve Brahlek. Newcastle upon Tyne, England: Cambridge Scholars, 2006. 103–19.

Eye, Stefanie Bates. "Fact, Not Fiction: Questioning our Assumptions about Crane's 'The Open Boat.'" *Studies in Short Fiction* 35.1 (1998): 65–76.

Frus, Phyllis. "Two Tales 'Intended to be After the Fact': 'Stephen Crane's Own Story' and 'The Open Boat.'" *Literary Nonfiction: Theory, Criticism, Pedagogy*. Ed. Chris Anderson. Carbondale: Southern Illinois UP, 1989. 125–51.

Gerstenberger, Donna. "Crane's Lapses of Style in 'The Open Boat' Are Purposeful." *Readings on Stephen Crane*. Ed. Bonnie Szumski. San Diego: Greenhaven, 1998. 160–66.

———. "'The Open Boat': Additional Perspective." *Modern Fiction Studies* 17 (1971): 557–61.

Greenfield, Stanley B. "The Unmistakable Stephen Crane." *PMLA: Publications of the Modern Language Association of America* 73.5 (1958): 562–72.

Hageman E. R. "'The Open Boat' Is a Study of Man against Nature." *Readings on Stephen Crane*. Ed. Bonnie Szumski. San Diego: Greenhaven, 1998. 128–40.

———. "'Sadder than the End': Another Look at 'The Open Boat.'" *Stephen Crane in Transition: Centenary Essays.* Ed. Joseph Katz and James Dickey. DeKalb: Northern Illinois UP, 1972. 66–85.

Kissane, Leedice. "Interpretation Through Language: A Study of the Metaphors in Stephen Crane's 'The Open Boat.'" *Rendezvous: Journal of Arts and Letters* 1.1 (1966): 18–22.

"Loss of the *Commodore.*" *The New York Times* 3 January 1897: 1.

Metzger, Charles R. "Realistic Devices in Stephen Crane's 'The Open Boat.'" *Midwest Quarterly* 4 (1962): 47–54.

Quinn, Brian T. "A Contrastive Look at Stephen Crane's Naturalism as Depicted in 'The Open Boat' and 'The Blue Hotel.'" *Studies in English Language and Literature* 42 (1992): 45–63.

Schaefer, Michael W. "'I . . . Do Not Say That I Am Honest': Stephen Crane's Failure of Artistic Nerve in 'The Open Boat.'" *Philological Review* 31.1 (2005): 1–16.

Shulman, Robert. "Community, Perception, and the Development of Stephen Crane: From *The Red Badge* to 'The Open Boat.'" *American Literature* 50.3 (1978): 441–60.

Spofford, William K. "Stephen Crane's 'The Open Boat': Fact or Fiction." *American Literary Realism* 12 (1979): 316–21.

Taylor, Thomas W. "Stephen Crane and the *Commodore:* A Prelude to the Spanish-American War." *Stephen Crane Studies* 5.1 (1996): 25–27.

"The Tug *Commodore* Sunk." *The New York Times* 2 January 1897: 1.

Warren, Robin O. "The Cuban Insurrection and Northeast Florida in 'Stephen Crane's Own Story' and 'The Open Boat.'" *Stephen Crane Studies* 8.1 (1999): 8–19.

Wright, Jonathan. "The Unpleasant 'Business' of Stephen Crane's 'The Open Boat.'" *A Class of Its Own: Re-Envisioning American Labor Fiction.* Ed. Laura Hapke and Lisa A. Kirby. Newcastle upon Tyne, England: Cambridge Scholars, 2008. 33–74.

"THE BLUE HOTEL"

READING TO WRITE

In January 1895 Stephen Crane convinced the Bacheller Syndicate to send him as a correspondent to explore the American West and parts of Mexico, a trip he had planned for some three years. Crane travelled to Lincoln, Nebraska, Kansas City, New Orleans, Texas, and into Mexico, and early in 1896 he used material gathered there for four western stories. Later he wrote four other western stories, including the well-known "The Bride Comes to Yellow Sky" and "The Blue Hotel," one of his best short stories. At the time Crane explored the West and wrote his stories, that part of the country had already been chronicled at length, especially in dime novels, but also in more serious literature by such well-known writers as James Fenimore Cooper, Owen Wister, Mark Twain, and Bret Harte. In most of these works the West had been romanticized as idyllic with humans thrust against the wilderness or in conflict with Native Americans. In "The Blue Hotel" Crane uses the concept of the dime novel to make a literary statement about romanticism and realism.

When you read this story, you should look for elements that are romantic and other elements that are realistic. Ask yourself about the importance of this juxtaposition of disparate elements. What does the story suggest about these elements? Look at the following description of the hotel itself, found in the first paragraph:

Pat Scully, the proprietor, had proved himself a master of strategy when he chose his paints. It is true that on clear days, when the great

> trans-continental expresses, long lines of swaying Pullmans, swept
> through Fort Romper, passengers were overcome at the sight, and the
> cult that knows the brown-reds and the subdivisions of the dark greens
> of the East express shame, pity, horror, in a laugh. But to the citizens
> of this prairie town, and to the people who would naturally stop there,
> Pat Scully had performed a feat. With this opulence and splendor,
> these creeds, classes, egotisms, that streamed through Romper on the
> rails day after day, they had no color in common. (142)

Which words seem particularly important? Start with the name of the
town: Fort Romper. What does that name suggest? Why is that important? After you realize that it is not a real name, but one made up to create an atmosphere, you also realize that perhaps Crane is being ironic,
even satiric. It is a town removed from the real West in the same way
that most popular fiction portrayed the West in a romanticized or melodramatic fashion, a "romp" through the imaginary West. The characters who live in Fort Romper feel that the hotel owner has "performed
a feat" by using this melodramatic blue to paint his hotel a color that
screams and howls against "the dazzling winter landscape of Nebraska"
(142). Crane carefully points out that the people who see the bright blue
color of the hotel have nothing in common, "no color in common," with
that "opulence and splendor." In other words, the hotel itself is just the
opposite of what they expect in the real life of their town. It has been
depicted in such a way as to attract attention, not to present ordinary life
in a western town.

"The Blue Hotel" is full of allusions to a romanticized West. Look for
other passages that contain events or characters typical of popular western stories. For example, note the specific people in the hotel, and note
how they differ from the people in the saloon. Once you realize that the
hotel itself is more akin to melodrama than to ordinary life, ask yourself
why this discrepancy is important. Is there anything to suggest that the
reader is being asked to think of literature itself? Why and how does
Scully entrap the Easterner? Later near the end of the story, Crane even
refers directly to language by his use of the grammatical terms *noun* and
adverb. Carefully reread any passages that seem to relate to literature and
language, or parts of literature or language. Do the allusions suggest that

some people are convinced that the West is the type of place where fights and killings are commonplace? Does it suggest that Crane believes that such romanticizing of real life is detrimental? Or does his tone undercut that suggestion? Why is the Swede killed in a saloon instead of the blue hotel? Why is the ending section in a completely different third locale? Why does the Easterner feel that both he and the cowboy are complicit in the Swede's death?

The careful reading and rereading of this short story will produce many questions, as is evidenced by the numerous critical pieces already written on the story. Choose one question that intrigues you as you read and reread and gather evidence to answer that question to your satisfaction. When you have sufficient evidence, look for common threads or patterns that will allow you to devise a specific thesis.

TOPICS AND STRATEGIES

Consider the following topics and essays as mere starting points to help you fashion your own ideas and answer your own questions. Let your imagination run wild, but bring yourself to a reality check by determining whether you can sufficiently support your own specific thesis. Continue to gather evidence, and then craft a logical thesis statement. Determine the major points needed to support that thesis, ending with the strongest point so that your essay will convince your reader. After you have drafted an essay, remember that you have more to do—revising, editing, and finally proofreading. The good writer never stops with the first draft.

Theme

Begin to think about this short story's themes by asking yourself what the big ideas or issues are. What do you think is the primary theme? What are some secondary themes? This particular story has a variety of main ideas: romanticism versus realism, the stereotypes of western fiction, the motivation of fear, the consequences of irrational fear, the consequences of feeling invulnerable, the limits of duty or responsibility, and the care for fellow humans. Once your argument is clear in your own mind and then in a written thesis statement, you are ready to plan and write your essay.

Sample Topics:

1. **The use of romantic elements of the Old West:** Identify elements of the Old West as it has been portrayed in fiction and film. Then analyze how these elements function in "The Blue Hotel."

   Start with the stereotypical characters in the hotel: the cowboy, the proprietor, the Easterner, and the Swede. How are these particular types generally portrayed in popular fiction? Do Crane's characters break that stereotype in any way? Why or why not? Why does the Swede expect to be killed in the hotel? What causes him to change his way of acting? Why is he killed in the saloon? How do the characters in the saloon vary from those in the hotel? Why are these differences important?

2. **The use of fear:** Analyze the Swede's fear and its function in this story.

   Of what is the Swede afraid? What has caused his fear? The others in the hotel seem surprised that he is frightened, but they are perhaps even more surprised when his fear turns into a foolish bravado. Later, when the Swede goes to the saloon, his boldness has increased even more. Was he more foolish to be afraid in the hotel or not to be afraid in the saloon? Why? Is he more vulnerable in one place or the other? Why?

3. **Responsibility for protecting fellow humans:** The Easterner states at the end of the story that he and the others in the hotel are responsible for the Swede's death, even though they were nowhere near the actual stabbing. Analyze his statement of responsibility and decide whether to support it or to deny it.

   Why does the Easterner believe he and the other hotel characters are responsible for the Swede's death? Do you believe their complicity in Johnnie's cheating is responsible for the Swede's demise? What about the men in the saloon? Are any of them, other than the gambler, responsible for the stabbing and the

Swede's consequent death? Why or why not? The Easterner actually accepts responsibility for a death in which he had no direct action. Agree or disagree with his acceptance of that responsibility, arguing for human responsibility in general.

Character

In "The Blue Hotel" a number of characters can be the subject of a profitable analysis, especially that of the Swede, Scully, the Easterner, Johnnie, and the bartender. Choose one of these or even one or two minor characters and see how they function in the story. Pay particular attention to what the character says, how he or she acts, and how others interact with that character. Is there a discrepancy between the character's words and actions? Can you determine his or her motivation for specific actions? What values does the character maintain? Since these characters appear in a short story instead of a novel, most are likely to be static. You might, however, argue that the Swede is a dynamic character and that he changes from a fearful tenderfoot to a loud braggart. If you choose such a topic, you will need to show how that change is important to an understanding of the story itself.

Sample Topics:

1. **The Swede:** Analyze the character of the Swede.

   How does the Swede develop during the course of the narrative? What motivates him to be so afraid in the hotel? Why is he sure he will be killed there? Is his nationality important? If so, in what way? Why does the cowboy refer to him at the beginning of section VII as a "Dutchman"? Why does the Swede leave the hotel? How has his attitude changed? What caused the change? Do you feel sorrow at the Swede's death? Why or why not?

2. **Scully:** Analyze Scully as the proprietor of the hotel.

   In what specific ways does Crane depict Scully as a hard-working entrepreneur? What actions does he perform that the average hotel owner might neglect? Why? With these specific actions in mind, now look at the following paragraph:

As soon as the door was closed, Scully and the cowboy leaped
to their feet and began to curse. They trampled to and fro, waving their arms and smashing into the air with their fists. "Oh,
but that was a hard minute!" wailed Scully. "That was a hard
minute! Him there leerin' and scoffin'! One bang at his nose
was worth forty dollars to me that minute! How did you stand
it, Bill?" (164)

What does this final anger reveal about Scully's previous
actions? What does it suggest about his earlier motivation?
Why does he lapse into a "sudden brogue" in his speech?

3. **The cowboy:** Analyze the character of the cowboy, following
   him through the story and paying particular attention to his
   role at the end.

The cowboy participates in the card game, and he admonishes
the Swede for calling Johnnie a cheat: "Quit, now! Quit, d'ye
hear—" (157). Although he is unable to squelch the Swede's
desire to fight, the cowboy seems more agitated than one
would expect: "The cowboy's brow was beaded with sweat
from his efforts in intercepting all sorts of raids. He turned in
despair to Scully 'What are you goin' to do now?'" (158). How
do you explain this obvious anxiety? Then in the last section
of the story, the cowboy suggests that the bartender should
have "cracked that there Dutchman on the head with a bottle in the beginnin' of it and stopped all this here murderin'"
(169). Why does the cowboy blame the bartender more even
than the gambler, who did the actual stabbing? Whom does he
ultimately blame? Why? Is there any significance to his name,
"Bill," a name which Scully uses three times?

History and Context

When "The Blue Hotel" was written in late 1897, the American West had
been explored and largely settled. Dime novels, however, continued to
depict the area as lawless and dangerous, with many of these popular
books devoted to Wild Bill Hickok and Buffalo Bill Cody, along with

other western adventurers intent on taming this supposedly lawless area of the country. Although Hickok and Cody were actual people, their actual deeds, and those of other fictional counterparts, were romanticized and exploited by the commercial writers and publishers of dime novels, a genre widely condemned by some clergy, by parents and teachers, by journalists, and even by literary periodicals such as *Harper's Weekly.* These inexpensively produced books filled with gunfights, gambling, saloons, cowboys, and Indians were extremely popular, especially with the audience of young men. How does Stephen Crane make use of the stereotypes of dime novel characters in this story? Does he seem to condemn such novels? Does he blame them and their influence for the Swede's death? Why or why not?

Sample Topics:

1. **The dime novel western and "The Blue Hotel":** What does the short story indicate about the dangers of reading dime novels?

   Familiarize yourself with information about dime novels, looking particularly at the excellent website showcasing the Stanford University collection of these books. Once you have looked at several examples, studying the illustrated covers and reading portions of the dialogues and narratives, reread "The Blue Hotel" to identify dime novel elements. How did the public react to dime novels in the nineteenth century? How did the literary community react to such books? What statement does the story seem to make about the genre of dime novels? How does Crane's tone in this story help you to arrive at an answer to that question?

2. **Literary debate about realism:** Research the literary debate about realism as opposed to romanticism, or sensationalist fiction, and show how "The Blue Hotel" incorporates features of this debate into the story.

   See, for instance, William Dean Howells's essay "Criticism and Fiction," which can be found online, with his comments about realism. Howells, considered the foremost literary critic at the time, makes his case about the important characteristics of literature. He asserts that "I think the time is yet far off . . . that the people who have been brought up on the ideal grasshopper, the heroic grasshopper, the impassioned grasshopper, the self-devoted, adventureful, good old romantic card-board grasshopper, must die out before the simple, honest, and natural grasshopper can have a fair field." How does this statement relate to the stereotypical characters found in the hotel as opposed to the more realistic characters found in the saloon?

Philosophy and Ideas

For an overview of the various philosophies Stephen Crane employs in his different writings, you can read Patrick K. Dooley's *The Pluralistic Philosophy of Stephen Crane*. In "The Blue Hotel," Dooley sees one important philosophy as that of caring for our fellow humans:

> The conclusion of "The Blue Hotel" reaffirms the moral position Crane took in *The Red Badge of Courage*. The Palace Hotel group refuses to acknowledge and aid a human being suffering from psychological injury. Fleming refuses to minister to the tattered man's physical trauma. Genuine needs are immorally and selfishly ignored in both cases. (92)

The core of many different religious beliefs, this philosophy of caring for each other can be traced back to Crane's Methodist upbringing. To discuss the Christian ethics in this story, you should analyze a few characters and their actions, determining what their world-views or philosophies seem to be. You might decide what motivates Scully to act as he does. Then look at the bartender, who does not interfere in the fatal confrontation. What is his motivation?

Another philosophy that contrasts with the above Christian doctrine of "Love thy neighbor" is that of existentialism, or a focus on the conditions of existence of the individual person and his or her emotions, actions, responsibilities, and thoughts as he looks for meaning in a meaningless world. The early nineteenth-century philosopher Søren Kierkegaard, usually regarded as the father of existentialism, asserted that the individual is responsible for giving his or her own life meaning in the midst of an uncaring universe. If you wish to write about existentialism, look for specific passages that seem to engage in philosophical discussion about the men and their surroundings. Why does the Swede look for companionship? What does he find instead?

If you decide to examine the character of the Swede using the philosophy of Christianity, you might decide on the following thesis: Because of a failure of the other characters to exhibit care for fellow humans, the Swede is killed. An existentialist analysis of the Swede's character may, however, take you to a completely different conclusion: In a hostile universe, the Swede is unable to exhibit the basic fundamentals of survival. In this particular analysis, you would place responsibility on the Swede to develop his own survival skills in a variety of settings and situations. For example, if he had not drunk the liquor in the hotel and later in the saloon, he would have thought more clearly about the dangers that lay in wait for him.

Sample Topics:

1. **Human ethics:** What does this story suggest about ethical values?

   What actions could each of the characters have taken to avoid the Swede's death at the end? Who is most responsible for that death? You might begin with Scully himself. How does Scully contribute to the Swede's demise? Then you might consider his son, Johnnie, and his actions. Are all of the people in the hotel responsible, as the easterner suggests? George Monteiro states,

   > The theory calling for communal guilt and social complicity, if accepted, implies the existence of shared responsibility and the potential for social efficacy. Indeed, this bit of theory—a parade of new knowledge—so puffs up the Easterner that he ignores several facts: that the cowboy had not seen anyone cheating, that perhaps he was alone in knowing that the Swede's accusation was warranted, and that, despite his knowledge of the cheating, he also wanted to see the upstart Swede thrashed. (302)

Since the Swede is actually killed in the saloon, are those in the saloon also responsible? What could they have done to prevent the stabbing? Finally, what attitude leads to the unfortunate end? Does the reader herself, as William B. Dillingham, has suggested, contribute to that attitude in her own feelings about the Swede?

2. **The philosophy of existentialism:** How does Stephen Crane incorporate existential philosophy into this story?

Consider this passage and its position in the text:

> He [the Swede] might have been in a deserted village. We picture the world as thick with conquering and elate humanity, but here, with the bugles of the tempest pealing, it was hard to imagine a peopled earth. One viewed the existence of man then as a marvel, and conceded a glamour of wonder to these lice which were caused to cling to a whirling, fire-smote, ice-locked, disease-stricken, space-lost bulb. (165)

This "whirling, fire-smote, ice-locked, disease-stricken, space-lost bulb" is obviously the Earth, and the Swede has left the protected but still hostile Palace Hotel to venture out into this negative space where he is no more than a despised parasite. Although there may be a causal force that relegated him to clinging to this whirling bulb of an Earth, the cause, or creator, seems far distanced from the humanity that inhabits the world. What is man, or in this case the Swede, supposed to do in such circumstances? How can he cope with such an existence? What protections are afforded a human being?

Form and Genre

This story is divided into three sections: the hotel, the saloon, and a ranch far away in Nevada. When this story was first analyzed by literary critics, the final section was often seen as somehow tacked on to the real story and not an integral part of it. You might consider how the three different parts of the story fit together, and in doing so, you might also consider how this fanciful story can fit into the literary period of realism.

Sample Topics:
1. **The division of "The Blue Hotel" into three parts:** Consider the tripartite nature of this short story, and explain the relationship among the three sections.

   Consider how each of the three sections functions: the hotel section, the saloon section, and the final section with the Easterner and the cowboy on a ranch near the Dakota line. If you believe the first section to be romanticized, the middle section realistic, then what is the function of the last section, which some critics see as being nonessential to the story? How does it bring the other two sections together and offer commentary on both romanticism and realism?

2. **"The Blue Hotel" as a work of literary realism:** Argue that this work belongs in this category.

   What are the realistic elements of this story? Have you ever been fearful of an unknown situation because you associate it with a rumor or legend? Are the Swede's feelings realistic? Can the story function both as realistic fiction and a commentary on realism?

Language, Symbols, and Imagery

Paying close attention to the details—the language—of a literary work can lead to revelations otherwise missed in a text. For "The Blue Hotel," you might start with the description of the hotel itself: "The Palace Hotel at Fort Romper was painted a light blue, a shade that is on the legs of a kind of heron, causing the bird to declare its position against any background" (142). This bird and the color seem to be unusual in the story's setting since herons are more typically found near large bodies of water and in warmer climates, not in Nebraska, a cold, snowy, landlocked state with no major lakes. Describing the color of the hotel by referring to this color of the leg of a heron, Stephen Crane gives us a hint that the hotel is as far removed from the reality of Nebraska as this particular bird would be. Crane then follows up this description with that of the hotel owner, Scully, as he "perform[s] the marvel of catching three men" (142). As you continue to read details of Scully's trapping of his visitors in the hotel, you will begin to see that the imagery surrounding him and his actions presents a portrait as imaginative as the hotel itself.

Sample Topics:

1. **The imagery depicting Scully and his actions:** Analyze the images used to describe Scully as a man who catches his customers and works diligently to keep them in his hotel.

   Make a list of Scully's features. What is the significance of his "two red ears [that] stick out stiffly, as if they were made of tin" (143)? Do they remind you of any imaginative creature? Why does Crane state that Scully conducts the new visitors through the "*portals* of the blue hotel" (143, emphasis added). Why is Scully's shoulder said to be "tender from an old fall" (155)? Trace the occurrences of the word *hell* to see if there is any significance to its usage. When you connect the imagery with the idea of hell, what does the connection suggest about the hotel proprietor?

2. **Imagery of language and grammar:** Analyze the use of terms referring to language, grammar, and paper. What does this pattern of imagery suggest?

   Look through the story for terms such as *words, complete sentences, deep significance to . . . words, noun,* and *adverb.* Why are these particular words chosen? These terms associated with writing and other details that suggest the act of writing indicate that Crane consciously brings our attention to the fact that the story is a constructed work. Why does he want us to be aware of that construction? Given the fact that the Swede thinks he's in the middle of a dime-novel scenario, what does the use of such terms imply?

3. **The cash register legend or sign:** What is the significance of the sign on top of the cash register, which reads, "This registers the amount of your purchase" (169)?

Throughout this story Scully has been clever in trapping and keeping his customers, and it is obvious that the purpose is commercial, one of making money. He does not care for the Swede as a person, but as a customer. The pecuniary nature of their relationship when connected to the dime-novel aspects of the story suggests that profit is an important motif both in the blue hotel itself and in the story named after this edifice. Analyze the references to money throughout the story, including the amount the bartender rang up on the cash register.

4. **The card games:** Analyze the imagery surrounding the two games of cards being played, one in the hotel and another in the saloon.

What are the differences in the two games? How are the cards emphasized in the hotel? Why are they less important in the saloon? What is the difference between Johnnie and the gambler in the saloon? How are they alike?

Compare and Contrast Essays

Comparisons and contrasts can serve to generate ideas about a text and often can become the basis for an entire essay. In Stephen Crane's short story "The Blue Hotel," several comparisons are already set up: the two settings, the two card games, the characters in the two different settings, and several other elements. You can choose any of these, or you may want to make a comparison with a work outside this text: a dime novel or another author's story of fear, such as Edgar Allan Poe's "The Tell-Tale Heart."

Sample Topics:

1. **The characters in the Palace Hotel and the characters in the saloon:** Compare and contrast the characters in the hotel with their counterparts in the saloon.

In the hotel are the Swede, Scully, Johnnie, the cowboy, and the easterner. In the saloon are the Swede, the bartender, two local businessmen, the district attorney, and a professional gambler. Reread the story, listing the characteristics of each. How are they similar? How are they different? Pay particular attention to Scully and the bartender and to Johnnie and the professional gambler.

2. **Comparison of a dime novel from the Stanford University online collection with "The Blue Hotel":** Consider, for example, the novel *Adventures of Buffalo Bill from Boyhood to Manhood* in its similarities and differences with Crane's story.

In Chapter 3 of this dime novel, the young Buffalo Bill first encounters competition with a gambler.

> But Nannie [Bill's girlfriend] had another lover, in fact a score of them from among the neighboring young settlers, but one in particular who bid fair to be Billy's most dangerous rival. This one was a dashing young fellow from Leavenworth, with a handsome face and fine form, and who always had plenty of money.
>
> Folks said he was very dissipated, was a gambler, and his name had been connected several times with some very serious affairs that had occurred in the town.

How does the representation of young Buffalo's Bill's rival differ from the representation of the gamblers in the hotel or the gambler in the saloon in "The Blue Hotel"? After reading the entire dime novel, you might wish to compare the characters: the young Buffalo Bill with the Swede or the various gamblers in both stories with each other. You might consider their motivations, their relationships, and their reputations in the town. What does this comparison reveal about the psychological reality of "The Blue Hotel"?

3. **The Swede and the narrator of Poe's "Tell-Tale Heart":** Compare and contrast the fear of the Swede with that of the narrator in Poe's story.

After carefully reading the Poe story, consider what causes the narrator's fear in the "Tell-Tale Heart" and what causes the Swede's fear in "The Blue Hotel." How are these motivations different? Then consider the manifestation of the fear. How is the Swede's fear demonstrated in the hotel? How is the Poe narrator's fear expressed? What is the outcome in each case? What does each story reveal about the emotion of fear? How do the similarities and differences in these explorations of fear affect our interpretations of the stories?

Bibliography and Online Resources for "The Blue Hotel"

Backman, Bunnar. *Meaning by Metaphor: An Exploration of Metaphor with a Metaphoric Reading of Two Short Stories by Stephen Crane.* Stockholm: Uppsala, 1991.

Church, Joseph. "The Determined Stranger in Stephen Crane's 'Blue Hotel.'" *Studies in the Humanities* 16.2 (1989): 99–110.

Collins, Michael J. "Realism and Romance in the Western Stories of Stephen Crane." *Under the Sun: Myth and Realism in Western American Literature.* Ed. Barbara Howard Meldrum. Troy, NY: Whitston, 1985. 138–49.

Cox, James Trammell. "Stephen Crane as Symbolic Naturalist: An Analysis of 'The Blue Hotel.'" *Modern Fiction Studies* 3 (1957): 147–58.

Crane, Stephen. "The Blue Hotel." *The Works of Stephen Crane: Tales of Adventure.* Ed. Fredson Bowers. Vol. 5. Charlottesville: UP of Virginia, 1970.

Dillingham, William B. "'The Blue Hotel' and the Gentle Reader." *Studies in Short Fiction* 1 (1964): 224–26.

Dooley, Patrick K. *The Pluralistic Philosophy of Stephen Crane.* Champaign: U of Illinois P, 1994.

Fultz, James R. "Heartbreak at the Blue Hotel: James Agee's Scenario of Stephen Crane's Story." *Midwest Quarterly: A Journal of Contemporary Thought* 21 (1980): 423–34.

Greenfield, Stanley B. "The Unmistakable Stephen Crane." *PMLA: Publications of the Modern Language Association of America* 73.5 (1958): 562–72.

Grenberg, Bruce L. "Metaphysics of Despair: Stephen Crane's 'The Blue Hotel.'" *Modern Fiction Studies* 14 (1968): 203–13.

Gross, David S. "The Western Stories of Stephen Crane." *Journal of American Culture* 11.4 (1988): 15–21.

Howells, William Dean. "Criticism and Fiction." http://www.gutenberg.org/files/3377/3377.txt Web. 21 October 2010.

Juan-Navarro, Santiago. "Reading Reality: The Tortuous Path to Perception in Stephen Crane's 'The Open Boat' and 'The Blue Hotel.'" *Revista Canaria de Estudios Ingleses* 19–20 (1989): 37–50.

Kazin, Alfred, et al. "On Stephen Crane and 'The Blue Hotel.'" *The American Short Story.* Ed. Calvin L. Skaggs and Robert Geller. New York: Dell, 1977. 77–81.

Keenan, Richard. "The Sense of an Ending: Jan Kadar's Distortion of Stephen Crane's 'The Blue Hotel.'" *Literature/Film Quarterly* 16.4 (1988): 265–68.

Kimball, Sue L. "Circles and Squares: The Designs of Stephen Crane's 'The Blue Hotel.'" *Studies in Short Fiction* 17 (1980): 425–30.

Kinnamon, Jon M. "Henry James, the Bartender in Stephen Crane's 'The Blue Hotel.'" *Arizona Quarterly: A Journal of American Literature, Culture, and Theory* 30 (1974): 160–63.

Klotz, Marvin. "Stephen Crane: Tragedian or Comedian: 'The Blue Hotel.'" *University of Kansas City Review* 27 (1961): 170–74.

Monteiro, George. "Crane's Coxcomb." *Modern Fiction Studies* 31.2 (1985): 295–305.

Nelson, Ronald J. "A Possible Source for the Palace Hotel in Stephen Crane's 'The Blue Hotel.'" *Stephen Crane Studies* 8.2 (1999): 2–12.

Nothstein, Todd W. "Performance and Perspective on a Space-Lost Bulb: The Value of Impressionism in Stephen Crane's 'The Blue Hotel.'" *EAPSU Online: A Journal of Critical and Creative Work* 5 (2008): 193–211.

Petite, Joseph. "Expressionism and Stephen Crane's 'The Blue Hotel.'" *Journal of Evolutionary Psychology* 10. 3–4 (1989): 322–27.

Pierce, J. F. "Stephen Crane's Use of Figurative Language in 'The Blue Hotel.'" *South Central Bulletin* 34.4 (1974): 160–64.

Pilgrim, Tim A. "Repetition as a Nihilistic Device in Stephen Crane's 'The Blue Hotel.'" *Studies in Short Fiction* 11 (1974): 125–29.

Proudfit, Charles L. "Parataxic Distortion and Group Process in Stephen Crane's 'The Blue Hotel.'" *Studies in Literature* 15.1 (1983): 47–54.

Quinn, Brian T. "A Contrastive Look at Stephen Crane's Naturalism as Depicted in 'The Open Boat' and 'The Blue Hotel.'" *Studies in English Language and Literature* 42 (1992): 45–63.

Satterwhite, Joseph N. "Stephen Crane's 'The Blue Hotel': The Failure of Understanding." *Modern Fiction Studies* 2 (1956): 238–41.

Standford University and Green Library Department of Special Collections. *Dime Novels and Penny Dreadfuls.* http://www-sul.stanford.edu/depts/dp/pennies/

Woryma, Piotr. "A Sample Contrastive Analysis of 'The Blue Hotel' by Stephen Crane and 'The Nigger of the 'Narcissus' by Joseph Conrad." *Studia Anglica Posnaniensia: An International Review of English Studies* 30 (1996): 159–68.

"THE BRIDE COMES
TO YELLOW SKY"

READING TO WRITE

Because "The Bride Comes to Yellow Sky" is frequently taught in high school, you may be tempted to think you already know all there is to know about this story. You should, however, read it carefully, looking for new insights as you consider the details of the piece. It is usually thought to be a simple story of the old way of western life passing away and a new, more peaceful existence replacing it. It is indeed all of that, but it may be more. Consider, for example, the following excerpt:

> Later, he [Jack Potter] explained to her [his new bride] about the trains. "You see, it's a thousand miles from one end of Texas to the other, and this train runs right across it and never stops but four times." He had the pride of an owner. He pointed out to her the dazzling fittings of the coach, and in truth her eyes opened wider as she contemplated the sea-green figured velvet, the shining brass, silver, and glass, the wood that gleamed as darkly brilliant as the surface of a pool of oil. At one end a bronze figure sturdily held a support for a separated chamber, and at convenient places on the ceiling were frescoes in olive and silver. (107)

Jack Potter's elaborate explanation of the train's route westward and his proud display of its accoutrements make us aware that trains were important at that time both as a means of transportation and as a conduit for opening the frontier of the United States. In this story trains are perhaps even more important symbolically for not only opening up the western part of the country to easterners but also bringing with them the trappings of the East. This encroaching of civilization seems quite clear in the story, but the connection of the trip westward to the sea may remain unnoticed without further close reading of the entire story.

Now consider this connection made by Paul Sorrentino as he explores the sea imagery in his essay on the story:

> Like Turner, Crane used nautical imagery in "The Bride Comes to Yellow Sky" as a visual reminder of this westward movement. In the passenger car with its "sea-green figured velvet," a waiter, like a "pilot," is "steering [Potter and his bride] through their meal." Contemplating the best way to sneak into Yellow Sky undetected, Potter envisions himself as a boat, "a plains-craft"—to use a phrase invented by Crane. In the past when Scratchy terrorized the town, Potter "would sail in and pull out all the kinks in this thing," though this time the boat-like Potter encounters resistance as he and his bride, like two boat sails, "put forth the efforts of a pair walking bowed against a strong wind." Confronted with the stormy Scratchy, the bride becomes a "drowning woman" and Potter, despite attempts to maintain his course of direction, is "stiffening and steadying" while "a vision of the Pullman floated" in his mind as a symbol of his new condition. After Scratchy reluctantly accepts the end of the child-like drama that he and the marshal have repeatedly enacted in the past, he picks up his "starboard revolver," "his throat [working] like a pump" of a steamboat, and drifts away, his feet creating the "funnel-shaped tracks" that form the wake of a boat symbolizing the funeral wake commemorating the passing of the frontier. (53–54)

Consider the difference between a train moving westward and the sea rushing in that direction—the immense power of the sea is a force not to be stopped, one that respects nothing in its forward motion. The difference in energy and force of this natural element is even more compelling as we look at the story as a whole. What has changed in this story? The marshal has taken a bride—how can this ordinary, everyday act be so important? The answer is, of course, that an official's marriage would not be that important to the town. This town as it has existed, however, is not realistic but is the stuff of dime novels with all the attendant stereotypical elements—the shootout, the saloon, the stranger. Connecting the natural force of the sea with the natural course of literature allows the reader to see that the story makes a statement about the dime novel as a form of literature. The dime novel's exaggerated diction, events, and drama are doomed to extinction when realists like Crane bring the civilizing force of the East into the picture. Remember that Crane had toured the West in 1895 and had seen it as it really existed—he witnessed no shootouts, no extreme differences from the East except for the terrain and the less dense population.

TOPICS AND STRATEGIES

As you consider a writing topic, remember that the following suggestions should only get you started to think of possible subjects to explore in this story. You should be able to come up with one that seems particularly compelling to you. Once you have an idea, reread the story closely to see if your thesis fits the entire story, marking passages that are suitable to use in your argument. When you have enough evidence to support the theme you have chosen, then consider the most appropriate way to organize that evidence to form a valid argument.

Themes

What major ideas are presented in this story? How does the story deal with these ideas? "The Bride Comes to Yellow Sky" obviously presents the idea of the Old West as contrasted with the East, but it also deals with the idea of the exaggerated West of dime novels and the realistic West. Notice what seems to cause this change—the marrying of the town marshal and his bride. What are the immediate results of his new status as a married man when he confronts Scratchy? You might choose the theme of the Old West, the exaggerations of the dime novel, the course of violence in the story, or some other theme.

Sample Topics:
1. **The passing of the Old West:** Consider the civilizing influence of the sheriff's marriage on the town drunk. What does Crane reveal about the town before Potter brings his bride home?

   Start, perhaps, with the young man who warns those in the Weary Gentlemen saloon.

He cried: "Scratchy Wilson's drunk, and has turned loose with both hands." The two Mexicans at once set down their glasses and faded out of the rear entrance of the saloon.

The drummer, innocent and jocular, answered: "All right, old man. S'pose he has. Come in and have a drink, anyhow."

But the information had made such an obvious cleft in every skull in the room that the drummer was obliged to see its importance. All had become instantly morose. "Say," said he, mystified, "what is this?" His three companions made the introductory gesture of eloquent speech, but the young man at the door forestalled them.

"It means, my friend," he answered, as he came into the saloon, "that for the next two hours this town won't be a health resort." (114)

What is the tone of this passage? What do you infer about Scratchy Wilson? How are the reactions of the Mexicans and the townspeople different from that of the drummer, who is merely passing through the area? Why? What do their actions tell about the Old West? How do the happenings in this story contrast with the expectations of the townspeople?

2. **Marriage:** Consider the effects of marriage in this story. Is there a general feeling that marriage is a taming influence on a man?

Rereading the story, note the effects of marriage on both the bride and the groom. Are these realistic effects? Will they be long lasting or temporary? Is there anything atypical about this union? Why has the town marshal not told his townspeople about his upcoming marriage?

3. **The nature of change:** Consider the inevitability of change. What elements other than marriage bring about change in this story?

Has the town already begun to change? If so, in what ways? We are told that "Yellow Sky had a kind of brass band which played painfully to the delight of the populace" (112). What does this indicate about the town? What does Potter fear most about reaching his destination? How has the town already changed from the stereotypical expectations of a frontier settlement? What do Wilson's "funnel-shaped tracks in the heavy sand" (120) indicate about change?

Character

Three main characters populate this story: the marshal, Jack Potter; the town drunk, Scratchy Wilson; and the bride, who remains unnamed. Consider how these characters are stereotypical of the tales of the Old West and how they differ from those stereotypes. Are the three main characters static or dynamic? How do you know? Then consider the minor characters: the young man, the two Mexicans, the three Texans, and the drummer. What is their function in the story?

Sample Topics:

1. **Jack Potter:** Analyze the character of the town marshal, deciding whether or not he changes in the course of the story.

   Potter is introduced as he sits in the train:

   > The man's face was reddened from many days in the wind and sun, and a direct result of his new black clothes was that his brick-colored hands were constantly performing in a most conscious fashion. From time to time he looked down respectfully at his attire. He sat with a hand on each knee, like a man waiting in a barber's shop. The glances he devoted to other passengers were furtive and shy. (109)

   It is later that the reader learns he is the town marshal of Yellow Sky. How does this description conceal that fact? Why? Why does he appear uncomfortable in this excerpt? At the ending of the story, do you think he has changed? Why or why not?

2. **The bride:** Analyze the character of the bride.

   The bride is introduced immediately after her husband, and she is never given a name:

> The bride was not pretty, nor was she very young. She wore a
> dress of blue cashmere, with small reservations of velvet here
> and there and with steel buttons abounding. She continually
> twisted her head to regard her puff sleeves, very stiff, straight,
> and high. They embarrassed her. It was quite apparent that
> she had cooked, and that she expected to cook, dutifully. The
> blushes caused by the careless scrutiny of some passengers as
> she had entered the car were strange to see upon this plain,
> under-class countenance, which was drawn in placid, almost
> emotionless lines. (109)

How does she differ from our expectations of brides? What
do the "reservations of velvet" and the numerous "steel but-
tons" suggest? Why is she described as a "drooping drowning
woman" (120) at the end of the story?

3. **Scratchy Wilson:** Analyze the character of the town drunk.

Scratchy is introduced after the young man in the saloon has
heralded his coming:

> A man in a maroon-colored flannel shirt, which had been pur-
> chased for purposes of decoration and made, principally, by
> some Jewish women on the east side of New York rounded a
> corner and walked into the middle of the main street of Yel-
> low Sky. In either hand the man held a long, heavy blue-black
> revolver. Often he yelled, and these cries rang through a sem-
> blance of a deserted village, shrilly flying over the roofs in a
> volume that seemed to have no relation to the ordinary vocal
> strength of a man. It was as if the surrounding stillness formed
> the arch of a tomb over him. These cries of ferocious challenge
> rang against walls of silence. And his boots had red tops with
> gilded imprints, of the kind beloved in winter by little sledding
> boys on the hillsides of New England. (116–17)

How does Scratchy's apparel differ from that expected of a
gunman in a shootout? What is significant about where the
clothing and boots were made? How do they contrast with his

"cries of ferocious challenge"? How does this description lead to the ending, with his picking up his "starboard revolver, and placing both weapons in their holsters" (120), and going away?

4. **Minor characters:** What is the function of the minor characters found in Yellow Sky: the young man, the barkeeper, the three Texans, the two Mexicans, and the drummer?

Although the other characters seem somewhat stereotypical of what we expect in a western story, the drummer's role is a bit more important. What specifically is a drummer? What is he doing in Yellow Sky? What do his ties with entrepreneurship suggest about his role in this story?

History and Context

When Stephen Crane wrote "The Bride Comes to Yellow Sky," some two years after his actual journey through the West and Mexico, he had learned perhaps that the West was little different from the rest of the country, and he had certainly learned that it was nothing like the West depicted in dime novels or traveling Wild West Shows, including those featuring Buffalo Bill Cody and Wild Bill Hickok. This particular story indicates an undeniable nostalgia for the vanishing frontier while also suggesting that the real West was never anything like its fictional counterparts anyway. Consider elements of the West as it must actually have been and elements of the West romanticized in both fiction and art, for instance, the paintings and sculptures of Frederick Remington. What discrepancies do you suppose Crane encountered on his westward trip? Having grown up with the tales of the Wild West, Crane himself enjoyed horseback riding, and he often had a gun with him. He may have even imagined himself in a town where a cowboy might challenge him to a fight, but he was enough of a realistic writer to question even his own nostalgia for a place that existed only in his imagination.

Sample Topics:

1. **Analyze the train ride historically:** Research a train called the Sunset Limited, which began the run from New Orleans to

Houston to San Antonio all the way to Los Angeles and then to San Francisco in 1894.

You might consider the actual Sunset Limited train, its accoutrements, its route, and its contribution to the settlement of the Southwest. On the other hand, you might also research the development of the westward-moving railroads in general. How important was this mode of transportation to the country? How was it perhaps detrimental? How does this story address these concerns?

2. **Analyze an actual gunman of the time:** Research John Wesley Hardin or another western outlaw, and show how this description informs Crane's writing.

Although Hardin was known to shoot men with little or no provocation, his eventual demise is quite different from that of Scratchy. What does the true story of Hardin reveal about the reality of shootouts and violence in the West? How does Hardin's life shed light on the characterization of Scratchy Wilson and the theme of violence in "The Bride Comes to Yellow Sky"?

Philosophy and Ideas

"The Bride Comes to Yellow Sky" explores the difference between civilization and lawlessness. Civilization is represented by Marshal Jack Potter and his new bride and lawlessness by Scratchy Wilson. Although this story is a humorous exploration of this issue, it still retains serious elements that can be both positive and negative.

Sample Topics:

1. **Civilization and its restrictions:** In what ways are the town marshal and his new bride representative of the restrictions of civilization?

Consider the negative traits of this pair. You might include timidity, embarrassment, and a general lack of vitality. What statement does the story seem to make about these consequences of civilization? Is Scratchy Wilson presented as a viable alternative? Does civilization appear to triumph or fail by the story's end? What might civilization do to the town of Yellow Sky, and by extension, what might it do to the character of the West?

2. **Racial representations:** Analyze the depictions of both African Americans and Mexicans in this story.

The porter and the waiters on the train are all black. How are they presented? In what ways do they seem somewhat superior to the newlyweds? Why? The two Mexicans in the saloon are seen only briefly. How are they portrayed? What are their actions? What implications do those actions have for the story?

Form and Genre

"The Bride Comes to Yellow Sky" has an interesting narrative structure. The reader first sees the newly married couple on the train and follows them to their arrival in Yellow Sky; then the story joins the inhabitants of Yellow Sky some twenty-one minutes *earlier* as they are anticipating Scratchy Wilson's arrival in the saloon. A third section then introduces Scratchy as he tries to make trouble at the saloon and later goes to the town marshal's house, where no one is at home. The fourth, and final, section recounts the confrontation between the town marshal and Scratchy.

Sample Topics:

1. **Significance of the four sections in the narrative:** Analyze what each section contributes to the movement of the story.

How do the sections work with one another? What does each contribute? How do the actions in each seem to anticipate the actions in the next? Is there another trajectory of movement of the characters as they progress to the final section; in other words, does there seem to be a movement of the marshal toward the gunmen? Does the clash in that section seem inevitable? If so, how is that inevitability undercut by the results?

2. **Objective narrator:** Analyze the position of the objective narrator.

You should never assume that the narrator is the author. This particular story has a narrator who does not intrude to tell the reader what to think. Instead, the author chooses particular details that assist the reader in that process. Identify some of those details, such as the clothing of the bride, and decide how the reader is expected to react to the bride. Would the details of her clothing be important if the narrator had already told the reader that the bride was dowdy and timid? Do these details suggest such a conclusion? You can follow this same procedure with other specific details, each time assessing how your reaction helps in interpreting the story.

Language, Symbols, and Imagery

Stephen Crane's use of language and imagery are important in all his writings, often leading the reader to see what is never literally explained. The sea imagery mentioned at the beginning of this chapter is an example. In this tightly constructed story, the patterns of language reveal much about the characters and the themes. Reread, looking for significant patterns and highlighting any that interest you. Consider, for example, the names of the characters and the town. Also consider any references to time, of which there are several. Time has brought, and continues to bring, changes to Yellow Sky. How are these changes anticipated in the language? Language related to violence is another possible fruitful area of inquiry. What words are associated with violence in the story? How do these patterns reinforce your interpretation of "The Bride Comes to Yellow Sky"?

Sample Topics:

1. **The significance of the title:** Analyze the language of the title of the story. Then follow the implications throughout the story.

Since there is no town in that, or any other, part of Texas named "Yellow Sky," Crane must have chosen those words for a specific reason. What associations do the two words have? Look at the following sentence: "But the hour of Yellow Sky, the hour of daylight, was approaching" (111). This sentence is most curious, since the train is pulling into the town at 3:42

in the afternoon. It is clear that the wedding took place that morning in San Antonio: "To the minds of the pair, their surroundings reflected the glory of their marriage that morning in San Antonio" (110). What is the implication of "daylight," given the facts of the situation? Also, why is the "bride" singled out in the title? Consider what this particular combination of words has to say about the story itself.

2. **Names of the characters:** Analyze the names of the two main characters, Jack Potter and Scratchy Wilson.

   What associations does the word *potter* have? Do any of these apply to the marshal? Research the name as it applies to Texas history. What connections do the men named Potter seem to have with Jack Potter? What implications does the name "Scratchy" have? If you go a step further and think of him as Old Scratch, a sobriquet, or nickname, sometimes applied to the devil, what implications might the name have? Consider the language that is connected to each man; for example, Potter is said to speak "from a constricted throat and in mournful cadence as one announcing death" (113). Later when Wilson yells into the saloon, "the surrounding stillness formed the arch of a tomb over him" (117). What is the significance of their names when connected to the allusions to death?

3. **Allusions to time:** Analyze the language that suggests time or a connection with time.

   The bride's wedding gift from her husband is a watch, and the couple seems almost obsessed with the exact time the train will pull into Yellow Sky. The last sentence in the story refers to Wilson's tracks as "funnel-shaped," as he walks through the sand. Imagine how those tracks look and put that shape together with sand—then explore the idea of that image suggesting time. When you have collected all the allusions to time, analyze their relationship to theme in the story.

Compare and Contrast Essays

Many opportunities for comparison are available, both inside and outside this story. You can choose another short story that is concerned with changes in culture, or you can choose another story by Stephen Crane that features Potter and Wilson: "Moonlight on the Snow." You can also compare characters within the story or compare a character in the story with a character in another story. In any case, you will need to show how your particular comparison aids in the interpretation of "The Bride Comes to Yellow Sky."

Sample Topics:

1. **Comparison with "Moonlight on the Snow."** Compare these two stories by Crane, paying special attention to the changes in the two characters.

   Strangely enough, the character Scratchy Wilson in "Moonlight on the Snow" is a deputy to Potter, who is now the county sheriff. What does this rise in status indicate about each man? About the town itself and the conditions of change? How do the characters differ from their earlier representations? How is this difference important?

2. **Compare Scratchy Wilson and Jack Potter in "The Bride Comes to Yellow Sky":** Analyze the similarities and the differences of these two characters.

   What are the important differences? Do the two men have any similarities? Consider their relationship to each other. Do they truly dislike each other? What causes their confrontations? How do these confrontations usually end? Why is this one different?

Bibliography and Online Resources for "The Bride Comes to Yellow Sky"

Bassan, Maurice. "The 'True West' of Sam Shepard and Stephen Crane." *American Literary Realism* 28.2 (1996): 11–17.

Burns, Shannon, and James A. Levernier. "Androgyny in Stephen Crane's 'The Bride Comes to Yellow Sky.'" *Research Studies* 45 (1977): 236–43.

Collins Michael, J. "Realism and Romance in the Western Stories of Stephen Crane." *Under the Sun: Myth and Realism in Western American Literature.* Ed. Barbara Howard Meldrum. Troy, NY: Whitston, 1985. 138–49.

Cook, Robert C. "Stephen Crane's 'The Bride Comes to Yellow Sky.'" *Studies in Short Fiction* 2 (1965): 368–69.

Crane, Stephen. "The Bride Comes to Yellow Sky." *The Works of Stephen Crane: Tales of Adventure.* Ed. Fredson Bowers. Vol. 5. Charlottesville: UP of Virginia, 1970.

Fultz, James R. "High Jinks at Yellow Sky: James Agee and Stephen Crane." *Literature/Film Quarterly* 11.1 (1983): 46–54.

Greenfield, Stanley B. "The Unmistakable Stephen Crane." *PMLA: Publications of the Modern Language Association of America* 73.5 (1958): 562–72.

Gross, David S. "The Western Stories of Stephen Crane." *Journal of American Culture* 11.4 (1988): 15–21.

Sorrentino, Paul. "Stephen Crane's Sources and Allusions in 'The Bride Comes to Yellow Sky' and 'Moonlight on the Snow.'" *American Literary Realism* 40.1 (2007): 52–65.

Teague, David. "Green Grass in Yellow Sky: Stephen Crane in Southwest Texas." *Isle: Interdisciplinary Studies in Literature and Environment* 1.2 (1993): 81–91.

Tibbetts, A. M. "Stephen Crane's 'The Bride Comes to Yellow Sky.'" *English Journal* 54 (1965): 314–16.

Vorpahl, Ben Merchant. "Murder by the Minute: Old and New in 'The Bride Comes to Yellow Sky.'" *Nineteenth-Century Fiction* 26.2 (1971): 196–218.

Zanger, Jules. "Stephen Crane's 'Bride' as Countermyth of the West." *Great Plains Quarterly* 11.3 (1991): 157–65.

"THE MONSTER"

READING TO WRITE

In late summer of 1897, Stephen and Cora Crane were living in England, where they found the atmosphere hospitable. They were friends with other writers, including Joseph Conrad, Henry James, and Harold Frederic, and there Crane generally found more respect for his writings than he had received in the United States. He was also for the first time far from the American way of life, with both its virtues and faults. While on vacation with the Frederics in Ireland and perhaps reflecting on his distant hometown, he wrote "The Monster," the first of his stories set in Whilomville, a small village similar to Port Jervis, where he had grown up. Unlike the other later Whilomville stories, which focus on the simple everyday occurrences in the lives of children, this tale is fully developed and complex, sometimes even being called a novella. This narrative begins with the child Jimmie, who has just carelessly broken a peony in the garden, but it develops into a story encompassing the themes of obligation and its consequences in a very adult world.

In 1897 many Americans perceived life in a small town as idyllic, but they often ignored the underlying problems, choosing instead to focus on the social activities. The opening of "The Monster" presents the ideal, but it also foreshadows the problem to come. The first two paragraphs of the story begin with little Jim after his accident:

> Little Jim was, for the time, engine Number 36, and he was making the run between Syracuse and Rochester. He was fourteen minutes behind time, and the throttle was wide open. In consequence, when he swung

around the curve at the flower-bed, a wheel of his cart destroyed a peony. Number 36 slowed down at once and looked guiltily at his father, who was mowing the lawn. The doctor had his back to this accident, and he continued to pace slowly to and fro, pushing the mower.

Jim dropped the tongue of the cart. He looked at his father and at the broken flower. Finally he went to the peony and tried to stand it on its pins, resuscitated, but the spine of it was hurt, and it would only hang limply from his hand. Jim could do no reparation. He looked again toward his father.

He went on to the lawn, very slowly, and kicking wretchedly at the turf. Presently his father came along with the whirring machine, while the sweet new grass blades spun from the knives. In a low voice, Jim said, "Pa!"

The doctor was shaving this lawn as if it were a priest's chin. All during the season he had worked at it in the coolness and peace of the evenings after supper. Even in the shadow of the cherry-trees the grass was strong and healthy. (9)

These paragraphs put the reader on guard that some ominous undercurrents of small-town America will be explored in this story.

A close reading of these opening paragraphs should cause the reader to ask questions such as these: Why is Jimmie so upset at having broken a simple flower? Why is there so much emphasis on the peace and lushness of the setting? Of what does this garden remind the reader? Why is cutting the lawn described in terms of shaving a priest's chin?

A rereading of this passage reveals that perhaps this garden is meant to remind us of an archetypal garden—perhaps the Garden of Eden in Genesis, the first book of the Bible. Yet there are extra features here, an imaginary locomotive hurrying westward from Syracuse to Rochester and a lawn mower, both machines that disturb the peaceful atmosphere of the garden and mark it as a contemporary scene. Then there is Jimmie, feeling guilty for having marred the beauty of the place and being unable to repair the damage. If this scene reminds us of Eden, then the father and the son must be important figures, but they do not seem to be parallels to God and Jesus. Instead, they seem to be an ordinary father, who questions his son about the cause of the accident. Jimmie's answer to how the accident happened is that he was "playin' train." When he is told not to play train anymore that day, Jimmie goes away with his head lowered.

Trains at that time had proved highly effective in the westward progress of the country, and certainly push-style lawn mowers were an improvement over hand clippers for keeping the grass in check. Any machine when used without appropriate care, however, can prove destructive to humanity. Is it possible that this kind of machination is being portrayed as a threat to human society when essential issues of nature and humanity are neglected?

After reading this passage carefully, you may feel that this scene with its juxtaposition of human emotions—such as the boy's eagerness, his resulting guilt, and the father's care—with the two machines is important to what follows in the story. As you read other passages, you may want to consider similar juxtapositions and the effects they produce. A close reading will suggest any number of topics in this complex short story, allowing you to choose one of those suggested below or one of your own invention.

TOPICS AND STRATEGIES

The following subsections suggest different types of topics one might write about on "The Monster." These suggestions should make you think of other possible topics, ones that you yourself consider important. You can either choose one of these or invent a topic of your own, realizing that you must then brainstorm, organize, and gather evidence from the story itself before you begin writing.

After considering the questions listed with each topic and analyzing other passages from the story, focus on a particular question that interests you. Then locate sufficient examples and details to support an answer and to arrive at an understanding of some critical feature in the story.

Theme

Since "The Monster" is longer and more fully developed than a typical short story, you will find several different themes. What do you think are the primary ideas? What are some secondary themes? Think about the relationship of Jimmie to his father, the relationship of Henry to his employer, and the relationship of the town to the doctor. Some possible themes are the following: compassion for one's fellow man, disfigurement and alienation, racial prejudice, the town's collective paranoia, and the limits of human responsibility. Choose one of these themes or another. Identify any passages that seem relevant to that theme, carefully reading and rereading each of the chosen passages. What question do these passages seem to pose? How do they indicate a possible answer? Once you are able to work out the answer to your question, then you're ready to organize the main points of that answer and begin drafting your essay.

Sample Topics:

1. **Compassion for one's fellow man:** Look at how compassion is portrayed in this story. Then analyze the results of that compassion.

   The servant Henry rushes into the burning house with no thoughts for his own safety. Then the doctor shows compassion for Henry by nursing him back to health when the town leaders warn him against trying to save the man who has worked hard for him for years. In each case the act of compassion has several complications, with both positive and negative results. Jimmie is saved, but Henry is horribly burned. Henry is saved, but the doctor is faced with losing his friends and his patients.

   Writing about Stephen Crane's early death at the age of twenty-eight, Keith Gandal says, "His death is the revenge of a wild soul upon a successful man who has forced upon himself the social bounds" (504). Crane, as both an individual and a writer was well aware of the limits placed upon him by society. Over and over again, he strained against them—defending a prostitute, living with Cora without being married, and remaining in Cuba after the war had ceased. Yet each time he went beyond conventional boundaries, he suffered consequences— being harassed by the New York police, lying to his family by hiding his relationship with Cora and eventually presenting her as his wife, and being forced back to England and the obligations he had left there. Such constraints probably hastened

Crane's early death with psychological pressure adding more stress to his already weakened physical condition. Understanding the price one must pay for not conforming, Stephen Crane then presents his character, Dr. Trescott, as one who will not be bound by the constraints of small-town America.

Keeping in mind that Crane himself resisted social pressures, you might ask if the doctor's compassion in saving and caring for Henry is justified or if it is misplaced? What are the doctor's alternatives? What then does the story have to say about compassion?

2. **Disfigurement and alienation:** Analyze the disfigurement of Henry.

How does Henry's badly burned face lead to problems in the community? Are townspeople other than the doctor alienated?

Lee Clark Mitchell shows that the story addresses disfigurement: "What does it mean to be defaced, deformed, or otherwise disfigured, to have a surface so marred as to render features *all but* unrecognizable?" (175). Henry Johnson is no longer considered the person he was because he has been deformed by the fire in Whilomville. Does that fact make him less of a person? Are there any differences in Henry other than his burned face? As a result of his disfigurement, Henry is treated very differently by all the townspeople, both black and white. Why do they fear him? What do they expect him to do? Why do they alienate him?

3. **Racial prejudice:** Is it important that Henry is black? Why or why not?

When the story opens, Henry is friendly with all the other characters, including his fiancée's family, Jimmie, and the other townspeople. No one speaks ill of him or shows any signs that they dislike him. Why is their subsequent treatment of him different? Is that treatment different than it would have been for a white man whose face was horribly burned? Why or why not?

Is evidence of the town's racism seen before Henry is burned? Why does the town glorify Henry when it is reported that he has died saving Jimmie? Why does the town's attitude change when it is learned that the stableman has survived? What does all of this have to do with race?

Character

The major characters in "The Monster" are Henry, Dr. Trescott, and Jimmie, all of whom appear admirable at the beginning of the story. You could analyze any of these three and their function in the story; on the other hand, you could look at any of the minor characters such as John Twelve; the men in Reifsnyder's barbershop; Bella, the supposed fiancée; or the sisters Martha and Kate. Once you have chosen a character to analyze, pay particular attention to what you know about that character and how you know it. What does he or she say? How does this character act? How does he or she interact with others? What do others say about the character? What are the character's motivations? If you choose one of the three main characters, you should decide whether that character remains static or changes in the course of the story. Since this story is longer and more complicated than most short stories, you may find that even some of the minor characters change. If the character changes, how and why does he change? You might argue, for example, that Jimmie changes in the course of the story, going from an innocent child who feels guilty for breaking a simple flower in the garden to a braggart who shows off Henry to his young friends, placing the deformed man on display in the backyard. What is Jimmie's motivation for this change? What does his motivation add to your understanding of the story?

Sample Topics:

1. **Dr. Trescott:** Analyze the character of Dr. Trescott.

Does Dr. Trescott change during the course of the story? Why is he so insistent that he must save Henry? Why is he so adamant that he continue to take care of him? What would you have done in his place? How does he differ from the other town leaders? If this had been a factual account, what do you think would have happened to the doctor next, after this story's ending?

After seeing the doctor disciplining Jimmie for breaking the flower, the reader next sees him driving homeward from a medical case:

> Doctor Trescott had been driving homeward, slowly smoking a cigar, and feeling glad that this last case was now in complete obedience to him, like a wild animal that he had subdued, when he heard the long whistle, and chirped to his horse under the unlicensed but perfectly distinct impression that a fire had broken out in Oakhurst, a new and rather high-flying suburb of the town which was at least two miles from his own home. But in the second blast and in the ensuing silence he read the designation of his own district. He was then only a few blocks from his house. He took out the whip and laid it lightly on the mare. Surprised and frightened at this extraordinary action, she leaped forward, and as the reins straightened like steel bands, the doctor leaned backward a trifle. When the mare whirled him up to the closed gate he was wondering whose house could be afire. The man who had rung the signal-box yelled something at him, but he already knew. He left the mare to her will. (25)

Both this passage and the opening paragraphs of the story describe a man very much in charge, one who has pride in keeping order both in the garden and in the sick room. Although he notes the fire whistle when he thinks it signals a different district, he does so without any fear or concern. The word *chirped* denoting his communication with his horse indicates a certain lightness of heart when he thinks the fire is not nearby. How does he change when he realizes it's in his own district? Why? Find other passages that focus on the doctor and read those closely, paying particular attention to his actions and words.

2. **Henry:** Analyze the character of Henry.

When Henry is first introduced, he plays a dual role, both as a friend of Jimmie who sympathizes with him for his punishment after breaking the flower and as a mentor who cautions the boy about his reckless behavior. Later Henry is seen as a man about town in his fancy clothes on his way to visit Bella, and then he is seen as a savior after he rescues Jimmie. Account for the change in his character or at least in the townspeople's acceptance of his character. Analyze his actions after the fire. How is he different? Are his actions different? Are his interests different?

3. **Jimmie:** Analyze the character of Jimmie.

Jimmie is first seen in the garden after confessing his sin to his father, who reprimands him: "During the delivery of the judgment the child had not faced his father, and afterward he went away, with his head lowered, shuffling his feet" (10). Although Jimmie has a few months to mature while the Trescott house is being rebuilt, that time period does not explain the change in his sense of empowerment or his actions toward Henry. That change is evident when the boy enjoys showing off the disfigured "monster" to his young friends: "Jimmie seemed to reap all the joys of the owner and exhibitor of one of the world's marvels, while his audience remained at a distance—awed and entranced, fearful and envious" (53)

How do you explain the change? Is it a good one or not? Why does he feel ownership of Henry at this point? Why does he dare the other boys to go up close to Henry as he sits on the box in the sun? Why is one boy's mother upset? Why is Dr. Trescott upset?

4. **The men in Reifsnyder's barbershop:** Analyze the function of these men.

The first mention of the men in the barbershop clarifies their position in the town:

Reifsnyder and his assistant instantly poised their razors high and turned toward the window. Two belathered heads reared from the chairs. The electric shine in the street caused an effect like water to them who looked through the glass from the yellow glamour of Reifsnyder's shop. In fact, the people without resembled the inhabitants of a great aquarium that here had a square pane in it. Presently into this frame swam the graceful form of Henry Johnson. (14)

Why are the men like viewers into an aquarium? Why is this position important? How do they first recognize Henry Johnson? Why is the source of that recognition important?

The next appearance of the men in the shop comes after Henry Johnson has been sent to the Williams house to live. They are discussing Henry's condition, and the barber asks, "How would you like to be with no face?" As the men continue to talk about what the doctor did and what he should do, Reifsnyder continues to emphasize the condition of being faceless.

Looking at these two episodes together, decide how the men function in the story. Why is their characterization included, since they do very little to develop the story's plot?

History and Context

In 1897 the idealistic concept of racial equality in the United States differed greatly from actual practice. Three decades after slaves had been given their freedom by Lincoln's Emancipation Proclamation, African-American citizens were still relegated to subservient status, their hopes of equality thwarted in their quest for equal political, economic, or educational opportunity and cultural acceptance. Stephen Crane's story "The Monster" was written in a decade marked by increasingly vicious racism exemplified by Jim Crow laws, by more than 2,500 lynchings, and by the Supreme Court's decision in *Plessy v. Ferguson,* which resulted in upholding the constitutionality of state laws requiring racial segregation under the doctrine of "separate but equal." Popular literary portrayals of blacks contained either the "happy darkies" of Joel Chandler Harris and Thomas Nelson Page or the savage monsters of Thomas Dixon. How does Stephen Crane portray his black characters? Does anything in the story suggest that the characterization of blacks there reflects the town's prejudices?

Sample Topics:

1. **Newspaper accounts of "Negroes" in 1897:** Search a newspaper index for 1897 using the search term *Negro*, and discuss how Crane uses the popular depiction of the black person or persons within this story.

   How does the article you chose present black Americans? How does that presentation differ from a similar newspaper story on white Americans? As you discover the characteristics of the factual presentations, decide how the public perception of black Americans at the time informs and clarifies the characterization of Henry, Williams, and Bella in "The Monster."

2. **Reactions to fires in 1897:** Search a newspaper index for 1897, using the search term *fire* to see how house fires were fought and how the incident is presented in that newspaper. Discuss how Crane incorporates the details into this story.

   What does the newspaper account reveal about how fires were fought in 1897? Are there examples of heroism? If so, how is the hero characterized? What type of destruction is typical of a house fire at that time? What information about fighting fires do you find that makes the problems and procedures in "The Monster" clearer?

Language, Symbols, and Imagery

"The Monster" abounds in its use of imagery, with the two most important images being the veil that Henry is forced to wear after his face is severely burned and the fifteen teacups at the end of the story. Other images, however, can also be found: Dr. Trescott's lawn being shaved like a priest's chin (9), Henry dressing himself like a "belle of a court circle" (13), and Mrs. Williams's protecting "all her sleeping ducklings" (44). A close reading of the language in any given passage reveals much about how the author expects us to interpret that passage. Stephen Crane as a realist using a third-person objective narrator presents various types of imagery to allow the reader to form an interpretation of a particular passage. Look especially for patterns of imagery that seem important, for example, all the color imagery used when Henry's face is being burned away. Typically, the reader would not expect such a horrendous event to be described in such exotic detail. Why, then, does Crane choose to make the scene beautiful, almost seductive? Look for other passages where the imagery seems especially important, and try to determine how the specific language provides clues to meaning.

Sample Topics:

1. **The significance of the title:** Analyze the use of the word *monster* as the title of this story.

   Imagine other possible appropriate titles for this story. Then consider why Stephen Crane chose his particular title. *Who* is the monster? Although most people consider Henry to be the monster suggested by the title, others view the town as more monstrous. Which do you believe is the monster of the title? Why? You might also consider other literary monsters—such as Frankenstein's creation.

2. **The image of the veil:** Analyze how the image of the veil functions in "The Monster."

   Find the passage where Henry is first presented with the veil:

   > One time the monster was seated on a box behind the stable basking in the rays of the afternoon sun. A heavy crêpe veil was swathed about its head. Little Jimmie and many companions came around the corner of the stable. They were all in what was popularly known as the baby class, and consequently escaped from school a half-hour before the other children. They halted abruptly at the sight of the figure on the box. Jimmie waved his hand with the air of a proprietor. (56)

   What is the effect of the veil on the boys? What is the effect on Henry? Have you encountered other veils in literature? Why is the veil important as an image?

3. **The fifteen teacups:** Analyze the function of the image of the fifteen unused teacups at the end of the story.

When Mrs. Trescott has her weekly open house, only one woman comes. After this depressing tea party, Dr. Trescott tries to comfort his wife. His eyes are drawn to the unsliced cake and the unused teacups.

> Glancing down at the cups, Trescott mechanically counted them. There were fifteen of them. "There, there," he said. "Don't cry, Grace. Don't cry."
>   The wind was whining around the house and the snow beat aslant upon the windows. Sometimes the coal in the stove settled with a crumbling sound and the four panes of mica flushed a sudden new crimson. As he sat holding her head on his shoulder, Trescott found himself occasionally trying to count the cups. There were fifteen of them. (65)

Why are the cups given so much emphasis? Why is the repetition of the number of cups important? The doctor cannot keep his attention from the unused cups. Why is that fact important? What does it say about Mrs. Trescott? What does it imply about the doctor himself?

4. **The liquid that burns Henry's face:** Analyze the imagery used in the description of the chemicals that fall onto Henry's face.

Crane describes the scene in colorful and exotic detail:

> At the entrance to the laboratory he confronted a strange spectacle. The room was like a garden in the region where might be burning flowers. Flames of violet, crimson, green, blue, orange, and purple were blooming everywhere. There was one blaze that was precisely the hue of a delicate coral. In another place was a mass that lay merely in phosphorescent inaction like a pile of emeralds. But all these marvels were to be seen dimly through clouds of heaving, turning, deadly smoke.

> Johnson halted for a moment on the threshold. He cried
> out again in the negro wail that had in it the sadness of the
> swamps. Then he rushed across the room. An orange-colored
> flame leaped like a panther at the lavender trousers. This ani-
> mal bit deeply into Johnson. There was an explosion at one
> side, and suddenly before him there reared a delicate, trem-
> bling sapphire shape like a fairy lady. With a quiet smile she
> blocked his path and doomed him and Jimmie. (24)

Why is the burning room described in terms of a garden? Why
is there such a display of colors and how are they related to the
image of emeralds? What is the importance of the fairy lady
and the panther?

Philosophy and Ideas

Essays on philosophy and ideas allow you to examine the text's relationship to philosophical values or intellectual currents. These essays
critique social values, affirm such values, or present a metaphorical ren-
dering of the belief or metaphysical system in question. As with essays
of history and context, you may need to do some outside research on the
philosophical concept in question. For instance, some critics have seen
the figure of the monster in this story as a representation of Darwinian
thought as it filtered down into the popular realm and into the social
sciences. You would need to research how social scientists and others
adapted the tenets of survival of the fittest to justify categories of race
and intelligence. Once you are familiar with the ideas of Francis Gal-
ton, who founded a pseudoscience called eugenics, you might explore
the manifestations of such ideas in the story. On the other hand, you
might analyze the religious implications of the story, provided you either
possess or can acquire a grasp of Christianity's basic tenets. Ask yourself
whether or not Stephen Crane seems to be advocating the use of Christian ethics in this work. On the contrary, you may discover antireligious
overtones in the novel.

Sample Topics:

1. **The use of eugenic theory in "The Monster":** Analyze how
   Crane makes use of the idea that some humans were seen at the
   time as being less fit to survive than others.

Those in the late nineteenth century who looked at the concept of race in terms of evolutionary theory often saw some races as being unequipped to function as well as others. Are the townspeople in this story guilty of making such assumptions? What evidence do you find for such beliefs? What does the story say about such beliefs?

2. **The use of the Golden Rule:** Analyze how Crane uses the idea of treating others as you want to be treated in "The Monster."

Which of the characters follows the biblical message of "do unto others as you would have them do to you"? Which ignore the supposed Golden Rule?

3. **The use of other biblical ideas:** Analyze biblical allusions or parallels in "The Monster."

Do you see any resemblance between the Martha in this story and the one in the biblical story of Lazarus, whose sisters are Mary and Martha? How does Henry reflect some of the accounts of Moses in the Bible? Do you see other biblical allusions or parallels? If so, what is their importance to the story?

Form and Genre

Depending upon which critic you consult, this story is variously called a short story or a novella. It is certainly longer than the average short story, and it is shorter than a novel. It is more complicated than a short story and almost as complicated as the ordinary novel. A productive essay could be written by evaluating its genre, especially if the essay asserts that that genre is important in an understanding of the piece. It is also realism. At the end of the nineteenth century, it would not have been unusual to have a man ostracized because of his race or his physical deformity.

Sample Topics:

1. **Short story or novella:** Argue that "The Monster" is a short story, or conversely argue that it is a novella. Give the char-

acteristics of the genre chosen and support your answer with examples from the piece.

Stephen Crane himself referred to the piece as a novelette in a letter to his brother Edmund. What elements of the piece make it more closely related to a novel? What elements make it more closely related to a short story? Into which genre do you prefer to place the piece? Why? Is the specific genre of importance to the piece? Why or why not?

2. **"The Monster" as realism:** Analyze this story as a work of literary realism.

If you follow one of the standard definitions of literary realism, how is "The Monster" realistic? How does it reflect some of the characteristics of realism; for example, is it true to the everyday experience of ordinary people? Are there real-life events that are similar to the events in this story? Does Crane use "things" to allow the reader to judge specific events or ideas? Does it describe such things in minute detail to add to an interpretation of the work? Is characterization more important than the plot? Does it present the main character with an ethical choice?

Compare and Contrast

"The Monster" has several facets that lend themselves to essays that compare and contrast with stories by other authors: its monster character, the use of a veil, its depiction of human compassion and tragedy, its use of disfigurement. Other comparisons can be made within the story itself, such as the major characters and the actions before and after the fire.

Sample Topics:

1. **"The Monster" and Herman Melville's "Bartleby, the Scrivener":** Compare and contrast these two stories of human compassion and alienation.

Although Bartleby is not viewed as a monster, he is certainly alienated from those around him. What important ideas of

caring for one's fellow man does each story include? Compare
the causes of Bartleby's alienation with those of Henry. How
are they similar? How are they different? How is the compassion displayed similar or different?

2. **The image of the veil or mask:** Choose another story with a
   veil or mask, such as Nathaniel Hawthorne's "The Minister's
   Black Veil," and analyze the similarities and differences with the
   veil in "The Monster."

   How do the two veils function in each story? How are they
   alike? How do they differ? What does each story have to say
   about alienation? Why are the differences important?

3. **Henry Johnson and Doctor Trescott:** Compare and contrast
   these two men as "saviors" of their fellow men.

   Both men manage to save another human, yet the results are
   very different. What are the important similarities and differences in their motivations? What are the important similarities and differences in the results? Who is the more admirable
   character? Why? What does this choice tell about the story?

4. **"The Monster" and "The Fire":** Compare and contrast "The
   Monster" with Crane's newspaper sketch for the New York *Press*
   of November 25, 1894, headlined "When Every One Is Panic
   Stricken" but called "The Fire" in his typescript and in the University of Virginia collection of his works.

   How is the newspaper piece similar to the story? How is it different? Pay specific attention to the people portrayed in each, to
   their emotions, and to the details used in describing each event.

Bibliography and Online Resources for "The Monster"

Anderson, Margaret P. "A Note on 'John Twelve' in Stephen Crane's *The Monster.*" *American Notes and Queries* 15 (1976): 23–24.

Cleman, John. "Blunders of Virtue: The Problem of Race in Stephen Crane's 'The Monster.'" *American Literary Realism* 34.2 (2002): 119–34.

Cooley, John R. "'The Monster': Stephen Crane's 'Invisible Man.'" *Markham Review* 5 (1975): 10–14.

Crane, Stephen. "The Monster." *The Works of Stephen Crane: Tales of Whilomville.* Ed. Fredson Bowers. Vol. 7. Charlottesville: UP of Virginia, 1969. 9–65.

———. "The Fire." *The Works of Stephen Crane: Tales, Sketches, and Reports.* Ed. Fredson Bowers. Vol. 8. Charlottesville: UP of Virginia, 1973. 338–44.

Evans, Mark W. "Messianic Inversion in Stephen Crane's 'The Monster.'" *American Literary Realism* 31.3 (1999): 58–62.

Foster, Malcolm. "The Black Crepe Veil: The Significance of Stephen Crane's *The Monster.*" *International Fiction Review* 3 (1976): 87–91.

Fried, Michael. "Realism, Writing, and Disfiguration in Thomas Eakins's *Gross Clinic,* with a Postscript on Stephen Crane's 'Upturned Faces.'" *Representations* 9 (1985): 33–104.

Gandal, Keith. "A Spiritual Autopsy of Stephen Crane." *Nineteenth Century Literature* 51 (1997): 500–30.

Gilkes, Lillian B. "Stephen Crane and the Biographical Fallacy: The Cora Influence." *Modern Fiction Studies* 16 (1970): 441–61.

Hafley, James. "'The Monster' and the Art of Stephen Crane." *Accent: A Quarterly of New Literature* 19 (1959): 159–65.

Kahn, Sy. "Stephen Crane and the Giant Voice in the Night: An Explication of *The Monster.*" *Essays in Modern American Literature.* Ed. Richard E. Langford. DeLand, FL: Stetson UP, 1963. 35–45.

Knapp, Daniel. "Son of Thunder: Stephen Crane and the Fourth Evangelist." *Nineteenth-Century Fiction* 24.3 (1969): 253–91.

Lolordo, Nick. "Possessed by the Gothic: Stephen Crane's 'The Monster.'" *Arizona Quarterly* 57.2 (2001): 33–56.

Marshall, Elaine. "Crane's 'The Monster' Seen in the Light of Robert Lewis's Lynching." *Nineteenth-Century Literature* 51.2 (1996): 205–24.

Mitchell, Lee Clark. "Face, Race, and Disfiguration in Stephen Crane's *The Monster.*" *Critical Inquiry* 17.1 (1990): 174–92.

Modlin, Charles E., and John R. Byers, Jr. "Stephen Crane's 'The Monster' as Christian Allegory." *Markham Review* 3 (1973): 110–13.

Monteiro, George. "Stephen Crane and the Antinomies of Christian Charity." *Centennial Review* 16 (1972): 91–104.

Morace, Robert A. "Games, Play, and Entertainments in Stephen Crane's 'The Monster.'" *Studies in American Fiction* 9.1 (1981): 65–81.

Morgan, William M. "Between Conquest and Care: Masculinity and Community in Stephen Crane's *The Monster*." *Arizona Quarterly* 56.3 (2000): 63–92.

Nagel, James. "The Significance of Stephen Crane's 'The Monster.'" *American Literary Realism* 31.3 (1999): 48–57.

Naito, Jonathan Tadashi. "Cruel and Unusual Light: Electricity and Effacement in Stephen Crane's *The Monster*." *Arizona Quarterly* 62.1 (2006): 35–63.

Nettels, Elsa. "'Amy Foster' and Stephen Crane's 'The Monster.'" *Conradiana: A Journal of Joseph Conrad Studies* 15.3 (1983): 181–90.

Petry, Alice Hall. "Stephen Crane's Elephant Man." *Journal of Modern Literature* 10.2 (1983): 346–52.

Pizer, Donald. "Stephen Crane's 'The Monster' and Tolstoy's *What to Do*? A Neglected Allusion." *Studies in Short Fiction* 20.2–3 (1983): 127–29.

Rowe John, Carlos. "Race, Gender, and Imperialism in Stephen Crane: A Monstrous Case." *Red Badges of Courage: Wars and Conflicts in American Culture*. Ed. Biancamarie Pisapia, Ugo Rubeo, and Anna Scacchi. Rome: Bulzoni, 1998. 37–68.

Schweik, Susan M. "Disability Politics and American Literary History: Some Suggestions." *American Literary History* 20.1–2 (2008): 217–37.

Warner, Michael D. "Value, Agency, and Stephen Crane's 'The Monster.'" *Nineteenth-Century Fiction* 40.1 (1985): 76–93.

Wilson-Jordan, Jacqueline. "Teaching a Dangerous Story: Darwinism and Race in Stephen Crane's 'The Monster.'" *Eureka Studies in Teaching Short Fiction* 8.1 (2007): 48–61.

WAR IS KIND

READING TO WRITE

In *Black Riders and Other Lines,* Stephen Crane the poet seems to revel in creating as much "anarchy" as possible, as pointed out by John Blair. In Crane's other volume of poetry, *War Is Kind,* the poems provide a wider perspective. Although they still reject tradition, these poems present a more complicated, thoughtful exploration of worship, war, and social institutions and practices. As Blair observes, the Crane of the later poems is more mature, more an observer than a poseur, or someone who is just trying to impress his audience.

The poems in *War Is Kind* tend to be longer and more imagistic, and the narrators seem to be more aware of the complications of life near the end of the nineteenth century and to anticipate the fractured existence of the twentieth. In poem 90, beginning with the line "When the prophet, a complacent fat man," the prophet has abandoned the polarized vision of *The Black Riders.* Instead of finding the "good white lands" and the "bad black lands," he discovers that "the scene is grey." This short poem avoids limiting perception to two opposing sides and intimates that every issue is complex.

> When the prophet, a complacent fat man,
> Arrived at the mountain-top
> He cried: "Woe to my knowledge!
> "I intended to see good white lands
> "And bad black lands—
> "but the scene is grey." (1–6)

A close reading of this poem makes us aware of the man's complacency, of his preconceived ideas. Not only is he smug, but he is also "fat," an adjective indicating a certain laziness and inaction on his part, as well as a comfortable economic position that supplies him with more than adequate food. The speaker does, however, ascend to a mountaintop, so we as readers may then realize that we are perhaps too judgmental of his appearance, thinking that because he is fat and complacent, he is also unaware of reality. Just when we are ready to condemn him for his limited vision, he surprises us with a full awareness of both his intentions and the reality that he ultimately faces.

Close readings of other poems in this collection reveal the multi-faceted nature of various topics, ranging from war to religious beliefs and rituals. Although the poems in *War Is Kind* were neither numbered nor titled in the original manuscript, the numbers here reflect those in the University of Virginia collection, continuing the numbering scheme associated with the poems in *Black Riders,* in which the poems are all titled with Roman numerals.

Themes

To begin thinking about the themes in this collection of poems, ask yourself what main ideas or issues are addressed. Although many poems will share the same themes, each deals with that theme somewhat differently. Given the title of the volume, war is an obvious theme, but actual war as a specific subject is limited to only two poems. In the other poems, Crane explores various themes relating to perception, religion, love, truth, and economic success, suggesting a different, more metaphorical condition of war.

Sample Topics:

1. **The theme of war:** Analyze how Stephen Crane uses the theme of war in this collection.

   Beginning with the title poem, poem 69, what main point does Crane make about war, which the poem suggests is "kind"? How is war seen by the survivors, the maiden, the babe, and the mother? How does Crane juxtapose the horror of war with the heroism often involved in war?

What is the reader to believe about the statement "War is kind"? To whom is it kind? Why or why not? Does poem 76, a poem about a knight who is fighting to save his lady, take a similar stance on the horror and heroism of battle? What do these poems have to say about the act of war?

2. **The theme of perception:** Analyze Crane's use of changing perception, or point of view.

Several poems—71 with a juxtaposition of a maiden and a wrecked sailor, 75 with its green spectacles, 77 with its candid man, 81 with the wayfarer, 84 with a wooden tongue, 90 with a fat man, 91 with some violets, and 94 with lantern voices and pebbles—all deal with either perception or truth or a combination of both. After reading these poems, try to decide what they say about perception or truth. Poem 71, for example, shows the difference between the maiden's fanciful perception of the sea and that of the wrecked sailor. What does location have to do with such differences in point of view? What other circumstances change a person's perception?

3. **The theme of love:** Analyze how Crane uses the theme of love in these poems.

Poems 74 and 79 deal with the theme of love, as do all the poems in the final section of the book, titled "Intrigue," poems 96 through 105. How does the "ship of love" (10) function in poem 74? What is the overall tone of this poem? Is poem 79, with its "whispering snakes" (12) more about love or seduction? Of what do the snakes remind you? How does the repeated refrain of "Woe is me" (6, 15, 22, 27, 32, 36, 41, 47, 52, 56, 61) function in poem 96?

4. **The theme of religion:** Analyze how Crane presents religion or God in the poems in this collection.

Poems 72 with religious trinkets, 78 with its printed list, 82 with its mighty hymn, 83 the man's shout from the rooftops,

86 with a transition from night to morning to evening to night, 89 with the man's insistence on his existence, and 92 with the poor soul all deal with either religion or the concept of God. Poem 72 is notable in its defining and questioning the concept of God as it asks, "You define me God with these trinkets?" (8). Then the poem ends with "Where is God?" (19). What seems to be the narrator's problem with the concept of God? Is the poem atheistic? Or does it call for a different way of defining God?

Carefully read the other poems that deal with religion and decide what stance each poem takes on that theme. As a unit, do these poems deny the existence of God, or do they criticize the worshipers' insistence on a particular view of God? You might notice that poem 78 distinctly condemns church rituals and concepts:

> You tell me this is God?
> I tell you this is a printed list,
> A burning candle and an ass. (1–3)

To what does the "printed list" refer? Although the candle reference is somewhat obvious, suggesting the use of candles both in church ritual and private prayers, the ass is not. Who or what is the ass? What biblical event is suggested? Why is the tone of this poem so angry? What does that anger suggest about the speaker?

Character

As is the case in Stephen Crane's earlier poetry collection, *The Black Riders and Other Lines,* it is somewhat difficult to identify specific characters. His earlier "little man," a man who faces a daunting world, shows up as a wayfarer or searcher in a few poems. A maiden or lady appears in a few others, and a somewhat cruel lover is the subject of appeal in the "Intrigue" suite at the end of the volume. Choose one of these characters and follow him or her through several poems. What does Crane seem to imply about each? How does that character or type of character interact with others? What do the poems imply about specific character types?

Sample Topics:

1. **The maiden or lady:** Analyze Crane's presentation of the maiden or lady in *War Is Kind*.

   In poems 69, 71, and 76, a maiden and a lady are included. What is the main characteristic of each of these women? What is the maiden doing in poem 69? What is the maiden doing in poem 71? What do these acts suggest about the two women? What is the function of the lady in poem 76? How do they function in relation to the soldier and the knight? Using these three depictions of women, can you make a statement about Stephen Crane's depiction of women in his poetry?

2. **The lover in the "Intrigue" suite:** Analyze the characterization of the female lover in these ten poems.

   The female lover in these poems is very different from the maiden and the lady. What are the major differences? How is the relationship between the lover and the speaker character- ized? How do the following lines from poem 101 clarify that relationship?

   > I was impelled to be a grand knight,
   > And swagger and snap my fingers,
   > And explain my mind finely. (8–10)

   What effect has the lover had on the speaker? What do these poems imply about the condition of love?

3. **The wayfarer or searcher:** Analyze the men portrayed as way- farers or searchers in *War Is Kind*.

   In poems 81, 89, and 91, some rather ordinary men are por- trayed, as are the candid men in poems 77 and 92. What char- acterizes these men? How do they approach life? The wayfarer in poem 81 is on a search for truth, but when he finds how dif- ficult the way is, he decides to find another way. Is this typical of the average human? What do these poems indicate about the human condition? Overall how do they reveal the insecurities and flaws of humanity?

History and Context

During 1897 Stephen Crane found himself settled in England with Cora living as his wife, a relationship he kept secret from his brothers and their families. In many ways Cora seems to have given him some stability, establishing a household for him for the first time in his life, and provided constant companionship. In other ways, she proved to add to his complicated obligations, spending money they did not have and hosting numerous people in their home as he furiously wrote to pay the bills. When he found himself far from that relationship as he reported the war in Cuba, he may have considered his romantic involvement in a different light. In *War Is Kind*, Crane's "Intrigue" poems deal with the difficulty of romantic love and all address a lover, probably one based on Cora. According to Fredson Bowers, Crane wrote the first five poems in this group before he left Cora in England to cover the war in Cuba in 1898 (212–14) and he wrote the others while in Cuba. The lovesick narrator in these poems seems to be tortured by his love and jealousy, expressing doubt in his lover, knowledge of her other affairs, and concern for his own peace of mind. To learn more about this period in his life, you might consult Stanley Wertheim and Paul Sorrentino's *The Crane Log* or their edition of his *Correspondence* for specific biographical facts of his life at this time. Then you might want to consider the following topics or others of your own choosing.

Sample Topics:

1. **The similarity between Stephen Crane and the narrator in the "Intrigue" poems:** Analyze how Crane's own romantic situation provides a background for these poems.

   In the sixth poem of this suite, the first written or revised in Havana, the tone becomes dramatically dark, with the narrator remembering when he had thought himself to be a "grand knight" with his beloved "Sweetheart." The poem then ends abruptly with an image of despair:

And we preserved an admirable mimicry
Without heeding the drip of the blood
From my heart. (15–17)

The image of the dripping blood implies more than the disillu-
sionment of a romantic lover. How does this poem suggest the
very real problems that Crane faced in his relationship with
Cora? What other domestic problems was Crane confronting
at this time? What were the circumstances of his remaining
in Cuba? How does Stephen Crane use his own biographical
facts in his poetry? Does such personalization strengthen or
undermine the poetry?

2. **Crane as a war reporter and a poet:** Analyze these poems in
   light of Crane's reporting of the wars in Greece and Cuba.

Going to Cuba as a reporter, Crane wrote his first known
Cuban war dispatch, a telegram headlined "The Terrible Captain of the Captured Panama," dealing with the fear exhibited
by the captain of a captured Spanish steamship. The article
appeared in the *New York World* and can be found in the
University of Virginia collection *Reports of War.* How is the
captain's display of excessive fear at odds with the bravery of
maimed or wounded soldiers in *War Is Kind*?

It is important to note that poem 69 was written long before
Crane went to either Greece in 1897 or Cuba in 1898. It first
appeared in the *Bookman* in February 1896, yet Crane decided
to use it as the title poem in the manuscript for *War Is Kind,*
which he sent from Cuba to Paul Revere Reynolds, his agent,
on September 14, 1898. At this point Crane had witnessed
both the Greek-Turkish War and the Spanish-American War,
but he still felt this earlier poem to be important enough to
open this new collection. How does the poem compare with
"Stephen Crane Tells of War's Horrors" (53–56), a report filed
from Athens on May 22, 1897?

Philosophy and Ideas

Stephen Crane's upbringing by religious parents provided him with a strong ethical foundation and a wide knowledge of the Bible. Crane himself pointed out that his poems present his philosophy of life, a philosophy that can be readily discerned in the collected poems in *War Is Kind*. His ethics included not putting his own welfare above that of others and not being hypocritical but instead caring for his fellow humans and avoiding monetary profit as his goal in life. Poem 85 combines all of these ethical facets into one piece in its condemnation of becoming wealthy through trampling upon others. Poem 88 speaks of the "impact of a dollar upon the heart" (1). Crane then shows that all people are "sinners," or flawed by their human condition, as in poem 92. In this poem the narrator's wares consist only of his sins, but he is treated compassionately by one "met upon the road" who looked at him "with kind eyes" (1–2).

At the same time Stephen Crane's poems reveal Christian ethics, they also explore the existential nature of life. After becoming familiar with the term *existentialism,* identify poems in this collection that include examples of the difficulty of finding meaning in a meaningless universe.

Sample Topics:

1. **Ethics in poems 85, 88, or 92:** Choose one or more of these poems and show how the poetry reflects Christian teachings.

   The successful man in poem 85 has become successful by trampling upon others as he "stands heavily on the dead" (19) and "declaims his trampling of babes" (21). Poem 88 similarly reviles "the impact of a dollar upon the heart" (1). In contrast to these two poems, poem 92 shows Christian charity. What do these poems suggest about economic success? How does the poem make the greedy men seem utterly despicable?

   The impact money has on character also becomes quite negative in poem 88. How does Crane show that negativity? How is it related to ethics? Why does the "impact" smile "warm red light" (1–2)? What other terms denote debauchery or dishonesty?

Poem 92 is different from the two above in that the one "met upon the road" (1) practices Christian ethics. He recognizes the humanity of the narrator but treats him kindly in spite of his "sins." How is this behavior productive? How does it reflect the actions of Jesus as portrayed in the Bible? How then does Stephen Crane both revile those who claim to be religious and acclaim those who practice Christian virtues or ethics?

2. **Existentialism in poem 89:** Analyze this poem in terms of the philosophy of existentialism.

Existentialism focuses on the conditions of existence of the individual and his or her emotions, actions, thoughts, and responsibilities. It is up to the individual to find or make meaning in his or her life. The man in the poem fervently insists on his own existence, but he does not get any affirmation from the "universe." What does the poem suggest about the futility of existence? What does it suggest about what the man should do to find meaning in his life? How does the fervor in his pronouncement contrast with the indifference of the universe?

Form and Genre

Stephen Crane's poetry was unlike the more readily accepted poetry of his day. It does not rhyme, and it does not have a fixed meter. His first book of poetry, *The Black Riders and Other Lines,* was widely parodied, receiving very little positive feedback, but it is now regarded more highly than this second collection. In spite of such generally negative reception, many of Crane's poems are still widely anthologized, and they speak to today's audience, especially to younger readers. His poetry anticipates the modernists with their memorable images, their short lyrics, and their attention to exterior objects that carry much meaning in the poem.

Sample Topics:

1. **Poem 93 as a precursor of modernism:** Analyze the modernist elements in this short poem that invoke a workman to make a dream of a garden.

What elements of this poem make it similar to the modernist poetry of the twentieth century? What is the central image? How does it evoke a more traditional garden? Who is the "workman" (1) mentioned in the poem? And who is the "man walking thereon" (7) the meadow? Finally, what does the poem say about creation?

2. **Analysis of poem 84:** Discuss how this poem calls attention to the act of writing.

Who is the "man with tongue of wood" (1)? Can he be seen as a reference to Crane himself as a poet? How does the poem express satisfaction with the song or poem that results from the crude efforts of "the man"? How does it anticipate modernist or even postmodernist concerns?

Language, Symbols, and Imagery

Stephen Crane is masterful in his use of memorable images. It is difficult to forget the little man in poem 89 who insists to the universe that he exists. What makes this image so unforgettable? Is it the subservient nature of the man or the formal reply of the universe? Anyone who has read this poem remembers this visual image even though there is no description whatever in the short poem. Crane's evocation of specific images marks him as an original poet who manages to influence his reader with very simple words in a very short lyric. You can write an effective essay that explores the language and the imagery in Crane's poetry. Choose one of the following topics or branch out on your own to another.

Sample Topics:

1. **The images of nature in poem 75:** Analyze not only the visual imagery but also the sound and tactile imagery in this poem about "the sunset song of the birches" (1).

Several aspects of nature are personified in this poem: the pines, the grasses, and the wind. How does this personification work with these natural elements? How do they contrast with the supposed listener who "don[s] green spectacles before [he] look[s] at roses" (10)? What does the last line suggest about the artificiality of the listener? How is this contrast important to an interpretation of the lyric?

2. **The color imagery in poem 94:** Analyze how the various colors give meaning to the poem.

   Three different lines speak of the "songs of carmine, violet, green, gold" (3). What is the significance of these particular colors? In what rituals are they traditionally displayed? How do they "[s]ing good ballads of God" (12)? What is the function of the "[l]ittle priests, little holy fathers" (14)? What is the tone of this poem? Finally, how can you arrive at an interpretation of the poem by paying attention to this color imagery?

3. **The image of love as an imp in poem 104:** Analyze the image of love as an imp and a bungler in this poem.

   Love has often been seen as the deity Cupid in traditional poetry. Stephen Crane carries this personification one step further in this poem by using the words *imp* and *bungler* (2, 6) to indicate the love god. Not only is he an imp, but he is also "reckless" (2). Then he becomes "stupid, simpering, eyeless" (7). Why does the poem portray love in this way? What does this wording imply about the narrator? How does the narrator feel about the situation in which he finds himself?

Compare and Contrast

You can arrive at an understanding of Stephen Crane's poems by comparing and contrasting them with each other or with those of another poet. Crane's poems have often been compared to those of Emily Dickinson, whose work he learned about from his mentor William Dean Howells. Both poets' works are similarly short and unconventional and their attitude toward religion and God more personal and spiritual than traditional. It might also be productive to compare his poems to a modernist poet such as Robert Frost or William Carlos Williams.

Sample Topics:

1. **Poem 81 and Robert Frost's poem "The Road Not Taken":**
   Analyze the similarities and differences in these two poems.

   Crane's poem 81 portrays a wayfarer examining the "pathway to truth" (2) and deciding that "[d]oubtless there are other roads" (11). Robert Frost has his traveler looking back on a choice between two different roads and wondering whether the choice "made all the difference" (20). What are the similarities in the two poems? How are the narrators different? How are they alike? What is the difference in perspective? What is the most important image in Crane's poem? In Frost's? How does each poem make an entirely different point? How does this comparison lend more understanding of the Crane poem?

2. **Crane's poem 99 and Emily Dickinson's poem that begins with "My life once stood a loaded gun":** Compare the outlooks on love in each of these poems.

   The most obvious difference is in the gender of the narrators, with Crane's a male and Dickinson's a female. Another difference is the image of the woman as rocking happily in Crane's poem and the woman as an actual gun with Dickinson's. What are other differences? What are some similarities? Consider especially the potential for violence, the extreme longing, and the sorrowful tone at the end of each.

Bibliography for *War Is Kind*

Basye, Robert C. "Color Imagery in Stephen Crane's Poetry." *American Literary Realism, 1870–1910* 13 (1980): 122–31.

Blair, John. "The Posture of a Bohemian in the Poetry of Stephen Crane." *American Literature: A Journal of Literary History, Criticism, and Bibliography* 61.2 (1989): 215–29.

Campbell, Donna. "Reflections on Stephen Crane." *Stephen Crane Studies* 15.1 (2006): 13–16.

Cavitch, Max. "Stephen Crane's Refrain." *ESQ: A Journal of the American Renaissance* 54.1–4 (2008): 33–54.

Crane, Stephen. "The Terrible Captain of the Captured Panama." *The Works of Stephen Crane: Reports of War.* Ed. Fredson Bowers. Vol. 9. Charlottesville: UP of Virginia, 1971. 103–05.

———. *The Works of Stephen Crane: Poems and Literary Remains.* Ed. Fredson Bowers. Vol. 10. Charlottesville: UP of Virginia, 1975.

Dooley, Patrick K. *The Pluralistic Philosophy of Stephen Crane.* Urbana: U of Illinois P, 1993.

Gandal, Keith. "A Spiritual Autopsy of Stephen Crane." *Nineteenth-Century Literature* 51.4 (1997): 500–30.

———. "Stephen Crane's 'Mystic Places.'" *Arizona Quarterly: A Journal of American Literature, Culture, and Theory* 55.1 (1999): 97–126.

Gillis, E. A. "A Glance at Stephen Crane's Poetry." *Prairie Schooner* 28 (1954): 73–79.

Griffith, Benjamin W. "Robinson Jeffers' 'The Bloody Sire' and Stephen Crane's 'War is Kind.'" *Notes on Contemporary Literature* 3.1 (1973): 14–15.

Hoffman, Daniel G. *The Poetry of Stephen Crane.* New York: Columbia UP, 1957.

Huang, Jiaxiu. "Stephen Crane's Poetry of the Absurd." *Re-Reading America: Changes and Challenges.* Ed. Weihe Zhong and Rui Han. Cheltenham, England: Reardon, 2004. 131–35.

Kuga, Shunji. "Momentous Sounds and Silences in Stephen Crane." *Stephen Crane Studies* 15.1 (2006): 17–19.

Marcus, Mordecai. "Structure and Irony in Stephen Crane's 'War is Kind.'" *College Language Association Journal* 9 (1966): 274–78.

Paschke-Johannes, J. Edwin. "Existential Moments in Stephen Crane's Poems." *Stephen Crane Studies* 15.1 (2006): 32–36.

Saunders, Judith P. "Stephen Crane: American Poetry at a Crossroads." *Teaching Nineteenth-Century American Poetry.* Ed. Paula Bernat Bennett, Karen L. Kilcup, and Philipp Schweighauser. New York: Modern Language Association of America, 2007. 185-99.

Sutton, Walter. "The Modernity of Stephen Crane's Poetry: A Centennial Tribute." *Courier: Syracuse University Library Associates* 9.1 (1971): 3–7.

Wertheim, Stanley, and Paul Sorrentino. *The Crane Log: A Documentary Life of Stephen Crane 1871–1900.* New York: G. K. Hall, 1994.

———, ed. *The Correspondence of Stephen Crane.* New York: Columbia UP, 1988.

Westbrook, Max. "Recognizing the Two Voices in Crane's Poetry." *Readings on Stephen Crane.* Ed. Bonnie Szumski. San Diego: Greenhaven, 1998. 191–96.

———. "Stephen Crane's Poetry: Perspective and Arrogance." *Bucknell Review: A Scholarly Journal of Letters, Arts and Sciences* 11.4 (1963): 24–34.

WHILOMVILLE
STORIES

READING TO WRITE

In April 1898 Stephen Crane made a deal with Pulitzer's *New York World* to report on the Spanish-American War in Cuba. Pulitzer had chartered *The Three Friends* as a press boat carrying several correspondents, including Crane. In the middle of pursuing stories of war in both Cuba and other islands in the Caribbean, Crane writes to his agent, Paul Revere Reynolds, that he is sending him "His New Mittens," in which he uses the same locale as that of "The Monster." The difference is that this story is "a short story of boy life in Whilomville" (*Correspondence* 360–61). Crane continued writing such stories, forwarding them to Reynolds to send on to *Harper's* for their magazine. Although typically seen as less literary than "The Monster" and his other works, these lighthearted stories also explore the human condition and ridicule hypocrisy and other human shortcomings. They also use the metaphor of war with domestic battles between the children themselves and between the adults and the children. Most of these stories were eventually collected into one volume titled *Whilomville Stories* (1900), omitting "His New Mittens" and excluding "The Monster," a very different type of fiction set in the same town but published in another collection.

The first story in this collection is "The Angel-Child," a story including Jimmie Trescott, his father, and his mother—all introduced in "The Monster"—as well as a distant cousin, "little Cora," a female character based loosely on Crane's ideas of his wife as a child. Cora, the little girl ironically referred to as the "angel-child," has come with her parents from the big city of New York to visit, and she immediately becomes both the focus of Jimmie's adoration and the catalyst for playground mischief. A close reading of the following passage will reveal the extent to which Cora is able to corrupt the other usually well-behaved children.

> Yes, they were all most excellent children, but, loosened upon this candy-shop with five dollars, they resembled, in a tiny way, drunken revelling soldiers within the walls of a stormed city. Upon the heels of ice-cream and cake came chocolate mice, butter-scotch, "everlastings," chocolate cigars, taffy-on-a-stick, taffy-on-a-slate-pencil, and many semi-transparent devices resembling lions, tigers, elephants, horses, cats, dogs, cows, sheep, tables, chairs, engines (both railway and for the fighting of fire), soldiers, fine ladies, odd-looking men, clocks, watches, revolvers, rabbits, and bedsteads. A cent was the price of a single wonder.
>
> Some of the children, going quite daft, soon had thought to make fight over the spoils, but their queen ruled with an iron grip. Her first inspiration was to satisfy her own fancies, but as soon as that was done she mingled prodigality with a fine justice, dividing, balancing, bestowing, and sometimes taking away from somebody even that which he had.
>
> It was an orgy. In thirty-five minutes those respectable children looked as if they had been dragged at the tail of a chariot. The sacred Margate twins, blinking and grunting, wished to take seat upon the floor, and even the most durable Jimmie Trescott found occasion to lean against the counter, wearing at the time a solemn and abstracted air, as if he expected something to happen to him shortly. (131)

The Whilomville children are not, of course, accustomed to having the kind of spending money that Cora has—five dollars, a large sum of money at that time—and the children revel in her freedom to buy all sorts of sweets. Crane exaggerates their debauchery by referring to them as "drunken revelling soldiers" and listing every possible sweet, or "wonder," in their "orgy" of excess: "ice-cream and cake . . . , chocolate mice, butter-scotch, 'everlastings,' chocolate cigars, taffy-on-a-stick, taffy-on-a-slate-pencil, and many semi-transparent devices resembling lions, tigers, elephants, horses, cats, dogs, cows, sheep, tables, chairs, engines (both railway and for the fighting of fire), soldiers, fine ladies, odd-looking men, clocks, watches, revolvers, rabbits, and bedsteads."

Although the consequences of eating so much sugar are not debilitating, Cora's next idea causes a more serious result. She has the sudden inspiration that all the children should get haircuts, and they do. When mothers see their precious children shorn of their long, curly locks, they become extremely upset, eventually settling the blame on Cora's father for having given his daughter five dollars for her birthday. Although the events in this story are not especially important, they suggest that similar attitudes toward overindulgence, money, and authority in adults can and do cause immense problems. As you read the other stories in the collection, you should look beneath the surface of these humorous tales for fundamental issues of human actions and responsibilities.

TOPICS AND STRATEGIES
Themes

Reading the *Whilomville Stories,* you will soon realize that quite serious themes underlie the adventures of these small children in a town which on the surface seems idyllic. These themes are not unlike those found in Crane's other fiction: courage and fear, pride, life as a battle, violence, truth and lies, and prejudice. A close reading of these stories will reveal that the idyllic town is finally not so edenic, with the children often imitating some of the worst actions of the larger adult world outside this small town.

Sample Topics:

1. **Pride:** Analyze the theme of pride in the *Whilomville Stories.*

   Look particularly at "The Angel-Child." Why do the children follow Cora's suggestions without giving any thought to what they are being asked to do? Crane even points out, "Little did they know if this were fun; they only knew that their small leader said it was fun" (133). Why do the parents become so upset when they see their children with short haircuts?

   What other stories reveal a false pride, a self-esteem based more on appearance than on actual substance? A close reading of "The Stove" will give you more evidence that pride is often the target of the humor in this series.

2. **Truth and lies:** Analyze the consequences of telling lies in these stories.

Read "Lynx-Hunting" and list the lies that Jimmie Trescott tells, beginning with the one that he relates to the other boys about being allowed to take his father's rifle whenever he wants. Then consider "The Lover and the Tell-Tale" and "Showin' Off." What other stories include lies? What are the consequences of lying? What do these stories overall indicate about the importance of telling the truth? How does this theme carry over into the adult world beyond the children?

3. **Courage:** Analyze the theme of courage in the *Whilomville Stories.*

Which stories contain childish ideas of courage that are really revelations of false bravado? How does Jimmie lose face in "Lynx-Hunting"? What are the sources of Homer Phelps's fear in the "Trial, Execution, and Burial of Homer Phelps?" How does the desire to conform cause the children in these stories to have false ideas about courage? What are those ideas? How are they overturned?

Character

The *Whilomville Stories* contain several recurring characters, including Jimmie Trescott, Cora, Willie Dalzel, and Dr. and Mrs. Trescott. Although the characterization is often not as complex as that in Crane's more serious fiction, the reader does learn a great deal about these recurring characters. In addition, there are occasional reappearances of characters from Crane's other fiction, for example, Henry Fleming from the *Red Badge.*

Consider how the recurring characters function. Do they change or do they remain static in the course of the stories? Are the characters who appear in other Crane stories similar or different in this collection? Why do you suppose they reappear here? Which character is most admirable? Which is least admirable?

Sample Topics:

1. **Jimmie:** Analyze the character of Jimmie Trescott.

   What features of Jimmie do you least admire? Most admire? Why? Is he a typical little boy or one of a kind?
   Jimmie was rescued from his burning house in "The Monster"? Does that rescue justify Crane's use of him in further stories? In what way? What makes Jimmie stand out from the other boys in Whilomville? How do the other characters interact with Jimmie? What is his most admirable trait? What is his worst trait? What do you suppose makes Jimmie the most frequently appearing child in all of Crane's fiction? How does Crane make a literary statement through the character of Jimmie?

2. **Willie Dalzel:** Analyze the character of Willie Dalzel.

   Crane characterizes Willie as someone who is the group's chieftain in the "Trial, Execution, and Burial of Homer Phelps," but he also says about Willie, "he felt, no doubt, that he must proceed according to the books but unfortunately the books did not cover the point precisely" (208). What does this quote suggest about Willie? In which other stories does he appear? How does Willie's character serve as a contrast to that of Jimmie or to Homer Phelps? What point about leadership or conformity does Crane seem to make through the character of Willie Dalzel?

3. **Cora:** Analyze the character of Cora, the so-called angel-child.

   Cora is very different from the children of Whilomville. She is accustomed to living in New York City, her family is rich compared to the local inhabitants, and she is a spoiled only child. How does she serve as a catalyst for all kinds of activities when she is in town? Why do the other children follow her lead? Why does Jimmie like her so much? How does she flaunt convention and get away with it? What point about life in a small town does Crane seem to be making through this character?

History and Context

At the time Crane was writing the *Whilomville Stories,* other "boy stories" had been quite popular: Frances H. Burnett's *Little Lord Fauntleroy,* Thomas Bailey Aldrich's *The Story of a Bad Boy,* George Wilbur Peck's famous "Peck's Bad Boy" stories, and the much more acclaimed *Adventures of Tom Sawyer* and *Adventures of Huckleberry Finn* by Mark Twain. Like Twain's stories, Crane's are much more realistic than the others, and they even expand to include girls as major characters. Unlike Twain's, however, Crane's stories have received little critical attention with Eric Solomon perhaps the only critic who credits them with genuine literary merit. Solomon points out that "all of the seven deadly sins, with the obvious exception of lechery, appear in the volume" (207).

Sample Topics:

1. **Analyze a Whilomville story in light of the "boy stories" of the late nineteenth century:** After reading a typical "boy story," show how Crane transcends this popular model.

   What aspects of Crane's stories give them more literary merit than the popular choice? Why would boys particularly enjoy the "boy stories"? Crane's stories have not been published specifically for boys. Do you think such a volume would be successful? Why or why not?

2. **Aspects of the Gilded Age:** Analyze the stories featuring Cora, the angel-child, as critiques of the excesses of what Mark Twain termed the Gilded Age.

   During the 1890s many businessmen amassed great quantities of wealth, spending the money in often ostentatious purchases. Research the wealthy of this time period, and note their acquisitions and activities. As you research the Gilded Age, with its quick accumulation of massive wealth and influence, consider the characterization of Cora as perhaps a parody of a wealthy

American. How does she acquire her money? How does she spend it? Which of her activities could be considered excessive in the same way that business tycoons of the time used their wealth and influence? Do you think Crane deliberately satirizes such excesses? If so, how and why?

Philosophy and Ideas

These seemingly lighthearted stories often deal with the same philosophical problems and ideas found in more serious tales of adults. Just as Stephen Crane reveals the hypocrisy of the town's prominent adult citizens in "The Monster," in *Maggie,* and in much of his poetry, he also reveals Jimmie Trescott's involvement with the church for all the wrong reasons. In "A Little Pilgrim," Jimmie is more interested in his Sunday school's traditional Christmas tree than he is in spending the money reserved for the tree to help earthquake victims. He is so disappointed that there will be no tree that he goes to another church—only to learn that his new Sunday school is following the model set by his previous church. They plan to give money earmarked for Christmas decorations to earthquake relief as well.

Sample Topics:

1. **Christianity:** Analyze Crane's use of Christian theology and morality in the stories.

   After closely reading these stories, find evidence that the children may be trained in the ways of the church, but they are often hypocritical. In "The Little Pilgrim," for example, Jimmie Trescott seems to enjoy the trappings of the church but subverts the idea of the Christian teaching of "love thy neighbor." Find other evidence of the children not behaving according to the Ten Commandments. Then determine how their actions and beliefs reflect those of the adults in that society. What point does Crane make about the church, its teachings, and its practices?

2. **The rules of society:** Analyze how the children break the rules of civilization.

What, for example, is Homer Phelps's "crime" in "The Trial, Execution, and Burial of Homer Phelps"? How are their skirmishes like those of adults, even those in positions of leadership? What makes them amusing when they are carried out by children? What do they reveal about adult society?

Form and Genre

The Whilomville tales were published individually in *Harper's New Monthly Magazine,* and they were published posthumously in August 1900 as *Whilomville Stories.* Although previously Stephen Crane had planned a differently configured collection, he realized that "The Monster" and "The Blue Hotel" did not fit with the other stories. Instead, he decided that the children's stories should be in their own volume, one following the chronological order of their serial publication. Omitting "His New Mittens," the final volume covers a more than two-year cycle, beginning in summer and ending in summer. Crane fashions Whilomville on his hometown of Port Jervis, New Jersey, where he lived from ages six to eleven. James Nagel makes the point that they have been given no real attention as a "short-story" cycle, and he points out the interconnected nature of these stories.

Sample Topics:

1. **The structure of the *Whilomville Stories:*** Analyze the structure of the stories in this volume.

   The *Whilomville Stories* include thirteen stories covering two and one-half years and including two Christmases. What significance do you find in that pattern? Is it significant that they begin in summer and end in summer? What characters tie the stories together? What themes tie the stories together? Which stories seem least like the others? Why? What overall importance is the structural organization of these stories?

2. **The *Whilomville Stories* as children's stories:** Analyze the audience of these stories.

   These stories are likely read by very few children today, and their original audience was that of *Harper's New Monthly*

Magazine, a magazine aimed at adults. The first story, "The Angel-Child" was published in the August 1899 issue of *Harper's,* complete with five illustrations: a tree-lined street with picket fences above the story title; an almost half-page illustration of the barber at work and the children closely watching; a half-page picture of Cora, her mother and father, and the whole Trescott family after the haircutting; a comic picture of the shorn Margate twins and a final three-quarter-page picture of Cora and her family at the train station as they are leaving to go back to New York City.

You might argue that these stories could have been written with the child audience in mind and that the illustrations would have drawn in children who read the popular magazine in their home. On the other hand, since *Harper's Young People,* a magazine published from 1879–1899, targeted a young audience, you might take the opposite point of view and argue that the stories were written for adults in spite of the emphasis on juvenile characters. In either case, you need to read the stories closely and determine what appeals are made for the audience you believe to be targeted.

Language, Symbols, and Imagery

Stephen Crane's writing is always filled with imagery, and the *Whilomville Stories* are no exception. Consider the following excerpt from "The Stove," in which Cora and Jimmie pretend to cook puddings but are actually burning turnips on Cora's toy stove in the cellar as Mrs. Trescott is presiding over a tea party in the parlor.

When a tea-party was to befall a certain house, one could read it in the manner of the prospective hostess who for some previous days would go about twitching this and twisting that and dusting here and polishing there; the ordinary habits of the household began then to disagree with her and her unfortunate husband and children fled to the lengths of their tethers. Then there was a hush. Then there was a tea-party. On the fatal afternoon, a small picked company of latent enemies would meet. There would be a fanfare of affectionate greetings during which everybody would measure to an inch the importance of what everybody else was wearing. Those who wore old dresses would wish then that they had not come and those who saw that, in the company, they were well-clad would be pleased or exalted or filled with the joys of cruelty. Then they had tea which was a habit and a delight with none of them, their usual beverage being coffee with milk. (199)

The women give great social importance to their ritualistic tea party, so it is easy to see how the stench of burning turnips could bring an abrupt halt to such a momentous affair. Crane sets the groundwork for the seemingly tragic disruption of the party by his use of words and phrases such as *befall, fatal,* and *latent enemies.* This imagery, more befitting a tragedy than a tea party, undercuts the seriousness of the children's actions and makes the reader question why everyone is so upset.

After the calamity, the usually calm and composed Dr. Trescott admonishes the always bewildered father of the "angel-child": "Spank her! Spank her, confound you man! She needs it. Here's your chance. Spank her and spank her good. Spank her!" (205). Crane shows Cora's behavior and demeanor to be such that the reader finds herself agreeing with Dr. Trescott, but Crane goes further with his imagery to suggest that the adults are just as foolish and savage as the children. Eric Solomon points out, "The foolishness and destructiveness of children are but a pale reflection of adults' stupidity and savagery" (222).

Sample Topics:

1. **Meaning of the title:** Analyze the use of Whilomville as the name of the town.

   You might start by reading Ellen A. Brown and Patricia Hernlund's essay on the source of the title, which they contend originates from a Crane family fife and drum corps of previous years. Even if these two scholars are accurate, the term seems much more meaningful than just that connection. What does the word *whilom* suggest to you? How is it different from a term with a similar meaning, such as *former*? How is even the sound of the term evocative of a certain type of town? Why are the sound and the connotations associated with the words important? How does the title work with the story to evoke a certain ambiance and meaning? Why is the collection named after the town and not a character or an event?

2. **War imagery:** Analyze the use of war imagery in one or more stories.

Crane's imaginary world is peopled with adults in discord with one another and children in imaginative feats of valor. Read one or more of the stories closely, making note of images such as "gladiator," "soldiers," "massacre," and others associated with or denoting violence. Then look at how Crane has used the terms, typically either inflating the importance of an event or often revealing the savagery inherent in human beings of all types.

Compare and Contrast Essays

As already mentioned, Crane's stories are similar to other stories of boys at the time, yet they are also quite different. You could locate and read a typical "bad boy" story and use it for a comparison. On the other hand, you might also compare elements within Crane's own writing. The possibilities are many, but a close reading of one or more stories can lead you to one that interests you.

Sample Topics:

1. **Tom Sawyer and Jimmie Trescott:** Compare and contrast the characterization of Mark Twain's Tom Sawyer with Jimmie Trescott.

Both of these boys are mischievous, often getting into trouble, yet both have features that make the reader identify with them and even admire their cunning. Begin by listing the similarities; then list the differences. Then group these features in meaningful ways, such as best features, worst features, or other appropriate categories. Once you have analyzed these groupings, decide what you think they reveal about meaning in the story or stories. Finally, what is the importance of this revelation in interpreting the Crane work?

2. **Henry Fleming in *The Red Badge*, "The Veteran," and "Lynx-Hunting":** Compare and contrast the characterization of Henry Fleming in each of these pieces

Again you will need to read the pieces closely, showing the chief characteristics of Fleming in each. How are they similar? How are they different? What is important about the differences? What does Crane imply about human nature in the changes we see in this character? How does "Lynx-Hunting" fit into the Whilomville collection?

Bibliography for *Whilomville Stories*

Brown, Ellen A. "Stephen Crane's Whilomville Stories: A Backward Glance." *Markham Review* 3 (1973): 105–09.

Brown, Ellen A., and Patricia Hernlund. "The Source for the Title of Stephen Crane's Whilomville Stories." *American Literature: A Journal of Literary History, Criticism, and Bibliography* 50.1 (1978): 116–18.

Crane, Stephen. *The Works of Stephen Crane: Tales of Whilomville.* Ed. Fredson Bowers. Vol. 7: Charlottesville: UP of Virginia, 1969.

Nagel, James. "The American Short-Story Cycle and Stephen Crane's Tales of Whilomville." *American Literary Realism* 32.1 (1999): 35–42.

Sieglen, John H. *The Metonymous World of the Child in Stephen Crane's Whilomville Stories.* Ann Arbor: U of Michigan P, 1969.

Soloman, Eric. *Stephen Crane: From Parody to Realism.* Cambridge: Harvard UP, 1966.

Sojka, Gregory S. "Stephen Crane's 'A Little Pilgrim': Whilomville's Young Martyr." *NMAL: Notes on Modern American Literature* 3 (1978): Item 3.

Westbrook, Max. "Whilomville: The Coherence of Radical Language." *Stephen Crane in Transition: Centenary Essays.* Ed. Joseph Katz and James Dickey. DeKalb: Northern Illinois UP, 1972. 86–105.

WOUNDS IN THE RAIN

READING TO WRITE

While Stephen Crane was in Cuba writing war dispatches for newspapers, he also began composing short stories based on what he observed there. Although the resulting collection, *Wounds in the Rain,* was published posthumously in September 1900, Crane himself had conceived, organized, and finished writing the volume of stories. An unsigned article in the *New York Times* on August 17, 1901, reports that the book had gone into its fourth edition, all within the period of one year from its first publication. Even though this successful selling suggests that the reading public welcomed the volume, the eleven stories included have received much less critical attention than most of Crane's other works. Each of the stories deals with a specific type of "wound," some physical and others not. Building on the success of the psychological realism in *The Red Badge* and *The Little Regiment,* both written before Crane had ever seen battle, these stories present a greater variety of realistic physical details gleaned from his observing both the Greek-Turkish War and then the Spanish-American War.

The following excerpt from the first story, "The Price of the Harness," displays this use of physical details to give the reader insight into the situation of the soldiers.

> Then suddenly every rifle in the firing line seemed to go off of its own accord. It was the result of an order, but few men had heard the order; in the main they had fired because they heard others fire, and their sense was so quick that the volley did not sound too ragged. These marksmen had been lying for nearly an hour in stony silence, their sights adjusted, their fingers fondling their rifles, their eyes staring at the intrenchments

[sic] of the enemy. The battalion had suffered heavy losses, and these losses had been hard to bear, for a soldier always reasons that men lost during a period of inaction are men badly lost.

The line now sounded like a great machine set to running frantically in the open air, the bright sunshine of a green field. To the prut of the magazine rifles was added the under-chorus of the clicking mechanism, steady and swift as if the hand of one operator was controlling it all. It reminds one always of a loom, a great grand steel loom, clinking, clanking, plunking, plinking, to weave a woof of thin red threads, the cloth of death. By the men's shoulders under their eager hands dropped continually the yellow empty shells, spinning into the crushed grass blades to remain there and mark for the belated eye the line of a battalion's fight.

All impatience, all rebellious feeling, had passed out of the men as soon as they had been allowed to use their weapons against the enemy. They now were absorbed in this business of hitting something, and all the long training at the rifle ranges, all the pride of the marksman which had been so long alive in them, made them forget for the time everything but shooting. They were as deliberate and exact as so many watchmakers. (109–10)

Notice in this passage the synchronicity of the soldiers, summed up in the last line: "They were as deliberate and exact as so many watchmakers." When the soldiers start shooting, each is shooting because someone else is shooting, the result of hearing shots. Crane's aural imagery is strong, indicating the overwhelming prevalence of sound on the battlefield with onomatopoeic words and phrases such as *prut* and *clinking, clanking, plunking, plinking,* which together "weave a woof of thin red threads, the cloth of death." While the imitations of the sounds themselves may seem to undercut the seriousness of the skirmish, the memorable metaphor of the cloth of death reminds the reader that these men are involved in very serious work indeed, that many of them will not live to go home again, yet this constant barrage is what they have been trained to do and what they must accomplish to survive.

TOPICS AND STRATEGIES

Your first task before choosing a topic is to read each story in the collection, looking for connections and inspirations as you read. This task is a bit more difficult with this group of short stories, where there are eleven different plots and many different characters. As you read, keep in mind the emphasis on "wounds," and observe how this metaphor links the stories to one another. You may decide to choose one element and trace it through two or more stories, or you may decide to choose just one story and analyze it. In any case, a thorough reading of all the stories will give you a strong background to make such a choice. As you read individual stories, take notes of the theme, the plotline, and the major characters. Also mark paragraphs that seem especially significant so that you can reread them after finishing all the stories. Then reread those passages, noting the specific language and word choices.

Themes

A variety of themes can be identified in *Wounds in the Rain,* ranging from the violence of war to the irresponsibility of "yellow journalism," that is, sensationalized news stories. Having the advantage of observing both war and correspondents and valuing truth as an ideal, Stephen Crane worked hard to be a reporter whose dispatches presented a realistic account of the Spanish-American War, as opposed to just a story calculated to sell more newspapers. Other reporters, especially Richard Harding Davis, found Stephen Crane top-notch at his work: "The best correspondent is probably the man who by his energy and resource sees more of the war, both afloat and ashore, than do his rivals, and who is able to make the public see what he saw. If that is a good definition, Stephen Crane would seem to have distinctly won the first place among correspondents in the late disturbance" (11). Davis and the other correspondents, then, recognized Crane's devotion to truth, to presenting what he saw in person to the public at large.

Using one of the themes suggested below or one of your own invention, write an essay on an important theme in this collection of stories.

Sample Topics:

1. **Yellow journalism:** Analyze how the stories in *Wounds in the Rain* expose the sensationalized reporting of some correspondents during the Spanish-American War.

Read the story "God Rest Ye, Merry Gentlemen," paying particular attention to the position in which Little Nell finds himself after he is told to locate the enemy's fleet. Little Nell, who can be seen as the representative or spokesman for Crane himself, is in the unfortunate position of having done what his editor has urged him to do, to locate and report on the enemy ships:

> If his unfortunate nine-knot craft should happen to find these great twenty-knot ships, with their two spiteful and faster attendants, Little Nell had wondered how he was going to lose them again. He had marveled, both publicly and in secret, on the uncompromising asininity of managing editors at odd moments, but he had wasted little time. (135)

If he were to find himself in the position of being fired upon, he does not have the weapons or the ability to fire back, and he knows that his newspaper, the fictional *New York Eclipse,* does not care. The editors only wanted a newspaper story, one that will sell many newspapers, even if at the moment the armies are doing nothing.

You might also consider Perkins in "The Lone Charge of William B. Perkins" and the correspondents in "The Revenge of the Adolphus" and in "Virtue in War." What is their attitude toward their newspapers? How do they feel they are being coerced instead of being allowed just to report the news? In "This Majestic Lie," how are the correspondents portrayed?

After reading the stories in which war correspondents are featured, formulate a question about their perceived role during the war. How does that role differ from the role that Crane implies they should play? What are the negative and positive attributes of the correspondents? Overall, what do these stories suggest about war reporting?

2. **Psychological wounds:** Analyze the psychological damage done to the soldiers involved in the Spanish-American War.

The most obvious psychological casualty of this war is Dryden in "The Serjeant's Private Mad-House." You might begin with that story, analyzing the causes and results of Dryden's plunge into insanity. Then you can examine other stories to assess the psychological problems that other military men face. What are some of these wounds? Who is involved? What seems to precipitate the damage? Does Crane indicate that these wounds are more or less important than the physical wounds? Why?

Character

Sample Topics:

1. **The soldier in the regular army:** Analyze how Crane portrays the regular servicemen, that is, the men who were career soldiers.

In "The Price of the Harness," a story set in San Juan during the American attack on July 1, 1898, the character of Michael Nolan represents the regular soldier simply doing his work as he has been trained.

> He sprang to his feet and, stooping, ran with the others. Something fine, soft, gentle, touched his heart as he ran. He had loved the regiment, the army, because the regiment, the army, was his life. He had no other outlook; and now these men, his comrades, were performing his dream-scenes for him. They were doing as he had ordained in his visions. It is curious that in this charge he considered himself as rather unworthy. (110)

Although Nolan gives his life in the process, he is not memorialized by the press as a volunteer from Theodore Roosevelt's Rough Riders might be.

Find other passages in this story that give a fuller understanding of the character of Nolan, and look for other accounts of regular soldiers, such as "Marines Signaling under Fire at Guantánamo." How do these soldiers differ from the typical idea of the hero? What are their major characteristics? What point does Crane make about heroism in the Spanish-American War?

2. **War correspondents:** Analyze one or more of the correspondents in *Wounds in the Rain*.

Paying particular attention to "This Majestic Lie," "The Lone Charge of William B. Perkins," and "God Rest Ye, Merry Gentlemen," what do you find are the major characteristics of the correspondents? What are the major components of their job? Is their danger more or less than the men in service? What motivates them to report on the war? How do they interact with the others? Overall what points does Crane make about reporting the war?

3. **Caspar Cadogan in "The Second Generation":** Analyze this character to see how Crane views power and privilege in the war situation.

As the son of a U.S. senator, Caspar expects, and often gets, special recognition or privileges. Show how Crane uses this character to reveal nepotism in assignments at that time. How does Caspar get his appointment as an army captain and commissary officer? What does he know about his job? What does he learn? How does he carry out his duties? When he is back at home, how does his father try to persuade him to choose the military as his career?

History and Context

At the end of the nineteenth century in the United States, the country was experiencing major changes. Certain segments of the population had become quite rich and influential, newspapers encouraged sensationalism, and government leaders felt they could easily overcome Spanish domination of Cuba and other parts of the Caribbean. You will need to do some research to find factual accounts of these phenomena. You might read Kenneth Whyte's *The Uncrowned King: The Sensational Rise of William Randolph Hearst,* covering the years from 1895 to 1898, to see how Hearst used the *New York Journal* to compete with a rival newspaper, Joseph Pulitzer's *New York World,* in a bid to capture the most newspaper circulation. On the other hand, you may want to learn more about the actual battle in Cuba. You can read historical accounts of the war, such as *The Spanish War: An American Epic 1898* by G.J.A. O'Toole, or you may want to explore the connection between these topics by reading

The War Lovers: Roosevelt, Lodge, Hearst, and the Rush to Empire, 1898
by Evan Thomas.

Sample Topics:

1. **Yellow journalism:** Discuss how Stephen Crane debunks so-
called yellow journalism, or sensationalized news accounts, in
Wounds in the Rain.

   Using the book by Kenneth Whyte, or some other account
   of "yellow journalism," examine one or more of the stories in
   which Crane shows his distaste for sensationalizing events and
   other tactics to sell more newspapers, especially the pressure
   from editors to have correspondents invent news when nothing
   significant was happening. In "This Majestic Lie," Crane writes:

   > The correspondents at Key West were perfectly capable of
   > adjusting their perspectives, but many of the editors in the
   > United States were like deaf men at whom one has to roar. A
   > few quiet words of information was not enough for them; one
   > had to bawl into their ears a whirlwind tale of heroism, blood,
   > death, victory or defeat—at any rate, a tragedy. The papers
   > should have sent play-wrights to the first part of the war. Play-
   > wrights are allowed to lower the curtain from time to time
   > and say to the crowd: "Mark, ye, now! Three or four months
   > are supposed to elapse." But the poor devils at Key West were
   > obliged to keep the curtain up all the time. "This isn't a con-
   > tinuous performance." "Yes, it is; it's got to be a continuous
   > performance. The welfare of the paper demands it. The people
   > want news." (204)

   How does this pressure to produce news continuously influence the correspondents? How does Crane show the correspondents responding to this pressure? Overall, what does
   Crane imply about the duties and responsibilities of news
   correspondents?

2. **The Spanish-American War in Cuba:** Analyze how Crane
   presents the war in terms of the actual history of the events.

After researching the war itself, choose one or more of the stories that present fictionalized accounts of actual war events. For example, you could choose "The Price of the Harness," a fictionalization of the July 1, 1898, American attack upon the fortifications of San Juan. How does Crane use this or another event? How does he present the Cubans who sided with Spain? How does he present the Spanish troops and officers? Do his stories seem to favor the Americans in such a way that the opposing forces are seen only as the enemy? Does the war serve as more than a backdrop for the story, or is it integral to the actions and characterizations?

Philosophy and Ideas

Although the twentieth century had not yet begun, Stephen Crane was already moving toward modernism—both in philosophy and technique. Some of the stories in this collection contain the idea of questioning reality—what is real and what is a result of perception. He also struggled with the representation of reality, like many of the modern artists and writers to follow him in the next century. In addition, Crane also begins to question duty in some of these stories. How much can a soldier be expected to endure? What is the value of exposing oneself to death? What is the duty of men fighting in this particular war or in any other war?

Sample Topics:

1. **The nature of reality in "War Memories":** Discuss Crane's presentation of reality as situational, anticipating later philosophers such as Edmund Husserl and Martin Heidegger.

    At the beginning of this story, Vernall, the main character, questions reality and how to represent it:

    > "But to get the real thing!" cried Vernall, the war correspondent. "It seems impossible! It is because war is neither magnificent nor squalid; it is simply life, and an expression of life can always evade us. We can never tell, one to another, although sometimes we think we can." (222)

Vernall's pronouncement sets the stage for his continued questioning of reality, as he realizes that he does not understand war or life, danger or safety. As he says, "I was a child who, in a fit of ignorance, had jumped into the vat of war" (226). What seems imminent danger becomes even less clear: "Our enemies? Yes—perhaps—I suppose so" (230). And even death is not always apparent: "one's eye could not pick the living from the dead until one saw that a certain head had beneath it a great dark pool" (227).

What other incidents or examples of ambiguous perception are given in the story? Does Vernall ever get to the point that he feels he understands what is real and what is not? What then does the story indicate about the nature of reality?

2. **A soldier's devotion to duty:** In "The Clan of No-Name," Crane presents Manolo Prat, a Cuban insurgent who is devoted to his duty. Discuss whether this story glorifies Manolo or presents his death as a foolish waste.

The ultimate value of Manolo's actions is somewhat ambivalent. While other stories in this collection portray soldiers dedicated to their duty and brave in their actions, this story shows Manolo bravely fighting but with the sure knowledge that his acts will be not only futile but also fatal:

> He knew that he was thrusting himself into a trap whose door, once closed, opened only when the black hand knocked, and every part of him seemed to be in panic-stricken revolt. But something controlled him; something moved him inexorably in one direction; he perfectly understood, but he was only sad, sad with a serene dignity, with the countenance of a mournful young prince. He was of a kind—that seemed to be it—and the men of his kind, on peak or plain, from the dark northern ice-fields to the hot wet jungles, through all wine and want, through all lies and unfamiliar truth, dark or light, the men of his kind were governed by their gods, and each man knew the law and yet could not give tongue to it; but it was the law, and

if the spirits of the men of his kind were all sitting in critical judgment upon him even then in the sky, he could not have bettered his conduct; he needs must obey the law, and always with the law there is only one way. (131)

What finally is the value of Manolo's heroism? What does Margharita's burning of his photograph signify?

Form and Genre

Some of the stories in *Wounds in the Rain* are much more advanced in their form than Crane's earlier stories and novels, with two in particular anticipating the narrative complexity of the later literary periods of modernism and postmodernism. The two most complex both in narrative form and genre are "The Clan of No-Name" and "War Memories."

Sample Topics:

1. **Narrative structure in "The Clan of No-Name":** Examine the structure of this story.

   Why is there a poem at the beginning of the story? How does the poem relate to the story? Why are the first and last lines of the poem the same? How many parts make up the story? How do the first and last parts serve as a type of frame? What parts make up the center of the story? Once you have discovered the thematic and metaphorical links that hold the tale together, decide how the overall narrative organization functions as an aid to interpretation.

2. **Narrative structure in "War Memories":** Examine the self-conscious awareness of the narrator as one telling a story and having difficulties with that recital.

   When Vernall, the narrator, finishes his narrative, he writes, "And you can depend upon it that I have told you nothing at all, nothing at all, nothing at all" (263). This authorial attitude about the difficulty of representation is decidedly far ahead of other narrative stances in Crane's writing, with such an attitude being obvious throughout this story. Find other instances of the narrative seeming to reshape itself in order to clarify what is impossible to represent fully. Another way to look at this narrative is as a mixed genre—both a short story and creative nonfiction, with the Vernall character representing the correspondent that was Crane in the actual war. Since Stephen Crane's era, genres of fiction have become more and more uncertain, with several genres sometimes permeating a work. How does this mixture present even more complications with the narrative structure?

Language, Symbols, and Imagery

Wounds in the Rain differs from earlier Crane fiction not only in its innovation in narrative but also in its use of less colorful imagery. Such imagery seems to be replaced with a conscious awareness of language and its limitations. Instead of having a literally colorful title such as his earlier *Red Badge* or "The Blue Hotel," Crane in this collection uses names with deeper psychological implications and less obvious sense appeal. Perhaps the sensationalized headlines that editors attached to his newspaper reports made him want to avoid similar tactics in his titles and his writings. Although he had never deliberately sensationalized any of his writings, he must have become much more aware of the temperance in language that he displays in these stories.

Sample Topics:

1. **"The Lone Charge of William B. Perkins" as satire on extravagant newspaper reporting:** Analyze the language in this story as satirical hyperbole.

   William B. Perkins is a correspondent with no knowledge of war. We are told in the first sentence, "He could not distinguish between a 5-inch quick-firing gun and a nickel-plated ice-pick, and so, naturally, he had been elected to fill the position of war correspondent" (114). His ineptitude having been enhanced by the imbibing of Scotch, Perkins proceeds to act even more outrageously:

> Now behold the solitary Perkins adrift in the storm of fight-
> ing, even as a champagne jacket of straw is lost in a great surf.
> He found it out quickly. Four seconds elapsed before he dis-
> covered that he was an almshouse idiot plunging through hot
> crackling thickets on a June morning in Cuba. *Sss-s-s-swing-
> sing-ing-Pop* went the lightning-swift metal grasshoppers over
> him and beside him beauties of rural Minnesota illuminated
> his conscience with the gold of lazy corn, with the sleeping
> green of meadows, with the cathedral gloom of pine forests.
> *Sshsh-swing-Pop*. Perkins decided that if he cared to extract
> himself from a tangle of imbecility he must shoot. The entire
> situation was that he must shoot. It was necessary that he
> should shoot. Nothing would save him but shooting. It is a
> law that men thus decide when the waters of battle close over
> their minds. So with a prayer that the Americans would not hit
> him in the back nor the left side, and that the Spaniards would
> not hit him in the front, he knelt like a suppliant alone in the
> desert of chaparral and emptied his magazine at his Spaniard
> before he discovered that his Spaniard was a bit of dried palm-
> branch. (116–17)

After this episode Perkins finds shelter in a rusty steam boiler
in the bushes. After closely reading how this supposedly brave
correspondent saves himself, examine the language to show
how Crane deflates Perkins's actions and makes him as ridiculous as some of the headlines made the war seem.

2. **Titles and their importance:** Choose one or more story titles
   and show how they fit with the story itself, setting the tone and
   the theme for the piece.

Stephen Crane could not control how his newspaper reports
were titled, but he could make such choices for his fiction.
The newspaper report that corresponds to "The Price of the
Harness" was titled "Regulars Get No Glory," and the incident
in his "Marines Signaling under Fire at Guantánamo" was
reported as "The Red Badge of Courage Was His Wig-Wag
Flag." The editors chose headlines that would sell when news-

papers were hawked on the street corners of New York and other large cities. They knew, for example, that Crane's most famous title would sell more papers than a more sedate headline similar to his later story title.

Compare and Contrast Essays

The stories in *Wounds in the Rain* can easily be compared to Stephen Crane's war reports on the same or similar events, to his earlier stories of war in *The Little Regiment,* or to other fictional or factual accounts of war. Appearing several months before Crane's stories were ready for publication, Teddy Roosevelt's *The Rough Riders* presents a very different picture of the war, with Roosevelt's part in the war later reenacted in Wild West shows such as Buffalo Bill's Wild West and Congress of Rough Riders of the World. William Frederick Cody, better known as Buffalo Bill, helped to create and preserve the dramatic myth of the Rough Riders. Drawing on Roosevelt's own account, these shows glamorized the war as exciting and dangerous. Roosevelt himself describes his feats as he and his khaki-uniformed troops rode forth:

> The instant I received the order I sprang on my horse and then my "crowded hour" began. The guerillas had been shooting at us from the edges of the jungle and from their perches in the leafy trees, and as they used smokeless powder, it was almost impossible to see them, though a few of my men had from time to time responded. We had also suffered from the hill on our right front, which was held chiefly by guerillas, although there were also some Spanish regulars with them, for we found their dead. I formed my men in column of troops, each troop extended in open skirmishing order, the right resting on the wire fences which bordered the sunken lane. Captain Jenkins led the first squadron, his eyes literally dancing with joyous excitement.

Roosevelt's use of terms such as *sprang, perches,* and *dancing with joyous excitement* make us feel his excitement, but they hide the death and misery that Crane's writing makes tangible.

Sample Topics:

1. **Duty in "Regulars Get No Glory" and "The Price of the Harness":** Compare Crane's presentation of the regular soldiers in

these two works, the first a newspaper report and the second a story in this collection.

What are the similarities in the two works? What are the differences? Which are more important? Why? How does the newspaper report aid in your understanding of the story?

2. **Teddy Roosevelt and Stephen Crane:** Compare an account of one event covered in both *The Rough Riders* and *Wounds in the Rain.*

You might choose, for example, the march into Santiago, covered in both "War Memories" and in a chapter in *Rough Riders.* What are the major similarities between the two accounts? What are the major differences? How do these points help in an analysis of "War Memories"? What insight do you gain about Crane's writing style?

Bibliography for *Wounds in the Rain*

Crane, Stephen. "Regulars Get No Glory" *The Works of Stephen Crane: Reports of War.* Ed. Fredson Bowers. Vol. 9. Charlottesville: UP of Virginia, 1971. 170–73.

———. *The Works of Stephen Crane: Tales of War.* Ed. Fredson Bowers. Vol. 6: Charlottesville: UP of Virginia, 1970.

Davis, Richard Harding. "Our War Correspondents in Cuba and Puerto Rico." *Harper's Monthly Magazine,* May 1899: 938–48. Rpt. in Joyce Caldwell Smith, volume ed., and Harold Bloom, series ed. *Stephen Crane: Bloom's Classic Critical Views.* New York: Chelsea House, 2009. 11–12.

Kunow, Rudiger. "'No Idea of a Grand Performance': Stephen Crane's Cuban War Stories as Revisionist Histories." *Re-Visioning the Past: Historical Self-Reflexivity in American Short Fiction.* Ed. Bernd Engler and Oliver Scheiding. Trier, Germany: Wissenschaftlicher, 1998.

O'Toole, G. J. A. *The Spanish War: An American Epic 1898.* New York: W. W. Norton, 1986.

Roosevelt, Theodore. *The Rough Riders.* 1899. http://www.bartleby.com/51/

Shaw, Mary Ann. *Crane's Concept of Heroism: Satire in the War Stories of Stephen Crane,* 1986.

Solomon, Eric. "Stephen Crane's War Stories." *Texas Studies in Literature and Language* 3 (1961): 67–80.

Thomas, Evan. *The War Lovers: Roosevelt, Lodge, Hearst, and the Rush to Empire, 1898*. New York: Little, Brown, 2010.

Whyte, Kenneth. *The Uncrowned King: The Sensational Rise of William Randolph Hearst*. Berkeley, CA: Counterpoint, 2009.

INDEX